Bed & B

S O U T H E A S T 1 9 9 7

B&Bs can be your home away from home! With hundreds of listings, all with reasonable rates, this indispensable directory gives you the keys to America's best alternatives to hotels and shows you why B&Bs are the *only* way to travel. Offering friendly, home-style places to stay for business travelers, family vacationers, and anyone who is looking for a way to really see the country, this information-packed book should be every traveler's constant companion.

◆

"A valuable source of information."

—*New York Times*

◆

PEGGY ACKERMAN is the co-director with her husband, Michael Ackerman, of the Tourist House Association, a national association of over 1,100 bed and breakfasts. She lives in Greentown, Pennsylvania.

Bed & Breakfast U.S.A.

Southeast 1997

PEGGY ACKERMAN

Tourist House Association of America, Inc.

A PLUME BOOK

PLUME
Published by the Penguin Group
Penguin Books USA Inc., 375 Hudson Street, New York, New York 10014, U.S.A.
Penguin Books Ltd, 27 Wrights Lane, London W8 5TZ, England
Penguin Books Australia Ltd, Ringwood, Victoria, Australia
Penguin Books Canada Ltd, 10 Alcorn Avenue, Toronto, Ontario, Canada M4V 3B2
Penguin Books (N.Z.) Ltd, 182–190 Wairau Road, Auckland 10, New Zealand

Penguin Books Ltd, Registered Offices:
Harmondsworth, Middlesex, England

Published by Plume, an imprint of Dutton Signet,
a division of Penguin Books USA Inc.

First Printing, January, 1997

10 9 8 7 6 5 4 3 2 1

LC card number: 86-649303

Printed in the United States of America

Set in Palatino and Optima
Designed by Stanley S. Drate/Folio Graphics Co. Inc.

If you want to be listed in future editions of this guide, DO NOT WRITE TO PLUME OR PENGUIN. See page 223 for a membership application, or write to:

Tourist House Association, Inc.
Greentown, PA 18426

Applications will be accepted until March 31, 1997.

The book you are holding is the result of one woman's hard work and big dreams. In 1974, my mother, Betty Revits Rundback, began thinking about how to celebrate the American Bicentennial in 1976. She decided to take her family of seven on a cross-country tour, but didn't like the idea of staying in motels night after night. She wanted her children to really see the country, and to get to know its people along the way. Remembering back to her own childhood, when the house down the road offered comfortable lodging and a bountiful breakfast to travelers, she set out to create a similar experience for us. She never expected to spend months at the New York Public Library doing it! But that's exactly what she did, going through every telephone directory in America to find listings of family-style guesthouses, contacting all the owners individually, and finally assembling them into a pamphlet in time for the Bicentennial. With the information Betty had gathered, she founded the Tourist House Association of America, which she ran enthusiastically and successfully until her death on July 4, 1990. My wife, Peggy, now continues her work of bringing together guests and hosts from around the world. We dedicate this book to her, in loving memory of her warmth, compassion, and spirit.

—Peggy & Michael Ackerman

Contents

Reservation service organizations appear here in boldface type.

FLORIDA

Reservation service organizations appear here in boldface type.

Reservation service organizations appear here in boldface type.

Reservation service organizations appear here in boldface type.

Reservation service organizations appear here in boldface type.

Reservation service organizations appear here in boldface type.

Reservation service organizations appear here in boldface type.

Reservation service organizations appear here in boldface type.

Reservation service organizations appear here in boldface type.

Preface

If you are familiar with earlier editions of *Bed & Breakfast U.S.A.*, you know that this book has always been a labor of love. It is very gratifying to see how it has grown from the first sixteen-page edition, titled *Guide to Tourist Homes and Guest Houses*, which was published in 1975 and contained forty individual listings. Twenty-one years later, the nineteenth revised edition lists 1,051 homes and 101 reservation agencies, giving travelers access to over 12,000 host homes. This spectacular success indicates how strongly the concept of the guest house has captured the fancy of both proprietors and travelers. In fact, the original book became so big, we divided it into three separate books in 1996.

Although we do not list grand hotels, rental properties, or campground compounds, we do list an exciting amount of smaller bed & breakfasts and inns, and a small percentage of higher-priced inns. But make no mistake—we still dedicate most of this book to meeting the needs of our readers, which will be to list only those B&Bs with reasonably priced accommodations. In the years of doing this book, we have found that you can pay a reasonable amount of money and enjoy the bed & breakfast experience just as much as a very chic inn, and in most cases enjoy more personal contact with your hosts. We have given a great deal of thought to what we feel a B&B should be and are focusing on our original definition: an owner-occupied residence with breakfast included at a fair rate, where a visitor is made to feel more like a welcome guest than a paying customer.

Because of personal experience and letters from our readers, *Bed & Breakfast U.S.A., Southeast* will not except properties where the host does not reside on the premises, rental properties, B&Bs with more than fifteen guest rooms, rates exceeding $35 where six people or more share a bath, rates exceeding $45 where five people share a bath, or rates without breakfast included. Higher-priced B&Bs and inns will only be included according to space availability.

This is not a project for which listings have been compiled just for the sake of putting a book together; bigger isn't necessarily better. *Bed & Breakfast U.S.A., Southeast* is a product of a membership organization whose credo is "Comfort, cleanliness, cordiality and fairness of cost." We solicit and rely on the comments of our readers. For this purpose, we include a tear-out form on page 233. We genuinely appreciate comments from guests—negative if necessary, positive when warranted—and we do follow up. We want to hear from you!

All of the B&Bs and inns described in this book are members of the Tourist House Association of America, Inc., Greentown, Pennsylvania 18426, phone: (888) 888-4068. THAA dues are $40 annually.

PEGGY ACKERMAN
Tourist House Association of America, Inc.

January 1997

Even after careful editing and proofreading, errors occasionally occur. We regret any inconvenience to our readers and members.

Acknowledgments

A special thanks to all the travel writers and reporters who have brought us to the attention of their audiences.

To my family, Mike Ackerman, Travis Kali, and Justin Ackerman, the three men in my life—thank you for all the encouragement and support you have shown; to Mary Kristyak Donnelly, a superb mother, grandmother, and best friend—I admire you so; to Bill Donnelly, dad and joke teller; to the grandmothers, Ann Revits and Helen Kristyak.

A final note of thanks to my editor, Leslie Jay, for her deeply appreciated assistance. Never too much, always a smile. And to editor Julia Moskin, I'm sad you're leaving. Thank you for all your help.

1

Introduction

Bed and Breakfast is the popular lodging alternative to hotel high-rises and motel monotony. B&Bs are either private residences where the owners rent spare bedrooms to travelers, or small, family-operated inns offering a special kind of warm, personal hospitality. Whether large or small, B&Bs will make you feel more like a welcome guest than a paying customer.

The custom of opening one's home to travelers dates back to the earliest days of Colonial America. Hotels and inns were few and far between in those days, and wayfarers relied on the kindness of strangers to provide a bed for the night. Which is why, perhaps, there is hardly a Colonial-era home in the mid-Atlantic states that does not boast: "George Washington Slept Here!"

During the Depression, the tourist home provided an economic advantage to both the traveler and the host. Travelers always drove through the center of town; there were no superhighways to bypass local traffic. A house with a sign in the front yard reading "Tourists" or "Guests" indicated that a traveler could rent a room for the night and have a cup of coffee before leaving in the morning. The usual cost for this arrangement was $2. The money represented needed income for the proprietor as well as the opportunity to chat with an interesting visitor.

In the 1950s, the country guest house became a popular alternative to the costly hotels in resort areas. The host compensated for the lack of hotel amenities, such as private bathrooms, by providing comfortable bedrooms and bountiful breakfasts at a modest price. The visitors enjoyed the home-away-from-home atmosphere; the hosts were pleased to have paying houseguests.

The incredible growth in international travel that has occurred over the past 30 years has provided yet another stimulus. Millions of Americans now vacation annually in Europe, and travelers have become enchanted with the bed and breakfast concept so popular in England, Ireland, and other parts of the Continent. In fact, many well-traveled Americans are delighted to learn that we "finally" have B&Bs here. But, as you now know, they were always here—just a rose by another name.

Bed and breakfasts are for:

- **Parents of college kids:** Tuition is costly enough without the added expense of Parents' Weekends. Look for a B&B near campus.
- **Parents traveling with children:** A family living room, playroom, or backyard is preferable to the confines of a motel room.
- **"Parents" of pets:** Many proprietors will allow your well-behaved darling to come, too. This can cut down on the expense and trauma of kenneling Fido.
- **Business travelers:** Being "on the road" can be lonely and expensive. It's so nice, after a day's work, to return to a home-away-from-home.
- **Women traveling alone:** Friendship and conversation are the natural ingredients of a guest house.
- **Skiers:** Lift prices are lofty, so it helps to save some money on lodging. Many mountain homes include home-cooked meals in your room rate.
- **Students:** A visit with a family is a pleasant alternative to camping or the local "Y."
- **Visitors from abroad:** Cultural exchanges are often enhanced by a host who can speak your language.
- **Carless travelers:** If you plan to leave the auto at home, it's nice to know that many B&Bs are convenient to public transportation. Hosts will often arrange to meet your bus, plane, or train for a nominal fee.
- **Schoolteachers and retired persons:** Exploring out-of-the-way places is fun and will save you money.
- **History buffs:** Many B&Bs are located in areas important to our country's past. A number have the distinction of being listed on the National Register of Historic Places.
- **Sports fans:** Tickets to championship games are expensive. A stay at a B&B helps to defray the cost of attending out-of-town events.
- **Antique collectors:** Many hosts have lovely personal collections, and nearby towns are filled with undiscovered antique shops.
- **House hunters:** It's a practical way of trying out a neighborhood.
- **Relocating corporate executives:** It's more comfortable to stay in a real home while you look for a permanent residence. Hosts will often give more practical advice than professional realtors.
- **Relatives of hospitalized patients:** Many B&Bs are located near major hospitals. Hosts will offer tea and sympathy when visiting hours are over.
- **Convention and seminar attendees:** Staying at a nearby B&B is less expensive than checking into a hotel.

And everyone else who has had it up to here with plastic motel monotony!

What It Is Like to Be a Guest in a B&B

The B&B descriptions provided in this book will help you choose the places that have the greatest appeal to you. A firsthand insight into local culture awaits you; imagine the advantage of arriving in New York City or San Francisco and having an insider to help you sidestep the tourist traps and direct you to that special restaurant or discount store. Or explore the countryside, where fresh air and home-cooked meals beckon. Your choice is as wide as the U.S.A.

Each bed and breakfast listed offers personal contact, a real advantage in unfamiliar environments. You may not have a phone in your room or a TV on the dresser. You may even have to pad down the hall in robe and slippers to take a shower, but you'll discover that little things count.

- In Williamsburg, Virginia, a visitor from Germany opted to stay at a B&B to help improve her conversational English. When the hostess saw that she was having difficulty understanding directions, she personally escorted her on a tour of Old Williamsburg.
- In Pennsylvania, the guests mistakenly arrived a week prior to their stated reservation date and the B&B was full. The hostess made a call to a neighbor who accommodated the couple. (By the way, the neighbor has now become a B&B host!)
- In New York City, a guest was an Emmy Award nominee and arrived with his tuxedo in need of pressing. The hostess pressed it; when he claimed his award over nationwide TV, he looked well groomed!

Expect the unexpected, such as a pot of brewed coffee upon your arrival, or fresh flowers on a nightstand. At the very least, count on our required standard of cleanliness and comfort. Although we haven't personally visited all of the places listed, they have all been highly recommended by chambers of commerce or former guests. We have either spoken to or corresponded with all of the proprietors; they are a friendly group of people who enjoy having visitors. They will do all in their power to make your stay memorable.

Our goal is to enable the traveler to crisscross the country and stay only at B&Bs along the way. To achieve this, your help is vital. Please take a moment to write us of your experiences; we will follow up on every suggestion. Your comments will serve as the yardstick by which we can measure the quality of our accommodations. For your convenience, an evaluation form is included at the back of this book.

Cost of Accommodations

Bed and Breakfast, in the purest sense, is a private home, often referred to as a "homestay," where the owners rent their spare bedrooms to travelers. These are the backbone of this book.

However, American ingenuity has enhanced this simple idea to include more spectacular homes, mansions, small inns, and intimate hotels. With few exceptions, the proprietor is the host and lives on the premises.

There is a distinction between B&B homestays and B&B inns. Inns are generally defined as a business and depend upon revenue from guests to pay expenses. They usually have six or more guest rooms, and may have a restaurant that is open to the public. The tariff at inns is usually higher than at a homestay because the owners must pay the mortgage, running expenses, and staff, whether or not guests come.

Whether plain or fancy, all B&Bs are based on the concept that people are tired of the plastic monotony of motels and are disappointed that even the so-called budget motels can be quite expensive. Travelers crave the personal touch, and they sincerely enjoy "visiting" rather than just "staying."

Prices vary accordingly. There are places listed in this book where lovely lodging may be had for as low as $40 a night, and others that feature an overnight stay with a gourmet breakfast in a canopied bed for $95. Whatever the price, if you see the sign ✪, it means that the B&B has guaranteed its rates through 1997 to holders of this book, so be sure to mention it when you call or write! (If there is a change in ownership, the guarantee may not apply. Please notify us in writing if any host fails to honor the guaranteed rate.)

Accommodations vary in price depending upon the locale and the season. Peak season usually refers to the availability of skiing in winter and water sports in summer; in the Sunbelt states, winter months are usually the peak season. Some B&Bs require a two-night weekend minimum during peak periods, and three nights on holiday weekends. Off-season rate schedules are usually reduced. Resorts and major cities are generally more expensive than out-of-the-way places. However, B&Bs are always less expensive than hotels and motels of equivalent caliber in the same area. A weekly rate is usually less expensive than a daily rate. Special reductions are sometimes given to families (occupying two rooms) or senior citizens. Whenever reduced rates are available, you will find this noted in the individual listings.

Meals

Breakfast: *Continental* refers to fruit or juice, rolls, and a hot beverage. Many hosts pride themselves on home-baked breads, homemade preserves, as well as imported teas and cakes, so their Continental breakfast may be quite deluxe. Several hosts have regular jobs outside the home, so you may have to adjust your schedule to theirs. A "full" breakfast includes fruit, cereal and/or eggs, breakfast meats, breads, and a hot beverage. The table is set family-style and is often the highlight of a B&B's hospitality. Either a Continental breakfast or full breakfast is included in the room rate unless otherwise specified.

Other Meals: If listed as "available," you can be assured that the host takes pride in his or her cooking skills. The prices for lunch or dinner are usually reasonable but are not included in the quoted room rate unless clearly specified as "included."

Making Reservations

- Reservations are a MUST or you may risk missing out on the accommodations of your choice. Reserve *early* and confirm with a deposit equal to one night's stay. If you call to inquire about reservations, please remember the difference in time zones. When dialing outside of your area, remember to dial the digit "1" before the area code.
- Many individual B&Bs now accept charge cards. This information is indicated in the listings by the symbols MC for MasterCard, AMEX for American Express, etc. A few have a surcharge for this service, so inquire as to the policy.
- Cash or traveler's checks are the accepted method of paying for your stay. Be sure to inquire whether or not tax is included in the rates quoted so that you will know exactly how much your lodging will cost.

- Rates are based on single or double occupancy of a room as quoted. Expect that an extra person(s) in the room will be charged a small additional fee. Inquire when making your reservation what the charge will be.
- If a listing indicates that children or pets are welcome, it is expected that they will be well behaved. All of our hosts take pride in their homes and it would be unfair to subject them to circumstances in which their possessions might be abused or the other houseguests disturbed by an unruly child or animal.
- Please note that many hosts have their own resident pets. If you are allergic or don't care to be around animals, inquire before making a reservation.
- In homes where smoking is permitted, do check to see if it is restricted in any of the rooms. Most hosts object to cigars.
- Where listings indicate that social drinking is permitted, it usually refers to your bringing your own beverages. Most hosts will provide ice; many will allow you to chill mixers in the refrigerator, and others offer complimentary wine and snacks. A few B&B inns have licenses to sell liquor. Any drinking should not be excessive.
- If Yes is indicated in the listings for airport/station pickup, it means that the host will meet your plane, bus, or train for a fee.
- Feel free to request brochures and local maps so that you can better plan for your visit.
- Do try to fit in with the host's house rules. You are on vacation; he or she isn't!
- A reservation form is included at the back of this book for your convenience; just tear it out and send it in to the B&B of your choice.

Cancellations

Cancellation policies vary from one B&B to another, so be sure to read the fine print on the reservation form. Many require a 15-day notice to refund the entire deposit, after which they will refund only if the room is rebooked. When a refund is due, most keep a processing fee and return the balance. A few keep the deposit and apply it to a future stay.

While these policies may seem harsh, please keep in mind that B&Bs are not hotels, which commonly overbook and where no-show guests can easily be replaced. Your host may have turned down a prospective guest, and may have bought special breakfast food in anticipation of your visit and should not be penalized. If you feel you've been unfairly treated in a cancellation situation, please do let us know.

B&B Reservation Services

There are many host families who prefer not to be individually listed in a book, and would rather have their houseguests referred by a coordinating agency. The organizations listed in this book are all members of the Tourist House Association. They all share our standards regarding the suitability of the host home as to cordiality, cleanliness, and comfort.

The majority do a marvelous job of matching host and guest according to age, interests, language, and any special requirements. To get the best match, it is practical to give them as much time as possible to find the host home best tailored to your needs.

Many have prepared descriptive pamphlets describing the homes on their rosters, the areas in which the homes are located, and information regarding special things to see and do. *Send a self-addressed, stamped, business-size envelope to receive a descriptive directory by return mail along with a reservation form for you to complete.* When returning the form, you will be asked to select the home or homes listed in the brochure that most appeal to you. (The homes are usually given a code number for reference.) The required deposit should accompany your reservation. Upon receipt, the coordinator will make the reservation and advise you of the name, address, telephone number, and travel instructions for your host.

A few agencies prepare a descriptive directory and *include* the host's name, address, and telephone number so that you can contact the host and make your arrangements directly. They charge anywhere from $2 to $11 for the directory.

Several agencies are *membership* organizations, charging guests an annual fee ranging from $5 to $25 per person. Their descriptive directories are free to members and many of them maintain toll-free telephone numbers for reservations.

Most reservation services have a specific geographic focus. The coordinators are experts in the areas they represent. They can often make arrangements for car rentals, theater tickets, and touring suggestions, and offer information in planning a trip best suited to your interests.

Most work on a commission basis with the host, and that fee is included in the room rates quoted in each listing. Some make a surcharge for a one-night stay; others require a two- or three-night minimum stay for holiday periods or special events. Some will accept a credit card for the reservation, but the balance due must be paid to the host in cash or traveler's checks.

All of their host homes offer a Continental breakfast, and some may include a full breakfast.

Many reservation services in the larger cities have, in addition to the traditional B&Bs, a selection of apartments, condominiums, and houses *without hosts in residence.* This may be appealing to those travelers anticipating an extended stay in a particular area.

Statewide services are listed first in the section for each state. City or regionally based organizations are listed first under the heading for that area. For a complete description of their services, look them up under the city and state where they're based.

NOTE: When calling, do so during normal business hours (for that time zone), unless otherwise stated. Collect calls are not accepted.

2

How to Start Your Own B&B

What It's Like to Be a Host

Hosts are people who like the idea of accommodating travelers and sharing their home and the special features of their area with them. They are people who have houses too large for their personal needs and like the idea of supplementing their income by having people visit. For many, it's a marvelous way of meeting rising utility and maintenance costs. For young families, it is a way of buying and keeping that otherwise-too-large house, as well as a way of furnishing it, since many of the furnishings may be tax deductible. Another advantage is that many state and local governments have recognized the service that some host families perform. In browsing through this book you will note that some homes are listed on the National Historic Register. Some state governments allow owners of landmark and historical houses a special tax advantage if they are used for any business purpose. Check with the Historical Preservation Society in your state for details.

If you have bedrooms to spare, if you sincerely like having overnight guests, if your home is clean and comfortable, this is an opportunity to consider. It is a unique business because *you* set the time of the visit and the length of stay. (Guest houses are not boarding homes.) You invite the guests at *your* convenience, and the extras, such as meals, are entirely up to you. You can provide a cup of coffee, complete meals, or just a room and shared bath. Remember that your income may be erratic and should not be depended upon to pay for monthly bills. However, it can afford you some luxuries.

Although the majority of hosts are women, many couples are finding pleasure in this joint venture. The general profile of a typical host is a friendly, outgoing, flexible person who is proud of his or her home and hometown. The following information and suggestions represent a guideline to consider in deciding whether becoming a B&B host is really for you.

There are no set rules for the location, type, or style of a B&B. Apartments, condos, farmhouses, town houses, beach houses, vacation cottages, houseboats, mansions, as well as the traditional one-family dwelling are all appropriate. The important thing is for the host to be on the premises. The setting may be urban, rural, or suburban, near public transportation or in the hinterlands. Location is only important if you want to have guests every night. Areas where tourism is popular, such as resort areas or major cities, are often busier than out-of-the-way places. However, if a steady stream of visitors is not that important or even desirable, it doesn't matter where you are. People will contact you if your rates are reasonable and if there is something to see and do in your area, or if it is near a major transportation route.

Setting Rates

Consider carefully four key factors in setting your rates: location, private versus shared bath, type of breakfast, and your home itself.

Location: If you reside in a traditional resort or well-touristed area, near a major university or medical center, or in an urban hub or gateway city, your rates should be at least 40 percent lower than those of the area's major motels or hotels. If you live in an out-of-the-way location, your rates must be extremely reasonable. If your area has a "season"—snow sports in winter, water sports in summer—offer off-season rates when these attractions are not available. Reading through this book will help you to see what the going rate is in a situation similar to yours.

The Bath: You are entitled to charge more for a room with private bath. If the occupants of two rooms share one bath, the rate should be less. If more than five people must share one bathroom, you may have complaints, unless your rates are truly inexpensive.

The Breakfast: Figure the approximate cost of your ingredients, plus something for your time. Allow about $2 to $3 for a Continental breakfast, $4 to $5 for a full American breakfast, and then *include* it in the rate.

Your Home: Plan on charging a fair and reasonable rate for a typical B&B home, one that is warm and inviting, clean and comfortable. If your home is exceptionally luxurious, with king-size beds, Jacuzzi baths, tennis courts, or hot tubs, you will find guests who are willing to pay a premium. If your home is over 75 years old, well restored, with lots of antiques, you may also be able to charge a higher rate.

The Three Bs—Bed, Breakfast, and Bath

The Bedroom: The ideal situation for a prospective host is the possession of a house too large for current needs. The children may be away at college most of the year or may have left permanently, leaving behind their bedrooms and, in some cases, an extra bath. Refurbishing these rooms does not mean refurnishing; an extraordinary investment need not be contemplated for receiving guests. Take a long, hard look at the room. With a little imagination and a little monetary outlay, could it be changed into a bedroom *you'd* be pleased to spend the night in? Check it out *before* you go any further. Are the beds comfortable? Is the carpet clean? Are the walls attractive? Do the curtains or shades need attention? Are there sturdy hangers in the closet? Would emptying the closet and bureau be an impossible task? Is there a good light to read by? A writing table and comfortable chair? Peek under the bed to see if there are dust balls or old magazines tucked away. While relatives and friends would "understand" if things weren't perfect, a paying guest is entitled to cleanliness and comfort.

Equip the guest bureau or dresser with a good mirror, and provide a comfortable chair and good reading light. The clothes closet should be free of your family's clothing and storage items, and stocked with firm, plastic hangers, a few skirt hangers, and some hooks. Sachets hung on the rod will chase musty odors. Provide room-darkening shades or blinds on the windows. And, if your house is located on a busy street, it is wise to have your guest bedrooms in the rear. Paying guests are entitled to a good night's rest! If your tap water is not tasty, it is thoughtful to supply bottled water.

If the idea of sprucing up the room has you overwhelmed, forget the idea and continue to be a guest rather than a host! If, however, a little "spit and polish," replacement of lumpy mattresses and sagging springs, and freshening the room in general present no problem, continue!

Mattresses should be firm, covered with a mattress pad, attractive linens, and bedspread. Although seconds are OK, good-quality linens are a wise investment, since cheap sheets tend to pill. Offer a selection of pillows of various firmnesses—a choice of down or fiberfill is the ultimate in consideration! Twin beds are often preferred, since many people do not wish to share a bed. Sofa beds are really not comfortable and should be avoided. Is there a bedside lamp and night table on each side of the bed? Bulbs should be at least 75 watts for comfortable reading. A luggage rack is convenient for guests and keeps the bedspread clean. Provide a varied assortment of books, current magazines in a rack, a local newspaper, and some information on what's doing in your town along with a map. If yours is a shared-bath accommodation, do provide a well-lit mirror and convenient electric outlet for makeup and shaving purposes. It will take the pressure off the bathroom! A fresh thermos of ice water and drinking glasses placed on an attractive dresser tray is always appreciated. Put it in the room while the guest is out to dinner, right next to the dish of hard candy or fruit. A fancy candlestick is a pretty accessory and a useful object in case of a power failure. Dresser drawers should be clean and lined with fresh paper. A sachet, flashlight, and a pad and pencil are thoughtful touches. For safety's sake, prohibit smoking in the bedroom. Besides, the odor of tobacco clings forever. Always spray the bedroom with air freshener a few minutes before the guest arrives. On warm or humid days, turn on the air conditioner as well.

From time to time sleep in each guest room yourself. It's the best test.

The Breakfast: Breakfast time can be the most pleasant part of a guest's stay. It is at the breakfast table with you and the other guests that suggestions are made as to what to see and do, and exchanges of experiences are enjoyed. From a guest's point of view, the only expected offering is what is known as a Continental breakfast, which usually consists of juice, roll, and coffee or tea.

Breakfast fare is entirely up to you. If you are a morning person who whips out of bed at the crack of dawn with special recipes for muffins dancing in your head, muffins to be drenched with your homemade preserves followed by eggs Benedict, an assortment of imported coffees or exotic teas—hop to it! You will play to a most appreciative audience. If, however, morning represents an awful intrusion on sleep, and the idea of talking to anyone before noon is difficult, the least you should do is to prepare the breakfast table the night before with the necessary mugs, plates, and silverware. Fill the electric coffeepot and leave instructions that the first one up should plug it in; you can even hook it up to a timer so that it will brew automatically!

Most of us fall somewhere in between these two extremes. Remember that any breakfast at "home" is preferable to getting dressed, getting into a car, and driving to some coffee shop. Whether you decide upon a Continental breakfast or a full American breakfast, consisting of juice or fruit, cereal or eggs, possibly bacon or sausage, toast, rolls, and coffee or tea, is up to you. It is most important that whatever the fare, it be included in your room rate. It is most awkward, especially after getting to know and like your guests, to present an additional charge for breakfast.

With so many of us watching calories, caffeine, and cholesterol, be prepared to offer unsweetened and/or whole grain breads, oat-bran cereals and muffins, and brewed decaf coffee or tea. It is also thoughtful to inquire about your guests' dietary restrictions and allergies. Whatever you serve, do have your table attractively set.

Some Suggestions

- Don't have a messy kitchen. If you have pets, make sure their food dishes are removed after they've eaten. If you have cats, make sure they don't walk along the countertops, and be certain that litter boxes are cleaned without fail. Sparkling clean surroundings are far more important than the decor.
- Let guests know when breakfast will be served. Check to see if they have any allergies, diet restrictions, or dislikes. Vary the menu if guests are staying more than one night.
- Do offer one nonsweet bread for breakfast.
- Consider leaving a breakfast order sheet in each room with a request that it be returned before guests retire. It might read:

We serve breakfast between 7 AM and 10 AM. Please check your preference and note the time at which you plan to eat.

☐ Coffee ☐ Tea ☐ Decaf ☐ Milk ☐ Toast ☐ Muffins
☐ Sweet Rolls ☐ Orange Juice ☐ Tomato Juice ☐ Fruit Cup

The Bath: This really is the third B in B&B. If you are blessed with an extra bathroom for the exclusive use of a guest, that's super. If guests will have to share the facilities with others, that really presents no problem. If it's being shared with your family, the family must always be "last in line." Be sure that they are aware of the guest's importance; the guest, paying or otherwise, always comes first. No retainers, used Band-Aids, or topless toothpaste tubes are to be carelessly left on the sink. The tub, shower, floor, and toilet bowl are to be squeaky clean. The mirrors and chrome should sparkle, and a supply of toilet tissue, fresh soap, and unfrayed towels goes a long way in reflecting a high standard of cleanliness. Make sure that the grout between tiles is free of mildew and that the shower curtain is unstained; add nonskid tape to the tub. Cracked ceilings should be repaired. Paint should be free of chips, and if your bath is wallpapered, make certain no loose edges mar its beauty.

Although it is your responsibility to check out the bath at least twice a day, most guests realize that in a share-the-bath situation they should leave the room ready for the next person's use. It is a thoughtful reminder for you to leave tub cleanser, a cleaning towel or sponge, and bathroom deodorant handy for this purpose. A wastepaper basket, paper towels, and paper cups should be part of your supplies. Needless to say, your hot water and septic systems should be able to accommodate the number of guests you'll have without being overtaxed. Call the plumber to fix any clogged drains or dripping faucets. Make sure that there are enough towel bars and hooks to accommodate the towels of all guests. Extra bathroom touches:

- Use liquid soap dispensers in lieu of bar soap on the sink.
- Provide a place for guests' personal toilet articles; shelves add convenience and eliminate clutter.
- Give different colored towels to each guest.
- Supply each guest room with its own bath soap in a covered soap dish.
- Provide guests with one-size-fits-all terry robes.

The B&B Business

Money Matters: Before embarking upon any business, it's a good idea to discuss it with an accountant and possibly an attorney. Since you'll be using your home for a business enterprise there are things with which they are familiar that are important for you to know. For instance, you may want to incorporate, so find out what the pros and cons are. Ask about depreciation. Deductible business expenses may include refurbishing, furnishings, supplies, printing costs, postage, etc. An accountant will be able to guide you with a simple system of record keeping. Accurate records will help you analyze income and expense, and show if you are breaking even or operating at a profit or a loss.

Taxes: Contact your state department of taxation requesting specific written information regarding tax collection and payment schedules. Get a sales tax number from your county clerk. If you rent rooms less than 15 days a year, you need not report the B&B income on your federal return. Income after the fourteenth day is taxable, and you can take deductions and depreciation allowances against it. If the revenues from running the B&B are insignificant, you can call it "hobby income" and avoid taxes. However, you can't qualify as a business and may lose other tax advantages.

Record Keeping: Open a B&B checking account and use it to pay expenses and to deposit all income, including sales tax associated with the B&B. Write checks whenever possible for purchases; get dated receipts when you can. Estimate the cost of serving breakfast and multiply it by the number of guests you feed annually; keep track of extra expenses for household supplies and utilities.

The Case for Credit Cards: Many guests prefer to stay now and pay later; business travelers like the easy record keeping for their expense sheets. Even if you don't wish to accept them on a regular basis, credit cards give you the opportunity to take a deposit over the phone when there isn't time to receive one by mail. The cost is negligible, generally 4 percent.

If you do accept a last-minute reservation without a credit card number to guarantee it, make certain the caller understands that if they don't show up, and you have held the room for them, you will have lost a night's rent. You may also remind the caller that if they aren't there by a mutually agreed upon time, you may rent the room to someone else. Needless to say, it is equally important for you to remain at home to receive the guests or to be on hand for a phone call should they get lost en route to your home.

Insurance: It is important to call your insurance broker. Some homeowner policies have a clause covering "an occasional overnight paying guest." See if you will be protected under your existing coverage and, if not, what the additional premium would be.

Every home should be equipped with smoke detectors and fire extinguishers. All fire hazards should be eliminated; stairways and halls should be well lit and kept free of clutter. If you haven't already done so, immediately post prominently the emergency numbers for the fire department, police, and ambulance service.

Safety Reminders: Equip guest bedrooms and bathrooms with nightlights. Keep a flashlight (in working order!) in each bedroom, in case of power failure. Bathrooms should have nonslip surfaces in the tub and shower, and handholds should be installed in bathtubs. Keep a well-stocked first aid kit handy and know how to use it. Learn the Heimlich Maneuver and CPR (cardiopulmonary resuscitation). Periodically test smoke detectors and fire extinguishers to make certain they are in working order.

Regulations: If you have read this far and are still excited about the concept of running a B&B, there are several steps to take at this point. As of this writing, there don't seem to be any specific laws governing B&Bs. Since guests are generally received on an irregular basis, B&Bs do not come under the same laws governing hotels and motels. And since B&Bs aren't inns where emphasis is on food rather than on lodging, no comparison can really be made in that regard either. As the idea grows, laws and regulations will probably be passed. Refer to the back of *Bed & Breakfast U.S.A., Southeast* to write to your state's office of tourism for information. The address and phone number are listed for your convenience. You might even call or write to a few B&Bs in your state and ask the host about his or her experience in this regard. Most hosts will be happy to give you the benefit of their experience, but keep in mind that they are busy people and it would be wise to limit your intrusion upon their time.

If you live in a traditional, residential area and you are the first in your neighborhood to consider operating a B&B, it would be prudent to examine closely the character of houses nearby. Do physicians, attorneys, accountants, or psychologists maintain offices in their residences? Do dressmakers, photographers, cosmeticians, or architects receive clients in their homes? These professions are legally accepted in the most prestigious communities as "customary house occupations." Bed and breakfast has been tested in many communities where the question was actually brought to court. In towns from La Jolla, California, to Croton-on-Hudson, New York, bed and breakfast has been approved and accepted.

Zoning boards are not always aware of the wide acceptance of the B&B concept. Possibly the best evidence that you could present to them is a copy of *Bed & Breakfast U.S.A., Southeast,* which indicates that it is an accepted practice throughout the entire country. It illustrates the caliber of the neighborhoods, the beauty of the homes, and the fact that many professionals are also hosts. Reassure the zoning board that you will accept guests only by advance reservation. You will not display any exterior signs to attract attention to your home. You will keep your home and grounds properly maintained, attractive, and in no way detract from the integrity of your neighborhood. You will direct guests to proper parking facilities and do nothing to intrude upon the privacy of your neighbors.

After all, there is little difference between the visit of a family friend and a B&B guest, because that is the spirit and essence of a B&B. Just as a friend would make prior arrangements to be a houseguest, so will a B&B guest make a reservation in advance. Neither would just drop in for an overnight stay. We are happy to share letters from hosts attesting to the high caliber, honesty, and integrity of B&B guests that come as a result of reading about their accommodations in this book. There are over 12,000 B&Bs extending our kind of hospitality throughout the United States, and the number is increasing geometrically every day.

You should also bring along a copy of *Bed & Breakfast U.S.A., Southeast* when you go to visit the local chamber of commerce. Most of them are enthusiastic, because additional visitors mean extra business for local restaurants, shops, theaters, and businesses. This is a good time to inquire what it would cost to join the chamber of commerce.

The Name: The naming of your B&B is most important and will take some time and consideration because this is the moment when dreams become reality. It will be used on your brochures, stationery, and bills. (If you decide to incorporate, the corporation needs a name!) It should somehow be descriptive of the atmosphere you wish to convey.

Brochure: Once you have given a name to your house, design a brochure. The best ones include a reservation form and can be mailed to your prospective guests. The brochure should contain the name of your B&B, address, phone number, best time to call, your name, a brief description of your home, its ambience, a brief history of the house if it is old, the number of guest rooms, whether or not baths are shared, the type of breakfast served, rates, required deposit, minimum stay requirement if any, dates when you'll be closed, and your cancellation policy. Although widely used, the phrase "Rates subject to change without notice" should be avoided. Rather, state the specific dates when the rates will be valid. A deposit of one night's stay is acceptable, and the promise of a full refund if cancellation is received at least two weeks prior to arrival is typical. If you have reduced rates for a specific length of stay, for families, for senior citizens, etc., mention it.

The Rate Sheet should be a separate insert so that if rates change, the entire brochure need not be discarded. Mention your smoking policy. If you do allow smoking inside the house, do you reserve any bedrooms for nonsmokers? Don't forget to mention the ages of your children, and describe any pets in residence. If you don't accept a guest's pet, be prepared to supply the name, address, and phone number of a reliable local kennel.

If you can converse in a foreign language, say so, because many visitors from abroad seek out B&Bs; it's a marvelous plus to be able to chat in their native tongue. Include your policy regarding children, pets, or smokers, and whether you offer the convenience of a guest refrigerator or barbecue. It is helpful to include directions from a major route and a simple map for finding your home. It's a good idea to include a line or two about yourself and your interests, and do mention what there is to see and do in the area as well as proximity to any major university. A line drawing of your house is a good investment since the picture can be used not only on the brochure but on your stationery, postcards, and greeting cards as well. If you can't have this taken care of locally, write the Tourist House Association. We have a service that can handle it for you.

Take your ideas to a reliable printer for his professional guidance. Don't forget to keep the receipt for the printing bill since this is a business expense.

Confirmation Letter: Upon receipt of a paid reservation, do send out a letter confirming it. You can design a form letter and have it offset printed by a printer, since the cost of doing so is usually nominal. Include the dates of the stay; number of people expected; the rate, including tax; the cancellation policy; as well as explicit directions by car and, if applicable, by public transportation. A simple map reflecting the exact location of your home in relation to major streets and highways is most useful. It is a good idea to ask your guests to call you if they will be traveling and unavailable by phone for the week prior to their expected arrival. You might even want to include any of the house rules regarding smoking, pets, or whatever.

Successful Hosting

The Advantage of Hosting: The nicest part of being a B&B host is that you aren't required to take guests every day of the year. Should there be times when having guests would not be convenient, you can always say you're full and try to arrange an alternate date. But most important, keep whatever date you reserve. It is an excellent idea at the time reservations are accepted to ask for the name and telephone number of an emergency contact should you have to cancel unexpectedly. However, *never* have a guest come to a locked door. If an emergency arises and you cannot reach your prospective guests in time, do make arrangements for someone to greet them, and make alternate arrangements so that they can be accommodated.

House Rules: While you're in the thinking stage, give some thought to the rules you'd like your guests to adhere to. The last thing you want for you or your family is to feel uncomfortable in your own home. Make a list of House Rules concerning arrival and departure during the guests' stay, and specify when breakfast is served. If you don't want guests coming home too late, say so. Most hosts like to lock up at a certain hour at night, so arrange for an extra key for night owls. If that makes you uncomfortable, have a curfew on your House Rules list. If smoking disturbs you, confine the area where it's permitted.

Some guests bring a bottle of their favorite beverage and enjoy a drink before going out to dinner. Many hosts enjoy a cocktail hour too, and often provide cheese and crackers to share with guests. B&Bs cannot sell drinks to guests since this would require licensing. If you'd rather no drinks be consumed in your home, say so.

Many hosts don't mind accommodating a well-behaved pet. If you don't mind, or have pets of your own, discuss this with your guests before they pack Fido's suitcase. Your House Rules can even be included in your brochure. That way, both host and guest are aware of each other's likes and dislikes, and no hard feelings are made.

Entertaining: One of the most appealing features of being a guest at a B&B is the opportunity to visit in the evening with the hosts. After a day of sightseeing or business, it is most relaxing and pleasant to sit around the living room and chat. For many hosts, this is the most enjoyable part of having guests. However, if you are accommodating several people on a daily basis, entertaining can be tiring. Don't feel you'll be offending anyone by excusing yourself to attend to your own family or personal needs. The situation can be easily handled by having a room to which you can retreat, and offering your guests the living room, den, or other area for games, books, magazines, and perhaps the use of a television or bridge table. Most guests enjoy just talking to one another since this is the main idea of staying at a B&B.

The Telephone: This is a most important link between you and your prospective guests. As soon as possible, have your telephone number included under your B&B name in the white pages. It is a good idea to be listed in the appropriate section in your telephone directory yellow pages. If your home phone is used for a lot of personal calls, ask the local telephone company about call-waiting service, or think about installing a separate line for your B&B. If you are out a lot, give some thought to using a telephone answering device to explain your absence and time of return, and record the caller's message. There is nothing more frustrating to a prospective guest than to call and get a constant busy signal, or no answer at all. Request that the caller leave his or her name and address so that you can mail a reservation form. This will help eliminate the necessity of having to return long-distance calls. If the caller wants further information, he or she will call again at the time you said you'd be home.

B&B guests don't expect a phone in the guest room. However, there are times when they might want to use your phone for a long-distance call. In your House Rules list, suggest that any such calls be charged to their home telephone. Business travelers often have telephone charge cards for this purpose. In either case, you should keep a telephone record book and timer near your instrument. Ask the caller to enter the city called, telephone number, and length of call. Thus, you will have an accurate record should a charge be inadvertently added to your bill. Or, if you wish, you can add telephone charges to the guest bill. A telephone operator will quote the cost of the per-minute charge throughout the country for this purpose.

Maid Service: If you have several guest rooms and bathrooms, you may find yourself being a chambermaid as part of the business. Naturally, each guest gets fresh linens upon arrival. If a guest stays up to three days, it isn't expected that bed linen be changed every day. What is expected is that the room be freshened and the bath be cleaned and towels replaced every day. If you don't employ a full-time maid you may want to investigate the possibility of hiring a high school student on a part-time basis to give you a hand with the housekeeping. Many guests, noticing the absence of help, will voluntarily lend a hand, although they have the right to expect some degree of service, particularly if they are paying a premium rate.

Keys: A great many hosts are not constantly home during the day. Some do "hosting" on a part-time basis, while involved with regular jobs. There are times when even full-time hosts have to be away during the day. If guests are to have access to the house while you are not on the premises, make extra keys and attach them to an oversize key chain. It is also wise to take a key deposit of $50 simply to assure return of the key. Let me add that in the 16 years of my personal experience, as well as in the opinions of other hosts, B&B guests are the most honest people you can have. No one has ever had even a washcloth stolen, let alone the family treasures. In fact, it isn't unusual for the guest to leave a small gift after a particularly pleasant visit. On the other hand, guests are sometimes forgetful and leave belongings behind. For this reason it is important for you to have their names and addresses so that you can return their possessions. They will expect to reimburse you for the postage.

Registering Guests: You should keep a regular registration ledger for the guest to complete before checking in. The information should include the full name of each guest, home address, phone number, business address and telephone, and auto license number. It's a good idea to include the name and phone number of a friend or relative in case of an emergency. This information will serve you well for other contingencies, such as the guest leaving some important article behind, an unpaid long-distance phone call, or the rare instance of an unpaid bill. You may prefer to have this information on your guest bill, which should be designed as a two-part carbon form. You will then have a record and the guest has a ready receipt. (Receipts are very important to business travelers!)

Settling the Bill: The average stay in a B&B is two nights. A deposit equal to one night's lodging is the norm; when to collect the balance is up to you. Most guests pay upon leaving, but if they leave so early that the settling of the bill at that time is inconvenient, you can request the payment the previous night. You might want to consider the convenience of accepting a major credit card, but contact the sponsoring company first to see what percentage of your gross is expected for this service. If you find yourself entertaining more business visitors than vacationers, it might be something you should offer. Most travelers are aware that cash or traveler's checks are the accepted modes of payment. Accepting a personal check is rarely risky, but again, it's up to you. You might include your preference in your brochure.

Other Meals: B&B means that only breakfast is served. If you enjoy cooking and would like to offer other meals for a fee, make sure that you investigate the applicable health laws. If you have to install a commercial kitchen, the idea might be too expensive for current consideration. However, allowing guests to store fixings for a quick snack or to use your barbecue can be a very attractive feature for families traveling with children or for people watching their budget. If you can offer this convenience, be sure to mention it in your brochure. (And be sure to add a line to your House Rules that the guest is expected to clean up.) Some hosts keep an extra guest refrigerator on hand for this purpose.

It's an excellent idea to keep menus from your local restaurants on hand. Try to have a good sampling, ranging from moderately priced to expensive dining spots, and find out if reservations are required. Your guests will always rely heavily upon your advice and suggestions. After all, when it comes to your town, you're the authority! It's also a nice idea to keep informed of local happenings that might be of interest to your visitors. A special concert at the university or a local fair or church supper can add an extra dimension to their visit. If parents are visiting with young children they might want to have dinner out without them; try to have a list of available baby-sitters. A selection of guidebooks covering your area is also a nice feature.

The Guest Book: These are available in most stationery and department stores, and it is important that you buy one. It should contain designated space for the date, the name of the guest, home address, and a blank area for the guest's comments. They generally sign the guest book before checking out. The guest book is first of all a permanent record of who came and went. It will give you an idea of what times during the year you were busiest and which times were slow. Second, it is an easy way to keep a mailing list for your Christmas cards and future promotional mailings. You will also find that thumbing through it in years to come will recall some very pleasant people who were once strangers but now are friends.

Advertising: Periodically distribute your brochures to the local university, college, and hospital, since out-of-town visitors always need a place to stay. Let your local caterers know of your existence since wedding guests are often from out of town. If you have a major corporation in your area, drop off a brochure at the personnel office. Even visiting or relocating executives and salespeople enjoy B&Bs. Hotels and motels are sometimes overbooked; it wouldn't hurt to leave your brochure with the manager for times when there's no room for their last-minute guests. Local residents sometimes have to put up extra guests, so it's a good idea to take an ad out in your local school or church newspaper. The cost is usually minimal. Repeat this distribution process from time to time so that you can replenish the supply of brochures.

Check the back of this book for the address of your state tourist office. Write to them, requesting inclusion in any brochures listing B&Bs in the state.

The best advertising is being a member of the Tourist House Association since all member B&Bs are fully described in this book, which is available in bookstores, libraries, and B&Bs throughout the United States and Canada. In addition, it is natural for THAA members to recommend one another when guests inquire about similar accommodations in other areas. The most important reason for keeping your B&B clean, comfortable, and cordial is that we are all judged by what a guest experiences in any individual Tourist House Association home. The best publicity will come from your satisfied guests, who will recommend your B&B to their friends.

Additional Suggestions

Extra Earnings: You might want to consider a few ideas for earning extra money in connection with being a host. If guests consistently praise your muffins and preserves, you might sell attractively wrapped extras as take-home gifts. If you enjoy touring, you can plan and conduct a special outing, off the beaten tourist track, for a modest fee. In major cities, you can do such things as acquiring tickets for theater, concert, or sports events. A supply of *Bed & Breakfast U.S.A., Southeast* for sale to guests is both a source of income and gives every THAA member direct exposure to the B&B market. Think about offering the use of your washer and dryer. You may, if you wish, charge a modest fee to cover the service. Guests who have been traveling are thrilled to do their wash or have it done for them "at home" rather than wasting a couple of hours at the laundromat.

Several hosts tell me that a small gift shop is often a natural offshoot of a B&B. Items for sale might include handmade quilts, pillows, potholders, and knitted items. One host has turned his hobby of woodworking into extra income. He makes lovely picture frames, napkin rings, and footstools that many guests buy as souvenirs to take home. If you plan to do this, check with the Small Business Administration to inquire about such things as a resale license and tax collection; a chamber of commerce can advise in this regard.

Transportation: While the majority of B&B guests arrive by car, there are many who rely on public transportation. Some hosts, for a modest fee, are willing to meet arriving guests at airports, train depots, or bus stations. Do be knowledgeable about local transportation schedules in your area, and be prepared to give explicit directions for your visitors' comings and goings. Have phone numbers handy for taxi service, as well as information on car rentals.

Thoughtful Touches: Guests often write to tell us of their experiences at B&Bs as a result of learning about them through this book. These are some of the special touches that made their visit special: fresh flowers in the guest room; even a single flower in a bud vase is pretty. One hostess puts a foil-wrapped piece of candy on the pillow before the guest returns from dinner. A small decanter of wine and glasses, or a few pieces of fresh fruit in a pretty bowl on the dresser are lovely surprises. A small sewing kit in the bureau is handy. Offer guests the use of your iron and ironing board, rather than having them attempt to use the bed or dresser. Writing paper and envelopes in the desk invite the guest to send a quick note to the folks at home. If your house sketch is printed on it, it is marvelous free publicity. A pre-bed cup of tea for adults and cookies and milk for children are always appreciated.

By the way, keep a supply of guest-comment cards in the desk, both to attract compliments as well as to bring to your attention the flaws in your B&B that should be corrected.

Join the Tourist House Association of America, Inc.: If you are convinced that you want to be a host, and have thoroughly discussed the pros and cons with your family and advisers, complete and return the membership application found at the back of this book. Our dues are $40 annually. The description of your B&B will be part of the next edition of *Bed & Breakfast U.S.A., Southeast,* as well as in the interim supplement between printings. Paid-up members receive one of the three *Bed & Breakfast U.S.A.* regional guides: *Northeast, Southeast,* and *West and Midwest.* You will also receive the THAA's newsletter; regional seminars and conferences are held occasionally and you might enjoy attending. And, as an association, we will have clout should the time come when B&B becomes a recognized industry.

Affiliating with a B&B Reservation Agency: There are 101 agencies listed in our three *Bed & Breakfast U.S.A.* books. If you do not care to advertise your house directly to the public, consider joining one in your area. Membership and reservation fees, as well as the degree of professionalism, vary widely from agency to agency, so do check carefully.

Prediction of Success: Success should not be equated with money alone. If you thoroughly enjoy people, are well organized, enjoy sharing your tidy home without exhausting yourself, then the idea of receiving compensation for the use of an otherwise dormant bedroom will be a big plus. Your visitors will seek relaxing, wholesome surroundings, and unpretentious hosts who open their hearts as well as their homes. Being a B&B host or guest is an exciting, enriching experience.

3

B&B Recipes

The recipes that follow are B&B host originals. They've been chosen because of the raves they've received from satisfied B&B guests. The most important ingredient is the heartful of love that goes into each one.

We always have a good response to our request for favorite breakfast recipes. Although we could not publish them all this time, we will use most of them in future editions.

Hewick B&B Pecan Coffee Cake

- ¾ c. brown sugar
- 1 pkg. of vanilla pudding (not instant)
- 1 tbsp. cinnamon
- 6 tbsp. margarine
- 1 c. pecans
- 1 12-oz. package refrigerated, unbaked dinner rolls

Preheat the oven to 350°F. Mix together the sugar, pudding, and cinnamon and set aside. Grease a Bundt pan with some of the margarine then coat it with the pecans. Put the rolls in the pan and sprinkle the dry mix over them. Dot with the remaining margarine and let the cake stand covered overnight. Remove the cover and bake for 30 minutes.

Hewick B&B, Urbana, Virginia

Baked Apples New England

- 6 baking apples (Cortland or MacIntosh)
- 6 heaping tsp. sugar mixed with 1 tsp. cinnamon
- 3 tbsp. butter
- 2 tbsp. water
- ½ cup raisins (optional)
- 2 tbsp. rum (optional)

Preheat the oven to 350°F. Core the apples and make a slit through the skin with a knife all the way around, stopping about a third of the way from the top; this keeps the apples from exploding. Place the apples in a glass pie plate. Spoon a heaping teaspoon of the sugar-cinnamon mixture into the center of each apple and top with a dab of butter. Pour water into pie plate. Bake 1 hour, basting after 30 minutes. Add water if necessary. You may add raisins to center of apple or a tablespoon of dark rum to the water for a slightly different flavor.

The Captain Ezra Nye House, Sandwich, Massachusetts

Peach Stratta

6 oz. peach baby food, no water added
1½ c. fresh peaches, diced
1⅓ c. sugar
¼ tsp. nutmeg
¾ tsp. cinnamon
4 eggs
7 c. French bread, crusts removed and cubed

Preheat the oven to 350°F. Mix the first six ingredients together until well blended. Pour over the bread and stir gently. Pour the mixture into a 1-quart casserole dish that has been sprayed with vegetable cooking spray. Bake for 50 to 60 minutes.

Joyce's Blueberry Muffins

1¾ c. flour
⅓ c. sugar
1 tbsp. baking powder
¾ c. milk
⅓ c. oil
1 tsp. grated lemon peel
1 egg, slightly beaten
1 8-oz. pkg. cream cheese, cut into ½-inch cubes
¾ c. fresh or frozen blueberries
1 tbsp. lemon juice
3 tbsp. sugar

Preheat the oven to 400°F. Mix the flour, sugar, and baking powder in a large bowl and set aside. Add the milk, oil, and grated lemon peel to the egg. Add the egg mixture to the flour mixture, blending until just moistened. Fold in the cream cheese and blueberries. Spoon the batter into greased or lined muffin tins until two-thirds full. Bake for 20 minutes. Mix together the lemon juice and sugar and brush over the muffins. Makes 12 muffins.

Miller's of Montana B&B Inn, Bozeman, Montana

Eggs Benedict Caledonia

1 pkg. Hollandaise sauce mix
3 tbsp. lemon juice
2 English muffins
2 tbsp. butter or margarine
4 slices Canadian bacon or ham
4 eggs
Garnish of choice

Preheat the oven to 160°F. Prepare Hollandaise sauce according to package directions, replacing 3 tablespoons of water with lemon juice and set aside. Toast or broil muffin halves and spread with the butter. Top with slices of the Canadian bacon or ham and keep warm in the oven. Poach the eggs for 3½ minutes in cups sprayed with vegetable oil. When the whites are set but the yolks are still loose, invert the eggs onto muffins. Cover the eggs with the sauce. Garnish with fresh parsley, kiwi slice, strawberry half, or a favorite garnish of your choice. Makes 2 servings.

Caledonia Farm B&B, Flint Hill, Virginia

Banana Butter

4 large ripe bananas, peeled and sliced
3 tbsp. lemon juice
1 tsp. pumpkin pie spice
1½ c. sugar

Place the bananas and lemon juice in a blender and process until smooth. Transfer to a large saucepan and stir in the pumpkin pie spice and sugar. Bring the mixture to a boil, lower the heat and simmer for 15 minutes, stirring frequently. Pour into sterilized jars and store in tightly covered containers in the refrigerator. Makes 3 cups.

Bannick's Bed & Breakfast, Dimondale, Michigan

Mountain Top Bacon

½ c. flour
¼ c. brown sugar
1 tsp. black pepper
1 lb. bacon, sliced

Preheat the oven to 300°F. Mix the flour, brown sugar, and pepper in a plastic bag. Add bacon slices one at a time and shake to coat. Lay the slices out in a baking pan. Bake for 20 to 25 minutes, or until crisp. Serves 4.

Von-Bryan Inn, Sevierville, Tennessee

Health Cereal

5 c. old-fashioned oats
2 c. wheat germ
½ c. sesame seeds, ground
1 c. shredded coconut (optional)
1 c. almonds or other nuts, chopped finely
½ tsp. cinnamon
¼ tsp. ground cloves
½ tsp. salt
1 c. brown sugar, or to taste
1 c. corn oil, or to taste
1 c. raisins

Preheat the oven to 350°F. In a large bowl, mix together all the ingredients except the raisins. Pour the mixture into a shallow pan and bake 30 minutes, stirring occasionally. Remove from the oven and stir in the raisins. Serve warm or at room temperature.

Honeysuckle Hill B&B, Madison, Connecticut

Aunt Dolly's Almost in the Country Quiche

¾ c. all-purpose flour
½ c. whole wheat flour
Pinch of salt
6 tbsp. butter
4 to 5 tbsp. ice water
5 slices bacon
1 large onion, chopped
2 large potatoes, thinly sliced
2 eggs
⅔ c. heavy cream
1 tbsp. each chopped parsley and chives
½ tsp. salt
¼ tsp. black pepper
½ sweet red pepper, seeded and chopped
¾ c. grated cheddar cheese

Preheat the oven to 375°F. In a large bowl, combine the flours and the pinch of salt and cut in the butter until the mixture turns to fine crumbs. Add enough water to make a firm dough. Knead lightly. On a lightly floured surface, roll out the pastry to a 10-inch circle. Ease the pastry into a 9-inch quiche pan, pressing evenly around the side; trim the edge. Prick all over with a fork; refrigerate for 30 minutes, or until the dough is firm. Line with foil, fill with dried beans and bake until set, 12 to 15 minutes. Remove the foil and beans and return the pastry to the oven for another 5 minutes. In a large frying pan, cook the bacon until crisp; remove it with a slotted spoon, allow it to cool, and crumble it. Add the onion and potatoes to the bacon drippings and cook until browned. Drain and set aside. Beat the eggs and cream together. Stir in the parsley, chives, the ½ teaspoon salt, and the black pepper and set aside. Spoon the potatoes and onion into the pastry shell and sprinkle with the bacon and red pepper. Pour in the egg mixture and sprinkle with the cheese. Bake for 20 to 25 minutes. Serve hot or cold.

Aunt Dolly's Attic B&B, Austin, Texas

Garden Harvest Muffins

4 c. all-purpose flour
2½ c. sugar
4 tsp. baking soda
4 tsp. cinnamon
1 tsp. salt
2 c. grated carrots
2 c. grated zucchini
1 c. raisins
1 c. chopped pecans
1 c. coconut
2 tart apples, peeled and grated
6 large eggs
1 c. vegetable oil
1 c. buttermilk
2 tsp. vanilla

Preheat the oven to 375°F. In a large bowl, sift together the flour, sugar, baking soda, cinnamon, and salt. Stir in the carrots, zucchini, raisins, pecans, coconut, and apples. In another bowl, whisk together the remaining ingredients and add to the flour-vegetable mixture. Stir the batter until just blended. Spoon the batter into well-buttered muffin tins (or use paper liners). Bake on the middle rack for 25 to 30 minutes, or until the muffins are springy to the touch. Let the muffins cool in the tins for 5 minutes, then turn them out onto a rack. Makes about 30 muffins.

Leland House, Durango, Colorado

Sausage en Croute

1 sheet frozen Pepperidge Farm puff pastry
1 lb. pork sausage
½ c. chopped onion
½ c. chopped green pepper
6 large mushrooms, sliced
1 large tomato, diced
1 c. total shredded Swiss and Cheddar cheese
3 tbsp. chopped parsley

Preheat the oven to 425°F. Thaw the puff pastry about 20 minutes. Meanwhile, brown the sausage in a skillet, breaking it into bits. Add the onion, green pepper, and mushrooms and cook until tender. Remove from the heat and pour off the drippings. Add the tomato, cheese, and parsley. Unfold the pastry sheet and roll it out on a lightly floured board to a 13 × 10-inch rectangle. Transfer to a baking sheet lined with brown paper (a grocery bag works well). Spread the sausage mixture on pastry. Roll up from the long side, jelly-roll fashion, and pinch the edges to seal. Bake for 20 minutes, or until golden brown. Serves 6 to 8 guests.

Grand Avenue Inn, Carthage, Missouri

4

Wheelchair Accessible Listings

Although this chapter is small, within a few years *Bed & Breakfast U.S.A., Southeast* hopes to have listings from all fifty states and Canada. The requirements are fairly simple. To be listed in this section, all B&Bs must have easy-access entrances and exits. Doorways must be wide enough to admit a wheelchair—36 inches should be wide enough. Toilets and tubs must have reach bars. If the bathroom has a shower, reach bars and a built-in seat are preferable. Wheelchairs should be able to fit under the breakfast table; 26 inches is high enough. It's also a good idea to check to see what kind of activities are available. Many parks, restaurants, shopping areas, museums, beaches, etc. have wheelchair accessibility.

Kern River Inn Bed & Breakfast ✪

P.O. BOX 1725, 119 KERN RIVER DRIVE, KERNVILLE, CALIFORNIA 93238

Tel: **(619) 376-6750; (800) 986-4382**
Best Time to Call: **8 AM–8 PM**
Hosts: **Jack and Carita Prestwich**
Location: **50 mi. NE of Bakersfield**
No. of Rooms: **1**
No. of Private Baths: **1**
Double/pb: **$89–$99**
Single/pb: **$79–$89**
Open: **All year**
Reduced Rates: **Available**
Breakfast: **Full**
Credit Cards: **AMEX, MC, VISA**
Pets: **No**
Children: **Welcome**
Smoking: **No**
Social Drinking: **Permitted**

Stay in a charming riverfront B&B in a quaint western town within Sequoia National Forest. Jack and Carita specialize in romantic, relaxing getaways. Their accessible room has a queen bed and a Piute-style, wood-burning fireplace. (Your hosts provide the wood.) Native American pictures and macramé wall hangings accent the room's Southwestern color scheme of beige, mauve, and sage green. The bathroom has grab bars; the full-size, mirror-doored closet has shelving that can be reached from a wheelchair.

San Francisco Bay Area B&B ✪

1636 CENTER ROAD, NOVATO, CALIFORNIA 94947

Tel: **(415) 892-9069**
Best Time to Call: **7–10 PM**
Hosts: **Russell and Joyce Woods**
Location: **25 mi. N of San Francisco**
Guest Apartment: **$55–$75**
Open: **April–mid-November**
Reduced Rates: **Available**
Breakfast: **Continental**
Pets: **Sometimes**
Children: **Welcome, crib & high-chair**
Smoking: **No**
Social Drinking: **Permitted**
Minimum Stay: **2 nights**

Located in a garden setting with an easy-access private entrance, this bed and breakfast offers a queen bed, kitchenette, living room, cable TV, and a bath equipped with grab bars for wheelchair users. It's near downtown Novato, Muir Woods, and Marine World Africa USA, and 25 miles from Napa-Sonoma wine country. Russell and Joyce are retired, native to San Francisco, and enjoy guiding guests to the many interesting places in the beautiful Bay Area.

Ferncourt Bed and Breakfast

P.O. BOX 758, PALATKA, FLORIDA 32187

Tel: **(904) 329-9755**
Best Time to Call: **Evenings**
Hosts: **Jack and Dee Morgan**
Location: **25 mi. W of St. Augustine**
No. of Rooms: **1**
No. of Private Baths: **1**
Double/pb: **$55–$65**
Open: **All year**
Breakfast: **Full**
Pets: **No**
Children: **No**
Smoking: **No**
Social Drinking: **Permitted**
Station Pickup: **Yes**

Ferncourt is a restored 1800s farm home, located in a tiny historic hamlet just a few minutes' drive from St. Augustine and Daytona Beach. Guests have use of several rooms and the wraparound veranda. Close by, restaurants serve excellent food. Cookies and tea are offered in the evening. Jack does woodworking and upholstery and many examples of his craft are on display throughout the inn. Dee dabbles in painting and loves antiques and flea markets, but her real passion is food, evidenced by the gourmet breakfast she serves. Discover North Central Florida, then retire to all the charm and hospitality of the Victorian era with your hosts. There is a long concrete wheelchair ramp, and one room is set up for the disabled, with a private bath and handrails installed. For hearing impaired guests, a smoke alarm has been installed. There are five additional rooms available not set up for wheelchair users.

Beautiful Dreamer ✪

440 EAST STEPHEN FOSTER AVENUE, BARDSTOWN, KENTUCKY 40004

Tel: **(800) 811-8312**
Host: **Lynell Ginter**
Location: **30 mi. SE of Louisville**
No. of Rooms: **1**
No. of Private Baths: **1**
Double/pb: **$85**
Open: **All year**
Breakfast: **Full**
Credit Cards: **MC, VISA**
Pets: **No**
Children: **Welcome, over 8**
Smoking: **No**

Decorated with antiques and cherry furniture, this Federal-style home, circa 1995, is located in the historic district. Relax on the porch and enjoy a breathtaking view of My Old Kentucky Home, or show off your talent on the baby grand piano. The Stephen Foster Room is wheelchair accessible, featuring a shower with rails and a double sink that can accommodate a wheelchair, air-conditioning, and queen-size bed. A hearty breakfast is included.

Amanda's B&B Reservation Service ✪

1428 PARK AVENUE, BALTIMORE, MARYLAND 21217

Tel: **(410) 225-0001; fax: (410) 728-8957**
Best Time to Call: **8:30 AM–5:30 PM Mon.–Fri.**
Coordinator: **Betsy Grater**
States/Regions Covered: **Annapolis, Baltimore, Delaware, District of Columbia, Maryland, New Jersey, Pennsylvania, Virginia, West Virginia**
Descriptive Directory of B&Bs: **$5**
Rates (Double):
Modest: **$85**
Luxury: **$100–$150**
Credit Cards: **AMEX, DISC, MC, VISA**

The roster of this reservation service includes seven sites designed for visitors with disabilities—five in downtown Baltimore, and two in Annapolis.

Jemez River Bed & Breakfast Inn ✪

16445 HIGHWAY 4, JEMEZ SPRINGS, NEW MEXICO 87025

Tel: **(505) 829-3262**
Best Time to Call: **Evenings**
Hosts: **Larry and Roxe Ann Clutter**
Location: **40 mi. NW of Albuquerque**
No. of Rooms: **2**
No. of Private Baths: **2**
Double/pb: **$99–$109**
Open: **All year**
Breakfast: **Full**
Credit Cards: **AMEX, CB, DC, DISC, MC, VISA**
Pets: **No**
Children: **Welcome**
Smoking: **No**
Social Drinking: **No**

A new, adobe-style home completed in 1994, Jemez River Bed & Breakfast Inn is nestled on 3½ acres in a valley below the Jemez Mountains Virgin Mesa. At night, the murmuring of the Jemez River—located in the B&B's backyard—will lull you to sleep. As you enjoy a hearty breakfast, you'll feast your eyes on breathtaking mountain views through the grand kitchen windows. Authentic Indian pottery, rugs, paintings, arrowheads, and kachina dolls decorate the bedrooms, which have individual access to a spacious garden plaza; there, a spring-fed birdbath draws hummingbirds and other wildlife. Stone-lined trails follow the spring around cottonwood trees, large rocks and crevices to secluded riverside rest spots. Two rooms are completely accessible for wheelchair users, four other rooms are not.

Bed & Breakfast—The Manor ✪

830 VILLAGE ROAD, P.O. BOX 416, LAMPETER, PENNSYLVANIA 17537

Tel: **(717) 464-9564; (800) 461-6BED [6233]**
Best Time to Call: **9 AM–9 PM**
Hosts: **Mary Lou Paolini and Jackie Curtis**
Location: **3 mi. SE of Lancaster**
No. of Rooms: **3**
No. of Private Baths: **3**
Double/pb: **$75**
Double/sb: **$65**
Open: **All year**
Reduced Rates: **Available**
Breakfast: **Full**
Other Meals: **Available**
Credit Cards: **MC, VISA**
Pets: **No**
Children: **Welcome**
Smoking: **No**
Social Drinking: **No**
Airport/Station Pickup: **Yes**

Set on 4½ acres of lush Amish farmland, this cozy farmhouse is just minutes away from Lancaster's historic sites and attractions. Guests delight in Mary Lou's delicious breakfasts, with specialties like eggs mornay, apple cobbler, and homemade breads and jams. This cozy inn features two ground-floor bedrooms decorated with country charm and antique beds. Both rooms are easily accessible to the parking area; no steps involved. Guests may join an Old Order Amish family for dinner. A conference room is available for groups. In summer a swim in the pool or a nap under one of the many shade trees is the perfect way to cap a day of touring.

Selby House Bed & Breakfast ✪

226 PRINCESS ANNE STREET, FREDERICKSBURG, VIRGINIA 22401

Tel: **(703) 373-7037**
Hosts: **Jerry and Virginia Selby**
Location: **54 mi. S of Washington, D.C.**
No of Rooms: **4**
No. of Private Baths: **4**
Double/pb: **$75**
Single/pb: **$65**
Open: **All year**
Reduced Rates: **Available**
Breakfast: **Full**
Credit Cards: **MC, VISA**
Pets: **No**
Children: **Welcome**
Smoking: **No**
Social Drinking: **Permitted**
Station Pickup: **Yes**

Selby House has two barrier-free, ground-level rooms. In 1986, Jerry designed and built this annex to fulfill his dream of extending hospitality to physically challenged guests. All doorways are 36 inches wide. The bedrooms have large baths with grab bars and other necessary adaptations. Both guest rooms connect to a large community area as well as the dining room, and their cement patios provide easy access to all inn facilities.

5

State-by-State Listings

ALABAMA

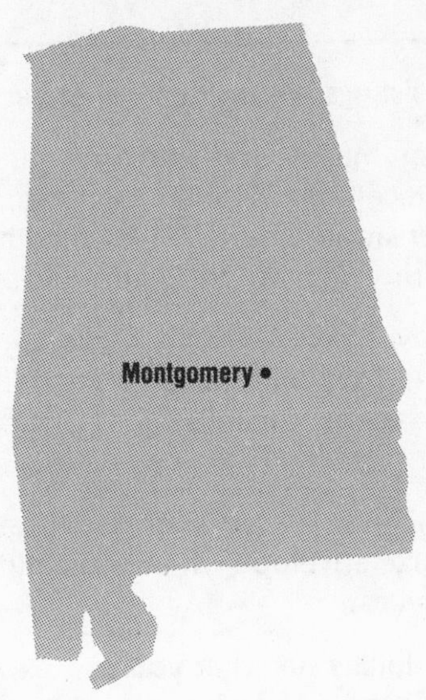

Red Bluff Cottage ✪

551 CLAY STREET, MONTGOMERY, ALABAMA
(MAILING ADDRESS: P.O. BOX 1026, MONTGOMERY, ALABAMA 36101)

Tel: **(334) 264-0056**
Best Time to Call: **9 AM–10 PM**
Hosts: **Anne and Mark Waldo**
No. of Rooms: **4**
No. of Private Baths: **4**
Double/pb: **$65**
Single/pb: **$55**
Suite: **$85**
Open: **All year**
Breakfast: **Full**
Pets: **No**
Children: **Welcome (crib)**
Smoking: **No**
Social Drinking: **Permitted**
Airport/Station Pickup: **Yes**

This raised cottage is high above the Alabama River in Montgomery's historic Cottage Hill District, close to the State Capitol, Dexter Avenue King Memorial Baptist Church, the First White House of the Confederacy, the Civil Rights Memorial, and Old Alabama Town. The Alabama Shakespeare Festival Theatre, the Museum of Fine Arts, and the expanded zoo are also nearby. The bedrooms are downstairs. Guests come upstairs to read or relax in the living rooms, to enjoy the front porch view, and to have breakfast in the dining room. Many interesting antiques and a music room, complete with harpsichord, add to the charm of this home.

For key to listings, see inside front or back cover.

✪ This star means that rates are guaranteed through December 31, 1997, to any guest making a reservation as a result of reading about the B&B in *Bed & Breakfast U.S.A.*—1997 edition.

Important! To avoid misunderstandings, always ask about cancellation policies when booking.

Please enclose a self-addressed, stamped, business-size envelope when contacting reservation services.

For more details on what you can expect in a B&B, see Chapter 1.

Always mention *Bed & Breakfast U.S.A.* when making reservations!

If no B&B is listed in the area you'll be visiting, use the form on page 231 to order a copy of our "List of New B&Bs."

We want to hear from you! Use the form on page 233.

ARKANSAS

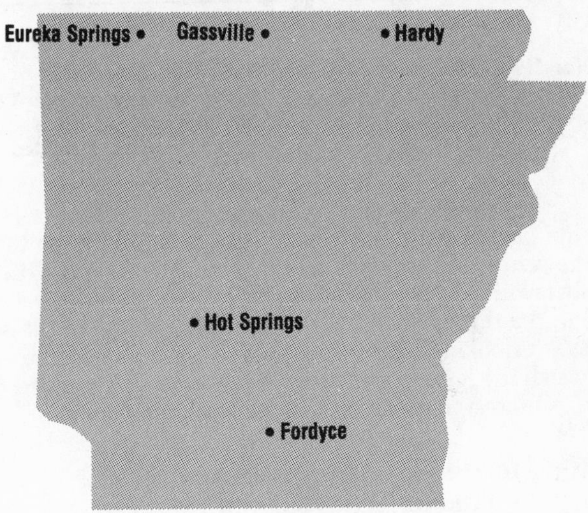

Crescent Cottage Inn

211 SPRING STREET, EUREKA SPRINGS, ARKANSAS 72632
E-mail: rbecker@alumni.uark.edu

Tel: **(501) 253-6022; fax: (501) 253-6234**
Best Time to Call: **10 AM–8 PM**
Hosts: **Ralph and Phyllis Becker**
Location: **On Rte. 62B, Historic Loop**
No. of Rooms: **4**
No. of Private Baths: **4**
Double/pb: **$75–$120**
Open: **All year**
Breakfast: **Full**
Credit Cards: **DISC, MC, VISA**
Pets: **No**
Children: **Welcome, under 1, over 13**
Smoking: **No**
Social Drinking: **Permitted**

Crescent Cottage Inn, built in 1881 for Arkansas' first post-Civil War governor, is listed on the National Register of Historic Places. This celebrated B&B has wonderful views of the mountains. All guest rooms are furnished with antiques; two have double Jacuzzi spas, and fireplaces. Ralph and Phyllis serve a full breakfast each morning. Then you'll be ready for the short walk to historic downtown Eureka Springs on a route that leads past lovely springs, shade trees, and a trolley stop.

Harvest House ✪

104 WALL STREET, EUREKA SPRINGS, ARKANSAS 72632

Tel: **(501) 253-9363; (800) 293-5665**
Best Time to Call: **9 AM–9 PM**
Hosts: **Bill and Patt Carmichael**
No. of Rooms: **4**
No. of Private Baths: **4**
Double/pb: **$75–$110**
Open: **All year**
Breakfast: **Full**
Credit Cards: **DISC, MC, VISA**
Pets: **Sometimes**
Children: **Welcome, over 12**
Smoking: **No**
Social Drinking: **Permitted**

Located in the historic district of Eureka Springs, Harvest House is a step off the beaten path, yet close to the bustle of downtown. This turn-of-the-century Victorian house is filled with antiques, collectibles, and family favorites. All guest rooms have private entrances. Breakfast is served in the dining room or, weather permitting, in the screened-in gazebo overlooking pine and oak trees. Bill is a native Arkansan and knows all the hidden treasures of the area. Patt is a shopper with a particular interest in antiques and the local attractions.

Singleton House Bed and Breakfast ✪

11 SINGLETON, EUREKA SPRINGS, ARKANSAS 72632

Tel: **(501) 253-9111; (800) 833-3394**
Best Time to Call: **Anytime**
Host: **Barbara Gavron**
No. of Rooms: **5**

No. of Private Baths: **5**
Double/pb: **$65–$75**
Single/pb: **$55–$65**
Suites: **$75–$95**
Open: **All year**
Reduced Rates: **After 3rd night**
Breakfast: **Full**
Credit Cards: **AMEX, DISC, MC, VISA**
Pets: **No**
Children: **Welcome**
Smoking: **No**
Social Drinking: **Permitted**

You'll find a hidden garden, winding stone paths, and more than fifty birdhouses on the grounds of this Victorian home in Eureka Springs' historic district. For help in identifying your various feathered friends, consult the titles in Singleton House's small nature library. Full breakfasts are served on the balcony overlooking the wildflower garden and lily-filled goldfish pond. After your meal, take a one-block stroll on the historic walking tour footpath to the city's shops, galleries, and cafes. If you prefer, there's an old-fashioned trolley that stops right at Singleton Street.

Wynne Phillips House ✪

412 WEST FOURTH STREET, FORDYCE, ARKANSAS 71742

Tel: **(501) 352-7202**
Best Time to Call: **Morning**
Hosts: **Colonel and Mrs. James H. Phillips**
Location: **60 mi. S of Little Rock**
No. of Rooms: **4**
No. of Private Baths: **4**
Double/pb: **$55**
Open: **All year**
Breakfast: **Full**
Credit Cards: **MC, VISA**
Pets: **No**
Children: **Yes**
Smoking: **No**
Social Drinking: **Permitted**

A gracious Colonial Revival mansion listed on the National Register of Historic Places, the Wynne Phillips House is filled with antiques and oriental rugs. Mrs. Phillips grew up here, and the bedrooms are furnished with family heirlooms. This is a place where you can enjoy old-fashioned pleasures, such as singing around the piano, or watching the sunset from the wraparound porch. A swimming pool is on the premises; tennis courts are nearby. The generous, Southern-style breakfasts feature fresh fruit, homemade biscuits, eggs, sausage, and grits.

Lithia Springs Bed & Breakfast Lodge ✪

RT. 1, BOX 77-A, HIGHWAY 126, GASSVILLE, ARKANSAS 72635

Tel: **(501) 435-6100**
Best Time to Call: **After 1 PM**
Hosts: **Paul and Reita Johnson**
No. of Rooms: **5**
No. of Private Baths: **3**
Max. No. Sharing Bath: **4**
Double/pb: **$50–$70**
Double/sb: **$50–$70**
Open: **All year, Dec.–Jan. special reservation only**
Breakfast: **Full**
Pets: **No**
Children: **Welcome, over 7**
Smoking: **No**

This 100-year-old former health lodge has been lovingly restored with an additional gift shop featuring many of the hosts' own fine handcrafts. The rooms are furnished with many antiques and period furniture. Breakfast is served in the dining room or on the large screened front porch. Lithia Springs is on 39 acres of meadows and woods. It is near the White and Buffalo Rivers, famous for fishing and canoeing, and between Bull Shoals and Norfork Lakes. It's 10 minutes from Mountain Home and a scenic drive to Blanchard Spring Caverns and Mountain View Folk Center.

Olde Stonehouse Bed & Breakfast Inn ✪

511 MAIN STREET, HARDY, ARKANSAS 72542

Tel: **(501) 856-2983; (800) 514-2983; fax: (501) 856-4036**
Best Time to Call: **10 AM–8 PM**
Host: **Peggy Johnson**
No. of Rooms: **7**
No. of Private Baths: **7**
Double p/b: **$59–$69**
Single p/b: **$55–$65**
Suites: **$89**
Open: **All year**
Reduced Rates: **10% seniors**
Breakfast: **Full**
Credit Cards: **AMEX, DISC, MC, VISA**
Pets: **No**
Children: **Welcome in suites, over 13 in main house**
Smoking: **No**
Social Drinking: **Permitted**
Minimum Stay: **2 nights, holiday weekends and special events**
Station Pickup: **Yes**

Recapture the romance of times past at the Olde Stonehouse. Unwind in lovely air-conditioned rooms decorated with period antiques, quilts, and old lace, plus a ceiling fan and queen-size bed. Curl up in the large rocking chairs on the front porch or take a walk to Old Hardy Town's antique and crafts shops. Stroll along the river or join other guests for conversation and games. Awaken to the aroma of freshly brewed coffee and bread baking. After breakfast, canoeing, golfing, shopping, and horseback riding are among the many activities to choose from.

Stillmeadow Farm ✪

111 STILLMEADOW LANE, HOT SPRINGS, ARKANSAS 71913

Tel: **(501) 525-9994**
Hosts: **Gene and Jody Sparling**
Location: **4 mi. S of Hot Springs**
No. of Rooms: **4**
No. of Private Baths: **2**
Max. No. Sharing Bath: **4**
Double/pb: **$65**
Single/pb: **$55**
Suites: **$80**
Open: **All year**
Breakfast: **Full**
Pets: **No**
Children: **Welcome, over 12**
Smoking: **No**
Social Drinking: **Permitted**

Stillmeadow Farm is a reproduction of an 18th-century New England saltbox, set in 75 acres of pine forest with walking trails and an herb garden. The decor is of early country antiques. Your hosts provide homemade snacks and fruit in the guest rooms. For breakfast, freshly baked pastries and breads are served. Hot Springs National Park, Lake Hamilton, the Mid-America Museum, and a racetrack are nearby.

Vintage Comfort B&B Inn ✪

303 QUAPAW AVENUE, HOT SPRINGS, ARKANSAS 71901

Tel: **(501) 623-3258; (800) 608-4682**
Host: **Helen Bartlett**
No. of Rooms: **4**
No. of Private Baths: **4**
Double/pb: **$65–$90**
Single/pb: **$55–$75**
Open: **All year**
Breakfast: **Full**
Credit Cards: **AMEX, MC, VISA**
Pets: **No**
Children: **Welcome, over 6**
Smoking: **No**
Social Drinking: **Permitted**
Airport/Station Pickup: **Yes**

This handsome turn-of-the-century Queen Anne–style home has been faithfully restored, attractively appointed, and air-conditioned. The theme here is comfort and Southern hospitality. Breakfast treats include biscuits and sausage gravy, grits, and regional hot breads. Afterwards, enjoy a short stroll to the famed Bath House Row or a brisk walk to the park, where miles of hiking trails will keep you in shape. Helen will be happy to direct you to the studios and shops of local artists and craftspeople. You are welcome to relax in the old-world sitting room and parlor or on the lovely veranda shaded by magnolia trees.

Williams House Bed & Breakfast Inn ✪

420 QUAPAW AVENUE, HOT SPRINGS, ARKANSAS 71901

Tel: **(501) 624-4275**
Hosts: **Mary and Gary Riley**
Best Time to Call: **Evenings**
Location: **50 mi. SW of Little Rock**
No. of Rooms: **4**
No. of Private Baths: **4**
Double/pb: **$70–$90**
Single/pb: **$65–$80**
Suites: **$85–$95**
Open: **All year**
Breakfast: **Full**
Credit Cards: **MC, VISA**
Pets: **No**
Smoking: **No**
Social Drinking: **Permitted**
Minimum Stay: **2 nights weekends Mar.–Apr.**

This Victorian mansion, with its stained glass and beveled glass windows, is a nationally registered historical place. The atmosphere is friendly, and the marble fireplace and grand piano invite congeniality. The breakfast menu may include quiche, toast amandine, or exotic

egg dishes. Mary and Gary will spoil you with special iced tea, snacks, and mineral spring water. World health experts recognize the benefits of the hot mineral baths in Hot Springs National Park. The Inn is within walking distance of Bath House Row.

FLORIDA

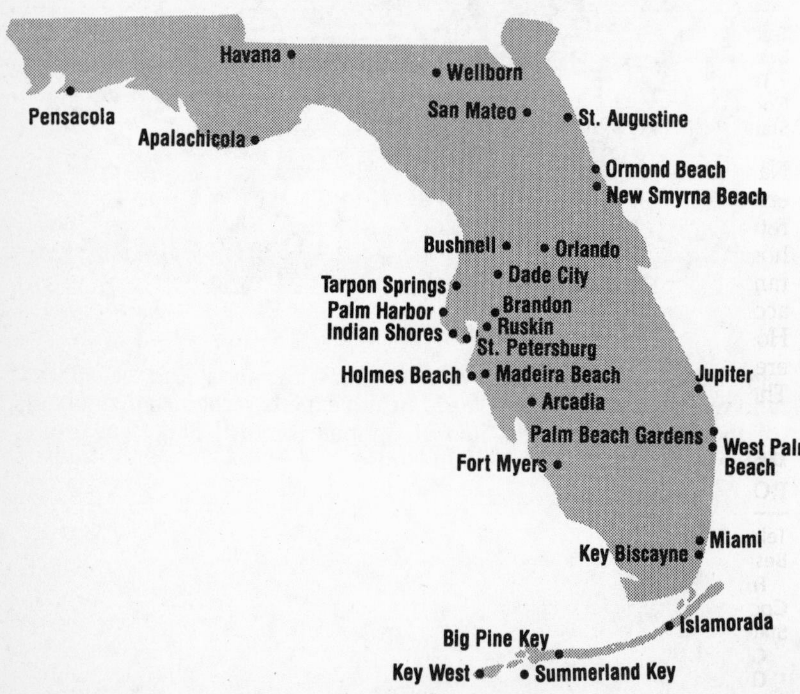

A & A Bed & Breakfast of Florida, Inc. ✪

P.O. BOX 1316, WINTER PARK, FLORIDA 32790

Tel: **(407) 628-0322**
Best Time to Call: **9 AM–6 PM**
Coordinator: **Brunhilde (Bruni) Fehner**
States/Regions Covered: **Orlando area—Disney World, Epcot; Altamonte Springs, Cape Canaveral (Kennedy Space Center), Maitland, New Smyrna Beach, Sea World, Winter Park, Delray Beach, Ft. Myers, St. Augustine**

Rates (Single/Double):
Modest: **$35 / $40**
Average: **$40 / $55**
Luxury: **$65 / $125**
Credit Cards: **No**
Minimum Stay: **2 nights**

You should allow several days to really savor all this area has to offer. Bruni's hosts will suggest hints on getting the most out of the major attractions, wonderful un-touristy restaurants, and tips on where to shop for unique gifts to take home. All of her homes have a certain "touch of class" to make you delighted with your visit. Rollins College is close by. There is a surcharge of $10 for one-night stays.

Bed & Breakfast Co.—Tropical Florida

P.O. BOX 262, SOUTH MIAMI, FLORIDA 33243

Tel: **(305) 661-3270**
Best Time to Call: **9 AM–5 PM Mon.–Fri.**
Coordinator: **Marcella Schaible**
States/Regions Covered: **Statewide**

Rates (Single/Double):
Modest: **$35–$38 / $35–$40**
Average: **$38–$55 / $40–$60**
Luxury: **$55–$150 / $60–$170**
Credit Cards: **AMEX, MC, VISA**

Native Floridians, Marcella's hosts live in mansions on historic properties, in homes along the ocean and Gulf of Mexico, in woodland retreats, and on private residential islands. They exude Southern hospitality and want you to come stay in their accommodations that range from a charming cottage to a contemporary condo to unhosted accommodations. The decor may be simple or wildly extravagant. Hosts are ready to direct you to famous attractions or to an undiscovered special restaurant or shop that only a resident knows about. There is a $5 surcharge for each night stayed less than three.

Bed & Breakfast Scenic Florida

P.O. BOX 3385, TALLAHASSEE, FLORIDA 32315-3385

Tel: **(904) 386-8196**
Best Time to Call: **9 AM–6 PM Mon.–Fri.**
Coordinator: **Dianne C. Mahlert**
States/Regions Covered: **Gainesville, Gulf Beaches, Jacksonville, Ocala, Orlando, Tallahassee**
Descriptive Directory of B&Bs: **Free**

Rates (Single/Double):
Modest: **$50–$60**
Average: **$75–$75**
Luxury: **$165–$165**
Credit Cards: **MC, VISA**

Bed & Breakfast Scenic Florida specializes in unique accommodations throughout North and Central Florida and beyond. This service's goal is to attract pleasure and business travelers to beautiful Florida and to help them select the best location to meet their needs and tastes. The people at Bed & Breakfast Scenic Florida inspect all locations and can answer very detailed questions about individual room decor and amenities. They are familiar with the cities and towns and can recommend things to do, where to eat, what to see. The service also provides written confirmation and directions to each accommodation.

Coombs House Inn ✪

80 SIXTH STREET, APALACHICOLA, FLORIDA 32320

Tel: **(904) 653-9199**
Best Time to Call: **Before noon, after 5 PM**

Hosts: **Marilyn and Charles Schubert**
Location: **75 mi. SW of Tallahassee**
No. of Rooms: **14**

No. of Private Baths: **14**
Double/pb: **$89–$99**
Single/pb: **$69–$79**
Suites: **$105–$115**
Open: **All year**
Breakfast: **Continental**
Credit Cards: **AMEX, MC, VISA**
Pets: **Sometimes**
Children: **Welcome**
Smoking: **No**
Social Drinking: **Permitted**

Elegantly restored, this 1905 Victorian mansion welcomes those special guests who appreciate the charm and historical authenticity of another era and an intimate homey atmosphere. The three-story mansion features high ceilings and nine fireplaces. Inside you'll admire antique furniture of the period, paintings, historical photographs, imported English chintz draperies that frame the large bay windows, and oriental carpets. Each guest room has a private bath and cable TV. Located only minutes from fishing, boating, the Apalachicola River, and from the white beaches of St. George Island.

Historic Parker House ✪

427 WEST HICKORY STREET, ARCADIA, FLORIDA 33821

Tel: **(941) 494-2499; (800) 969-2499**
Best Time to Call: **8 AM–10 PM**
Hosts: **Bob and Shelly Baumann**
Location: **45 mi. E of Sarasota**
No. of Rooms: **4**
No. of Private Baths: **2**
Max. No. Sharing Bath: **4**
Double/pb: **$75**
Single/pb: **$75**
Double/sb: **$60**
Single/sb: **$60**
Open: **All year**

Reduced Rates: **10%**
Breakfast: **Continental**
Credit Cards: **AMEX, MC, VISA**
Pets: **No**
Children: **Welcome, over 10**
Smoking: **No**
Social Drinking: **Permitted**

Once you step inside the Historic Parker House you become acquainted with a much grander, yet simpler life. The 6000-square-foot home is chock full of antiques, old clocks, and Florida's past. The original section of the home dates to the mid 1890s; a large addition was put in in 1914 by the original owners, the Parkers, Florida cattle barons. Located in historic downtown Arcadia, recently named one of the one hundred best small towns in America, the home is close to antique and gift shopping and the Peace River for canoeing. Nearby are all of South Central Florida's attractions.

The Barnacle ✪

1557 LONG BEACH DRIVE, BIG PINE KEY, FLORIDA 33043

Tel: **(305) 872-3298; (800) 465-9100; fax: (305) 872-3863**
Best Time to Call: **10 AM–8 PM**
Hosts: **Jane and Tim Marquis**
Location: **Mile marker 33**
No. of Rooms: **4**
No. of Private Baths: **4**
Double/pb: **$105–$140**
Open: **All year**
Breakfast: **Full**
Pets: **No**
Children: **Welcome, over 16**
Smoking: **No**

Tim and Jane welcome you to their Caribbean-style home, where tranquility and leisurely breezes prevail. Enjoy the private beach, where you can scuba dive, snorkel, and swim. Then take a nature walk, soak in the hot tub, ride a bicycle or paddle boat, or nap in the hammock between the palms. Here, your time is your own. The ultimate in privacy is the self-contained cottage, a tropical treehouse with stained glass windows and a private terrace. The rooms overlook the ocean or open to the atrium, with a hot tub, waterfall, and lush plants. The Ocean room has a private entrance and opens to the patio on the beach. Special attention is given to the detail of the villa, decorated with artistic flair. The Barnacle puts emphasis on the sun and sea with warm hospitality.

Bed & Breakfast-on-the-Ocean "Casa Grande" ✪

P.O. BOX 378, BIG PINE KEY, FLORIDA 33043

Tel: **(305) 872-2878**
Host: **Kathleen Threlkeld**
Location: **30 mi. E of Key West**
No. of Rooms: **3**
No. of Private Baths: **3**
Double/pb: **$95**
Open: **All year**
Breakfast: **Full**
Pets: **No**
Children: **No**
Smoking: **Permitted**
Social Drinking: **Permitted**

This spectacular Spanish-style home, facing the ocean, was custom-designed to suit the natural beauty of the Keys. The large landscaped garden patio, with panoramic beach views, is where you'll enjoy Jon and Kathleen's bountiful breakfast. It is also the site of the hot tub/ Jacuzzi for relaxing by day or under a moonlit sky. The large and airy guest rooms are comfortably cooled by Bahama fans or air-conditioning. Key deer and birds abound. From the private beach, you'll enjoy swimming, fishing, snorkeling, bicycling, and jogging. There's a picnic table, gas grill, hammock, and Windsurfer for guests to use, compliments of the gracious hosts.

Canal Cottage Bed & Breakfast

P.O. BOX 430266, BIG PINE KEY, FLORIDA 33043

Tel: **(305) 872-3881**
Best Time to Call: **Evenings**
Hosts: **Dean and Patti Nickless**
Suites: **$95 for 2**
Open: **All year**
Breakfast: **Continental**

Pets: **No**
Children: **Welcome**
Smoking: **Permitted**
Social Drinking: **Permitted**
Minimum Stay: **2 nights**

Get away and relax! You can be self-sufficient in this unusual wood stilt house. Your accommodations are nestled in the trees and consist of a bedroom with a queen-size bed, a bathroom, a living room with sleeping space for two, and a kitchen stocked for your breakfast, which you can prepare at leisure and enjoy on the porch. Take advantage of local diving, snorkeling, and fishing charters, or bring your own boat to launch at the neighborhood ramp and tie it up at your backyard dock. There are bicycles for those so inclined, and a gas grill to cook your catch. You'll probably see a Key deer, too.

Vacation in Paradise ✪

31316 AVENUE J, BIG PINE KEY, FLORIDA 33043

Tel: **(305) 872-9009**
Host: **Joan Thoman**
Location: **30 mi. E of Key West**
Guest Cottage: **$85, for two**
Open: **All year**
Breakfast: **Continental**
Pets: **Sometimes**
Children: **Welcome**
Smoking: **Permitted**
Social Drinking: **Permitted**

True to its name, Vacation in Paradise is located six miles from Bahia Honda State Park (one of the best beaches in the country) and the famed Looe Key Reef. This spacious two-bedroom unit sleeps six and has a large kitchen and living room. Joan offers free dockage twenty feet from your door, a barbecue grill for cooking your dinner, and cable TV. Guests can enjoy fishing, scuba diving, snorkeling and the great nightlife in Key West.

Behind the Fence ✪

1400 VIOLA DRIVE AT COUNTRYSIDE, BRANDON, FLORIDA 33511

Tel: **(813) 685-8201**
Best Time to Call: 2–8 PM
Hosts: **Larry and Carolyn Yoss**
Location: 15 mi. E of Tampa
No. of Rooms: **5**
No. of Private Baths: **3**
Max. No. Sharing Bath: **4**
Double/pb: **$69–$72**
Single/pb: **$49–$59**
Double/sb: **$59–$69**
Single/sb: **$49–$59**
Suites: **$72–$79**
Open: **All year**
Reduced Rates: **10% seniors, June–Aug.; weekly**
Breakfast: **Continental, plus**
Pets: **Sometimes**
Children: **Welcome**
Smoking: **No**
Social Drinking: **Permitted**
Airport/Station Pickup: **Yes**

As the name suggests, this inn is nestled in the trees behind a fence on a quiet secluded lot. The ambiance of another era is reflected in the authentic country furnishings from the 1800s—you will feel as if you have entered another world. The house was built in 1976 in early saltbox style. The interior was finished in county salvage material from before the turn of the century. Art League tours of the house for groups interested in early lifestyles or antiques began in 1978 and are still available today. Nearby are restaurants, canoeing, fishing, horseback riding, golf, bike tours, and Florida's largest mall. Within driving distance is downtown Tampa, the Florida Aquarium, Florida State Fairgrounds, Busch Gardens, Adventure Island, Museum of Science and Industry, University of South Florida, west coast beaches, and Disney World.

Cypress House Bed and Breakfast ✪

5175 SOUTHWEST 90 BOULEVARD, C.R. 476B, BUSHNELL, FLORIDA 33513

Tel: **(352) 568-0909**
Best Time to Call: **8 AM–10 PM**
Hosts: **Jan Fessler and Thelma Schaum**
Location: **50 mi. N of Tampa**
No. of Rooms: **6**
No. of Private Baths: **3**
Max. No. Sharing Bath: **4**
Double/pb: **$70**
Double/sb: **$50**
Suite: **$85**
Open: **All year**
Reduced Rates: **Available**
Breakfast: **Continental, buffet**
Other Meals: **Available**
Pets: **Horses ($10 per night)**
Children: **Welcome, over 5**
Smoking: **Restricted**
Social Drinking: **Permitted**

A new log home built in the gracious old Florida style, Cypress House is set on wooded farmland. From the oak rockers on the wide wraparound veranda, you can see oak trees draped with moss. The Webster Flea Market (Mondays only) and Brooksville's Christmas House are nearby, and Disney World and Busch Gardens are an hour away. You won't have to travel far to browse for antiques, fish, hike, or go canoeing. To bolster your energy, your hosts offer a generous breakfast buffet, plus afternoon snacks and evening dessert. Your hosts have seven horses and offer one- to six-hour trail rides. There's a pool 15 × 40 feet, long enough for lap swimming.

Azalea House Bed & Breakfast ✪

37719 MERIDIAN AVENUE, DADE CITY, FLORIDA 33525

Tel: **(904) 523-1773**
Best Time to Call: **8 AM–10 PM**
Hosts: **Nancy and Grace Bryant**
Location: **40 mi. NE of Tampa**

No. of Rooms: **3**
No. of Private Baths: **3**
Double/pb: **$65–$85**
Single/pb: **$65–$75**
Suites: **$115, sleeps 4**
Open: **All year**
Reduced Rates: **10% seniors**
Breakfast: **Continental**
Credit Cards: **AMEX, MC, VISA**
Pets: **No**
Children: **Welcome, over 5**
Smoking: **No**
Social Drinking: **Permitted**
Station Pickup: **Yes**

Step back into time and enjoy true Southern hospitality. The Azalea House Bed & Breakfast is a beautifully restored, vintage 1906 home nestled in a setting of old oak trees, azaleas, hibiscus, and bamboo. The interior is a harmonious blend of traditional, Oriental, and country decor. Wood floors, fireplaces, high ceilings, and soft colors create an enjoyable atmosphere of relaxation and comfort. Dade City has antique stores, specialty shops, and the well-known restaurant, Lunch on Limoges.

Windsong Garden & Art Gallery

5570–4 WOODROSE COURT, FORT MYERS, FLORIDA 33907

Tel: **(813) 936-6378**
Host: **Embe Burdick**
No. of Rooms: **2**
No. of Private Baths: **2**
Double/pb: **$75**
Suite: **$75**
Open: **All year**
Breakfast: **Continental**
Pets: **No**
Children: **No**
Smoking: **No**
Social Drinking: **Permitted**
Minimum Stay: **2 nights**

This modern clear-shake-and-brick town house has a private courtyard and balcony for your enjoyment. The spacious combination bedroom-and-sitting room is most comfortable. Embe's varied interests include arts, crafts, music, and her household cats. It's close to Sanibel and Captiva Islands, Ft. Myers Beach, fine shopping, good restaurants, and the University of Florida. You are welcome to use the pool.

Gaver's Bed & Breakfast ✪

301 EAST SIXTH AVENUE, HAVANA, FLORIDA 32333

Tel: **(904) 539-5611**
Hosts: **Shirley and Bruce Gaver**
Location: **12 mi. N of Tallahassee**
No. of Rooms: **2**
No. of Private Baths: **2**
Double/pb: **$65–$75**
Open: **All year**
Breakfast: **Full**
Pets: **No**
Children: **Welcome, over 8**
Smoking: **No**
Social Drinking: **Permitted**

This B&B, situated on a quiet residential street two blocks from the center of town, is a likely stop for collectors—at last count, Havana had thirty antique shops plus many related businesses. Tallahassee, the state capital and home of Florida State University, is only fifteen minutes away by car. A restored 1907 frame house, Gaver's has a large screened porch, and guests are welcome to watch cable TV in the common area. For breakfast, your hosts will design a menu to suit your preferences.

Harrington House B&B Inn ✪

5626 GULF DRIVE, HOLMES BEACH, FLORIDA 34217

Tel: **(941) 778-5444, 778-6335; fax: (941) 778-0527**
Best Time to Call: **Noon–7 PM**
Host: **Jo Davis**
Location: **40 mi. SW of Tampa**
No. of Rooms: **12**
No. of Private Baths: **12**
Double/pb: **$99–$189**
Open: **All year**
Breakfast: **Full**
Credit Cards: **MC, VISA**
Pets: **No**
Children: **Welcome, over 12**
Smoking: **No**
Social Drinking: **Permitted**
Minimum Stay: **2 nights weekends**
Airport/Station Pickup: **Yes, local**

Surrounded by tropical foliage and the Gulf's blue waters, this gracious Florida home, built in 1925, has the beach for its backyard. Each of the twelve eclectically furnished guest rooms has its own charm and character. Relax by the pool, baste on the beach, take a moonlight stroll, or just let the sound of the surf lull you to sleep. Whatever your pleasure, the warm hospitality will ensure that your stay is a memorable one.

Meeks B&B on the Gulf Beaches ✪

19418 GULF BOULEVARD, #408, INDIAN SHORES, FLORIDA 34635

Tel: **(813) 596-5424; fax: (813) 593-0065**
Best Time to Call: **7 AM–10 PM**
Hosts: **Greta and Bob Meeks**
Location: **35 min. from Tampa Airport**
No. of Rooms: **7**
No. of Private Baths: **5**
Double/pb: **$60–$75**
Single/pb: **$50–$55**
Suites: **$75–$110**
Open: **All year**
Breakfast: **Continental**
Pets: **No**
Children: **Welcome**
Smoking: **No**
Social Drinking: **Permitted**

Beach! Pool! Sunsets! Enjoy your stay in this beach condo overlooking the Gulf of Mexico. A beach cottage is sometimes available. Choose your breakfast, then bask in the sun, swim in the gulf, and catch spectacular sunsets from your balcony. Dine at nearby seafood restaurants and visit the local seabird sanctuary, sunken gardens, and the Dali Museum. Other nearby attractions are Busch Gardens in Tampa and sponge diving in Tarpon Springs. This B&B is located between Clearwater and St. Petersburg Beach, only two hours from Walt Disney World. Your hostess is a real estate broker.

Bed & Breakfast of Islamorada ✪

81175 OLD HIGHWAY, ISLAMORADA, FLORIDA 33036

Tel: **(305) 664-9321**
Host: **Dottie Saunders**
Location: **87 mi. S of Miami**
No. of Rooms: **2**

No. of Private Baths: **2**
Double/pb: **$50–$65**
Single/pb: **$50**
Open: **All year**
Reduced Rates: **Available**
Breakfast: **Full**
Credit Cards: **MC, VISA**
Pets: **Sometimes**
Children: **Welcome**
Smoking: **Permitted**
Social Drinking: **Permitted**

Make the most of the Florida Keys while staying in this one-story house. Bicycles and snorkeling gear are at your disposal, and sailing trips on a historic old boat can be arranged. John Pennecamp Coral Reef State Park, 40 minutes away, is a great place for snorkeling and diving, and the whole family can ride in the glass-bottomed boats. Your hostess has had a varied career, from cooking on a freighter to selling real estate; she enjoys waterfront activities, gardening, and photography.

Innisfail ✪

134 TIMBER LANE, JUPITER, FLORIDA 33458

Tel: **(407) 744-5905**
Best Time to Call: **Evenings**
Hosts: **Katherine and Luke Van Noorden**
Location: **20 mi. N of Palm Beach**
No. of Rooms: **2**
Max. No. Sharing Bath: **4**
Double/sb: **$51–$60**
Open: **All year**
Reduced Rates: **10% weekly; 10% seniors**
Breakfast: **Continental**
Other Meals: **Available**
Pets: **Welcome**
Children: **Yes**
Smoking: **No**
Social Drinking: **Permitted**
Airport/Station Pickup: **Yes**

A contemporary ranch framed by palm trees, Innisfail—Gaelic for "the abode of peace and harmony"—doubles as a gallery. The Van Noordens are sculptors, and guests are welcome to watch them work in their home studio. While you don't have to be an art lover to visit, it helps to be a pet lover; Katherine and Luke's four-footed family comprises three dogs and two cats. Jupiter has wonderful beaches, but you can get an equally good tan lounging by the Van Noordens' swimming pool. In the morning, a Continental breakfast of coffee or tea, fresh citrus fruit, and muffins or cereal is served.

Hibiscus House ✪

345 WEST ENID DRIVE, KEY BISCAYNE, FLORIDA 33149

Tel: **(305) 361-2456**
Best Time to Call: **9 AM–5 PM**
Hosts: **Bernice and Earl Duffy**
Location: **10 mi. SE of Miami**
No. of Rooms: **2**
No. of Private Baths: **2**
Double/pb: **$65**
Single/pb: **$60**
Open: **All year**
Reduced Rates: **May 1–Dec. 15**
Breakfast: **Full**
Pets: **No**
Children: **No**
Smoking: **Permitted**
Social Drinking: **Permitted**
Minimum Stay: **2 nights**

Welcome to an island paradise only 15 minutes from downtown Miami and 20 minutes from Miami International Airport. Key Biscayne features two lushly landscaped parks, a championship golf course, and miles of white sandy beaches; your hosts offer private beach privileges. Tennis courts and bicycle paths are in plentiful supply. Add to this the famous Miami Seaquarium and easy access to Greater Miami's many attractions and you have all of the ingredients for a very pleasant visit.

Center Court Historic Inn & Cottages ✪

916 CENTER STREET, KEY WEST, FLORIDA 33040

Tel: **(305) 296-9292; (800) 797-8787**
Best Time to Call: **9 AM–9 PM**
Host: **Naomi Van Steelandt**
Location: **120 mi. S of Miami**
No. of Rooms: **7**
No. of Private Baths: **7**
Double/pb: **$118–$138**
Guest Cottage: **$138–$298, sleeps 2–6**
Suites: **$148**
Open: **All year**
Reduced Rates: **May 1–Dec. 15, 5% seniors**
Breakfast: **Continental, plus**
Credit Cards: **AMEX, DISC, MC, VISA**
Pets: **Sometimes**
Children: **Welcome in cottages, over 12 in main house**
Smoking: **No**
Social Drinking: **Permitted**
Minimum Stay: **2 nights weekends, cottages**

Center Court is located in the heart of Key West's Historic District, within walking distance to every major attraction. All rooms have been recently renovated with loving care and have lightweight comforters, feather pillows, hair dryers, TV, telephones, fans and air-conditioning. Amenities include private sundecks, an eight-person Jacuzzi, heated pool, exercise room and a private courtyard with outdoor dining and barbecue grills. In the morning, enjoy breakfast at your leisure.

Lighthouse Bed & Breakfast ✪

13355 2ND STREET, MADEIRA BEACH, FLORIDA 33708

Tel: **(813) 391-0015; (800) 241-0334**
Hosts: **Joyce and John Dickinson**
Location: **4 mi. W of St. Petersburg**
No. of Rooms: **5**
No. of Private Baths: **5**
Double/pb: **$45–$85**
Open: **All year**
Breakfast: **Full (Winter), Continental (Summer)**
Credit Cards: **MC, VISA**
Pets: **Sometimes**
Children: **Welcome, over 5**
Smoking: **Permitted**
Social Drinking: **Permitted**

Lighthouse Bed & Breakfast is located only 50 steps from the Intracoastal Waterway and 300 steps from white sand on the Gulf of Mexico's beaches. Guests enjoy the comfort of the Key West–style surroundings with a palm-filled courtyard, a gazebo for dining or relaxing, and a sundeck atop the lighthouse—for lying in the sun or watching the sunrise or sunset. If you want to cook your own supper, there's a barbecue grill. It's an easy walk to the famous John's Pass Boardwalk and village where shopping, restaurants, jet skiing, parasailing, chartered fishing boats, and casino cruises are available. St. Petersburg Pier, Dali Museum, and the Florida International Museum are within ten minutes. Busch Gardens in Tampa is approximately thirty minutes away. In 1995 St. Petersburg was awarded a major league baseball team. The Lighthouse is a quiet retreat from the city's traffic and commercial buildings, yet close enough to join in the rush if you want to. Breakfast specialties include pancakes, waffles, and omelettes. For those flying in, airport door-to-door service is available.

Redland's Bed and Breakfast ✪

19521 SOUTHWEST 128 COURT, MIAMI, FLORIDA 33177

Tel: **(305) 238-5285**
Hosts: **Tim and Marianne Hamilton**
Location: **18 mi. S of Miami**
No. of Rooms: **1**
No. of Private Baths: **1**
Guest cottage: **$65**
Open: **All year**
Reduced Rates: **10% seniors**
Breakfast: **Continental**
Pets: **Sometimes**
Children: **Welcome**
Smoking: **No**
Social Drinking: **Permitted**

This romantic tropical guest house has a private entrance, kitchen, living room, TV, air-conditioning, pool, and Jacuzzi. Enjoy breakfast at your leisure by the pool or at the gazebo. Bicycles are available for the nearby bike trails. Centrally located near Miami's farming community, Redland's is twenty-five minutes from the Miami airport, Florida Keys, and Everglades National Park.

Night Swan Intracoastal Bed & Breakfast ✪

512 SOUTH RIVERSIDE DRIVE, NEW SMYRNA BEACH, FLORIDA 32168

Tel: **(904) 423-4940**
Best Time to Call: **9 AM–9 PM**
Hosts: **Martha and Charles Nighswonger**
Location: **15 mi. S of Daytona Beach**
No. of Rooms: **8**
No. of Private Baths: **8**
Double/pb: **$59–$79**
Suites: **$99–$129; sleeps 4**
Open: **All year**
Reduced Rates: **Available**
Breakfast: **Continental, Full**
Credit Cards: **AMEX, DISC, MC, VISA**
Pets: **No**
Children: **Welcome**
Smoking: **No**
Social Drinking: **Permitted**
Airport/Station Pickup: **Yes**

Come sit on Night Swan's wraparound porch or by its windows and watch pelicans, dolphins, sailboats, and yachts ply the Atlantic Intracoastal Waterway. Then enjoy the waterfront yourself: surf, swim, fish, drive, or bicycle along the bathing beach two miles to the east. This spacious three-story home in New Smyrna's historic district has a central fireplace and intricate, natural woodwork in every room, and some rooms overlook the Indian River. Breakfast is served in the dining room; low-cholesterol dishes are a house specialty.

PerriHouse Bed & Breakfast Inn

10417 CENTURION COURT, ORLANDO, FLORIDA 32836
Internet: http://www.iag.net/-perrihse

Tel: **(407) 876-4830; (800) 780-4830; fax: (407) 876-0241**
Best Time to Call: **9 AM–9 PM**
Hosts: **Nick and Angi Perretti**
Location: **3 mi. N of I-4 Exit 27, Lake Buena Vista, on SR 535N**
No. of Rooms: **6**
No. of Private Baths: **6**
Double/pb: **$85–$95**
Single/pb: **$75**
Open: **All year**
Reduced Rates: **Seniors, weekly**
Breakfast: **Continental**
Credit Cards: **AMEX, DISC, MC, VISA**
Pets: **No**
Children: **Welcome (crib)**
Smoking: **No**
Social Drinking: **Permitted**
Airport/Station Pickup: **Yes**

PerriHouse is a quiet, private country estate inn secluded on 20 acres of land adjacent to the Walt Disney World Resort complex. Because of its outstanding location, Disney Village and Pleasure Island are only 3 minutes away; EPCOT center is only 5 minutes. It's the perfect vacation setting for families who desire a unique travel experience with a comfortable, convenient home away from home. An upscale Continental breakfast awaits you each morning, and a refreshing pool relaxes you after a full day of activities. Each guest room features its own spa and private bath, entrance, TV, telephone, ceiling fan, and central air/heat. The PerriHouse grounds are being developed and landscaped to create a future bird sanctuary and wildlife preserve. Come bird-watch on the peaceful, tranquil grounds of the PerriHouse estate and wake up to bird songs outside your window. Your hosts, Nick and Angi, instinctively offer their guests a unique blend of cordial hospitality, comfort, and friendship!

Bed 'n Breakfast of Greater Daytona Beach

P.O. BOX 1081, ORMOND BEACH, FLORIDA 32175

Tel: **(904) 673-2232**
Coordinator: **Rusty Reed**
States/Regions Covered: **Daytona Beach, Ormond Beach, Pt. Orange**
Rates (Single/Double):
Average: **$35–$75**
Credit Cards: **No**
Minimum Stay: **4 nights Speed Bike weeks in Feb. and Mar.**

The host homes, each with its own special amenities and charm, are located throughout the greater Daytona area and pride themselves on catering to the needs of each guest. The Space Center and Disney World are within 60 miles. Closer to home, Daytona offers deep-sea fishing, golf, tennis, jai alai, dog racing, theater, and Halifax River cruises. A Daytona International Speedway tour and a drive on "the world's most famous beach" are a must. Yacht enthusiasts will be interested in the new 600-slip Halifax Marina, where they can dock, and then bed-and-breakfast nearby. Rates are slightly higher Feb. and March.

Heron Cay ✪

15106 PALMWOOD ROAD, PALM BEACH GARDENS, FLORIDA 33410

Tel: **(407) 744-6315; fax (407) 744-6315**
Best Time to Call: **10 AM–12 noon; after 7 PM**
Hosts: **Randy and Margie Salyer**
Location: **15 mi. N of Palm Beach International Airport**
No. of Rooms: **9**
No. of Private Baths: **7**
Max. No. Sharing Bath: **4**
Double/pb: **$85–$115**
Guest Yacht: **$175–$250, sleeps 2–6**
Suites: **$135–$185**
Open: **All year**
Reduced Rates: **Available**
Breakfast: **Full**
Pets: **Borzoi dogs only**
Children: **By arrangement**
Smoking: **Restricted**
Social Drinking: **Permitted**

At Heron Cay you'll think you're in Key West. This island-style home is quietly nestled on two tropical acres overlooking the Intracoastal Waterway. Randy and Margie's private half-acre island is fun to explore—it protects their harbor that accommodates boats to 55 feet, plus a boat ramp for smaller water toys. All guest rooms open to a balcony leading to the sundeck and several patio areas for relaxation beside the 10-foot-deep pool or heated spa. Guests are provided with refrigerators in rooms and may use the recreation room and barbecue area poolside. Fine restaurants, major shopping, and miles of natural ocean beaches are just minutes away. Margie and Randy are avid boaters who regularly invite guests aboard their 48-foot sportsfisherman, *Waterfront Lady*, for Palm Beach area cruises.

Bed & Breakfast of Tampa Bay ✪

126 OLD OAK CIRCLE, OAK TRAIL, PALM HARBOR, FLORIDA 34683

Tel: **(813) 785-2342**
Best Time to Call: **7–9 AM; 6–10 PM**
Hosts: **Vivian and David Grimm**
Location: **18 mi. W of Tampa**
No. of Rooms: **4**
No. of Private Baths: **2**
Max. No. Sharing Bath: **4**
Double/pb: **$60**
Single/pb: **$40**
Double/sb: **$45**
Single/sb: **$30**
Suite: **$75**
Open: **All year**
Breakfast: **Full**
Pets: **Sometimes**
Children: **Welcome**
Smoking: **No**
Social Drinking: **Permitted**

A premier facility in a premier location: this new Art Deco residence is 1½ miles from the Gulf of Mexico and 25 minutes from Busch Gardens, Dali Museum, and Weeki-Wachee Springs. Shopping, restaurants, churches, and public transportation are within easy walking

distance. The Grimms' home has an ivory stucco exterior, with front pillars, a tile roof, and stained glass doors. Inside, artifacts from their world travels are shown to advantage under 12-foot ceilings. Amenities include a pool and Jacuzzi, a grand piano, and bicycles for local excursions.

Gulf Beach Inn ✪

10655 GULF BEACH HIGHWAY, PENSACOLA, FLORIDA 32507

Tel: **(904) 492-4501**
Hosts: **M.J. and Lisa Krause**
Location: **50 mi. E of Mobile**
Guest Cottage: **$65**
Open: **All year**
Breakfast: **Full**
Pets: **No**
Children: **Welcome**
Smoking: **No**
Social Drinking: **Permitted**
Airport/Station Pickup: **Yes**
Foreign Languages: **German**

The Gulf Beach Inn is on the Intracoastal Waterway. Because it is located on your own private beach, it is the ideal spot for sunning, swimming, and watching sailboats, sunrises and sunsets. The Naval Aviation Museum, excellent seafood restaurants, and an outlet mall with over 100 stores are nearby. Perdido Key and the Emerald Coast of Florida are just minutes away.

Sunshine Inn ✪

508 DECATUR AVENUE, PENSACOLA, FLORIDA 32507

Tel: **(904) 455-6781**
Best Time to Call: **Early mornings**
Hosts: **The Jablonskis**
Location: **8 mi. from I-10; 4 mi. from beach**
No. of Rooms: **2**
No. of Private Baths: **1**
Max. No. Sharing Bath: **4**
Double/sb: **$45**
Suites: **$35 for 2**
Open: **All year**
Breakfast: **Full**
Pets: **No**
Children: **Welcome**
Smoking: **No**
Social Drinking: **Permitted**
Airport/Station Pickup: **Yes**
Foreign Languages: **German**

Sun and swim in the Gulf of Mexico, on the beautiful Emerald Coast of northwest Florida. Your knowledgeable hosts will provide you with all the touring advice you seek. Sunshine Inn is only minutes from the Naval Aviation Museum and the beach. The breakfast specialty is blueberry pancakes.

Ruskin House Bed and Breakfast ✪

120 DICKMAN DRIVE S.W., RUSKIN, FLORIDA 33570

Tel: **(813) 645-3842**
Best Time to Call: **Anytime**
Host: **Arthur M. Miller, Ph.D.**
Location: **25 mi. S of Tampa; 30 mi. N of Sarasota**
No. of Rooms: **3**
No. of Private Baths: **1**
Max No. Sharing Bath: **4**
Double/pb: **$65**
Double/sb: **$45**
Suites: **$65**
Open: **All year**
Reduced Rates: **7th day free**
Breakfast: **Continental**
Credit Cards: **MC, VISA**
Pets: **No**
Children: **Welcome, over 6**
Smoking: **No**
Social Drinking: **Permitted**
Minimum Stay: **2 nights**
Foreign Languages: **French**

A waterfront home listed on the State Register of Historic Places, this B&B, built in 1910, is graced with verandas and furnished with period antiques. The property abounds in citrus trees, and guests can help themselves to fruit in season. Your host, a poet, editor, and literature professor at New College in Sarasota, is a third-generation inhabitant of Ruskin; his grandfather cofounded the town as a Christian Socialist venture complete with Ruskin College, tuition-free for residents and their families. (The college's only surviving building, just a block from Ruskin House, is enrolled on the National Register of Historic Places.) Ruskin is no longer a utopian community, but the beach and playground are nearby, and it's an easy drive to either Tampa or Sarasota.

Casa de la Paz

22 AVENIDA MENENDEZ, ST. AUGUSTINE, FLORIDA 32084

Tel: **(904) 829-2915**
Best Time to Call: **9 AM–9 PM**
Host: **Jan Maki**
Location: **7 mi. from I-95**
No. of Rooms: **6**
No. of Private Baths: **6**
Double/pb: **$85–$145**
Suites: **$85–$145**
Open: **All year**
Breakfast: **Full**
Credit Cards: **AMEX, MC, VISA**
Pets: **No**
Children: **No**
Smoking: **No**
Social Drinking: **Permitted**

Overlooking historic Matanzas Bay in the heart of Old St. Augustine is this three-story Mediterranean-style stucco home. The rooms are comfortably furnished in a pleasant blend of the old and new. Amenities in each room include ceiling fans, central air-conditioning and heat, high-quality linens, cable TV, and complimentary sherry or wine. The veranda rooms have private entrances. Guests are welcome to use the private, walled courtyard, well-stocked library, and delightful parlor. It is central to all attractions and convenient to fine restaurants and shops.

Castle Garden ✪

15 SHENANDOAH STREET, ST. AUGUSTINE, FLORIDA 32084

Tel: **(904) 829-3839**
Best Time to Call: **9 AM–6 PM**
Hosts: **Bruce Kloeckner and Kimmy VanKooten**
Location: **10 mi. from I-95**
No. of Rooms: **6**
No. of Private Baths: **6**
Double/pb: **$75–$150**
Open: **All year**
Reduced Rates: **20% weekly, $20 less Sun.–Thurs.; 10% seniors**
Breakfast: **Full**
Credit Cards: **AMEX, DISC, MC, VISA**
Pets: **No**
Children: **Welcome, over 5**
Smoking: **No**
Social Drinking: **Permitted**
Airport/Station Pickup: **Yes**

The only Moorish-revival dwelling in St. Augustine, Castle Garden dates to the late 1800s; the unusual coquina stone exterior has remained virtually untouched since its completion. The completely renovated interior features two beautiful and unique bridal suites, each complete with a sunken bedroom, in-room Jacuzzi, cathedral ceiling, and other wonderful details. Park your car in the B&B's fenced lot and borrow bikes to tour the city, one of the nation's oldest. When you return, rest on the sunporch or stroll the lovely grounds. The hosts give each guest complimentary wine, and pride themselves on preparing mouthwatering country breakfasts "just like Mom used to make."

Kenwood Inn

38 MARINE STREET, ST. AUGUSTINE, FLORIDA 32084

Tel: **(904) 824-2116**
Best Time to Call: **10 AM–10 PM**
Hosts: **Mark, Kerrianne, and Caitlin Constant**
Location: **40 mi. S of Jacksonville**
No. of Rooms: **14**
No. of Private Baths: **14**
Double/pb: **$75–$105**
Single/pb: **$45–$65**
Suite: **$135**
Open: **All year**
Breakfast: **Continental**
Credit Cards: **DISC, MC, VISA**
Pets: **No**
Children: **Welcome, over 8**
Smoking: **No**
Social Drinking: **Permitted**

If you are to discover a Victorian building in Florida, how appropriate that it should be in the historic section of St. Augustine, one of the oldest cities in the U.S. This New England–style inn is a rarity in the South; this one has old-fashioned beds with color-coordinated touches right down to the sheets and linens. Breakfast may be taken in your room, in the courtyard surrounded by trees, or by the swimming pool. Tour trains, waterfront shops, restaurants, and museums are within walking distance. Flagler College is three blocks away.

St. Francis Inn ✪

279 ST. GEORGE STREET, ST. AUGUSTINE, FLORIDA 32084

Tel: **(904) 824-6068; (800) 824-6062**
Host: **Joe Finnegan**
Location: **2 mi. from US 1**
No. of Rooms: **14**
No. of Private Baths: **14**
Double/pb: **$55–$98**
Guest Cottage: **$160; sleeps 4–6**
Suites: **$75–$125**
Open: **All year**
Breakfast: **Continental, plus**
Credit Cards: **MC, VISA**
Pets: **No**
Children: **Welcome (crib)**
Smoking: **No**
Social Drinking: **Permitted**

Built in 1791, the Inn is a Spanish Colonial structure with a private courtyard and garden, located in the center of the restored part of town. Balconies are furnished with rocking chairs, and the swimming pool is a great cooling-off spot. The building is made of coquina, a limestone made of broken shells and coral. Due to its trapezoidal shape, there are no square or rectangular rooms. All of St. Augustine's historic and resort activities are within a three-mile radius.

Bayboro House on Old Tampa Bay ✪

1719 BEACH DRIVE SOUTHEAST, ST. PETERSBURG, FLORIDA 33701

Tel: **(813) 823-4955**
Hosts: **Gordon and Antonia Powers**
Location: **½ mi. from I-275, Exit 9**
No. of Rooms: **4**
No. of Private Baths: **4**
Double/pb: **$85–$145**
Open: **All year**
Breakfast: **Continental**
Credit Cards: **MC, VISA**
Pets: **No**
Children: **No**
Smoking: **No**
Social Drinking: **Permitted**

Richly appointed in antiques and collectibles, the historic Bayboro House is what you would expect in a luxury waterfront bed and breakfast. All rooms have a water view, air-conditioning, TV, VCR, and a morning paper is delivered to your door. Breakfast includes fresh fruits, juice, rolls, muffins, homemade breads, cereal, coffee and tea served in the formal dining room.

The Frog Pond Guesthouse ✪

145 29TH AVENUE NORTH, ST. PETERSBURG, FLORIDA 33704

Tel: **(813) 823-7407**
Host: **Wendy Roberts**
Location: **2 mi. from Rte. I-275**
No. of Rooms: **1**
No. of Private Baths: **1**
Suites: **$55–$65**
Open: **All year**
Breakfast: **Continental**

Credit Cards: **MC, VISA**
Pets: **No**
Children: **No**
Smoking: **No**
Social Drinking: **Permitted**
Minimum Stay: **2 nights**

Located in the historical district of St. Petersburg's Old Northeast, the Frog Pond offers guests a relaxing atmosphere in a unique setting. The room features a queen bed, hardwood floors, French doors, cable TV, VCR, and a private entrance. Enjoy the spacious patio with garden pond, play billiards in the game room, take a sunset stroll along the water, or watch the sailboats at the Pier. Frog Pond is conveniently located near the Gulf beaches, Florida International and Dali museums, Busch Gardens, and Florida Aquarium in Tampa. It's just a 90-minute drive to Disney World and other major attractions in Orlando.

Ferncourt Bed and Breakfast ✪

150 CENTRAL AVENUE, SAN MATEO, FLORIDA 32187

Tel: **(904) 329-9755**
Hosts: **Jack and Dee Morgan**
Location: **25 mi. W of St. Augustine**
No. of Rooms: **5**
No. of Private Baths: **5**
Double/pb: **$55–$75**
Suites: **$100**
Open: **All year**
Breakfast: **Full**
Pets: **No**
Children: **No**
Smoking: **No**
Social Drinking: **Permitted**

Ferncourt is a restored 1800s farm home, located in a tiny historic hamlet just a few minutes' drive from St. Augustine and Daytona Beach. Guests have use of several rooms and the wraparound veranda. Close by, restaurants serve excellent food. Cookies and tea are offered in the evening. Jack does woodworking and upholstery and many examples of his craft are on display throughout the inn. Dee dabbles in painting and loves antiques and flea markets, but her real passion is food, evidenced by the gourmet breakfast she serves. Discover North Central Florida, then retire to all the charm and hospitality of the Victorian era with your hosts.

Florida Keys House ✪

P.O. BOX 41, SUMMERLAND KEY, FLORIDA 33042

Tel: **(305) 872-4680**
Best Time to Call: **8 AM–8 PM**
Hosts: **Capt. Dave and Camille Wiley**
Location: **27 mi. E of Key West**
Suites: **$79–$125**
Open: **All year**
Breakfast: **Continental**
Pets: **No**
Children: **Welcome**
Smoking: **Restricted**
Social Drinking: **Permitted**
Minimum Stay: **2 nights**
Foreign Languages: **French, Spanish**

Set among an abundance of coconut palm trees, your private guest quarters can accommodate up to four people and consist of one or two bedrooms, a bathroom, living room, and large kitchen stocked with breakfast selections which you may prepare at your convenience. Florida Keys House is canal front with a dock where you can fish, swim, barbecue or just relax in the hammock under the shade trees. Dave and Camille also offer snorkeling and diving trips to beautiful Looe Key Reef. Ask about their specialty, "backcountry flats fishing" for Tarpon Bonefish, and Permit for the Great White Heron Wildlife Refuge.

Knightswood ✪

P.O. BOX 151, SUMMERLAND KEY, FLORIDA 33042

Tel: **(305) 872-2246; (800) 437-5402**
Hosts: **Chris and Herb Pontin**
Location: **26 mi. E of Key West**
No. of Rooms: **2**
No. of Private Baths: **2**
Double/pb: **$85**
Single/pb: **$70**
Open: **All year**
Breakfast: **Continental, plus**
Pets: **No**
Children: **No**
Smoking: **No**
Social Drinking: **Permitted**
Minimum Stay: **2 nights**

Knightswood boasts one of the loveliest water views in the Keys. The guest apartment is self-contained and very private. Snorkeling, fishing, and boating can be enjoyed right from the Pontins' dock. You are welcome to swim in the freshwater pool, relax in the spa, or sunbathe on the white sand beach. Trips to protected Looe Key Coral Reef can be arranged. Fine dining and Key West nightlife are within easy reach.

Fiorito's Bed & Breakfast ✪

421 OLD EAST LAKE ROAD, TARPON SPRINGS, FLORIDA 34689

Tel: **(813) 937-5487**
Best Time to Call: **8 AM–9 PM**
Hosts: **Dick and Marie Fiorito**
Location: **2 mi. E of US 19**
No. of Rooms: **1**
No. of Private Baths: **1**
Double/pb: **$40**
Single/pb: **$35**
Open: **All year**
Breakfast: **Full**
Pets: **No**
Children: **No**
Smoking: **Restricted**
Social Drinking: **Permitted**
Airport/Station Pickup: **Yes**

Just off a quiet road that runs along Lake Tarpon's horse country, this meticulously maintained home on two-and-a-half acres offers respite for the visitor. The guest room and bath are decorated in tones of blue, enhanced with beautiful accessories. Fresh fruit, cheese omelette, homemade bread and jam, and a choice of beverage is the Fioritos' idea of breakfast. It is beautifully served on the tree-shaded, screened terrace. They'll be happy to direct you to the Greek Sponge Docks, deep-sea fishing opportunities, golf courses, beaches, and great restaurants.

Heartsease ✪

272 OLD EAST LAKE ROAD, TARPON SPRINGS, FLORIDA 34689

Tel: **(813) 934-0994**
Best Time to Call: **After 7 PM**
Hosts: **Gerald and Sharon Goulish**
Suite: **$55–$60**
Open: **All year**
Reduced Rates: **Available**
Breakfast: **Continental**
Pets: **No**
Children: **No**
Smoking: **No**
Social Drinking: **Permitted**
Airport Pickup: **Yes**

You'll find plenty of "heartsease," meaning peace of mind and tranquility, at Gerald and Sharon's guest cottage. Wicker and pine furniture and a green and mauve color scheme create a light, airy feeling. Amenities include a private entrance, a mini-kitchen stocked with a microwave and breakfast fixings, cable TV, private bath, tennis court, and a deck overlooking the in-ground pool. Pluck an orange or a grapefruit from one of the many fruit trees and then settle in the gazebo, an ideal place for observing the bald eagles that nest nearby. Golf courses, Tampa's Old Hyde Park, Harbour Island, and Tarpon Springs' famed sponge docks are all within a short drive.

B&B on the Bayou ✪

P.O. BOX 1545, TARPON SPRINGS, FLORIDA 34688

Tel: **(813) 942-4468**
Hosts: **Al and Chris Stark**
Location: **15–20 mi. NW of Tampa**
No. of Rooms: **3**
No. of Private Baths: **1**
Max. No. Sharing Bath: **2**

Double/pb: **$55**
Single/pb: **$50**
Double/sb: **$55**
Single/sb: **$50**
Suite: **$99**
Open: **All year**
Reduced Rates: **Available**
Breakfast: **Continental**
Pets: **No**
Children: **Welcome, over 7**
Smoking: **No**
Social Drinking: **Permitted**
Airport Pickup: **Yes**

Come stay at this beautiful, contemporary home situated on a quiet bayou. Fish for a big red or watch the blue herons and pelicans nesting in a bird sanctuary behind the B&B. Go for a swim in your host's solar-heated pool or soak your cares away in a whirlpool spa. Then take a stroll through the famous sponge docks and do some antiquing in town. The Inn is located just minutes from a white sandy beach with breathtaking sunsets. Busch Gardens and Adventure Islands are close by. Private tours with transportation are available.

1909 McLeran House Bed & Breakfast and Collectibles Shoppe ✪

12408 CR 137, WELLBORN, FLORIDA 32094

Tel: **(904) 963-4603**
Hosts: **Robert and Mary Ryals**
Location: **50 mi. N of Gainesville**
No. of Rooms: **2**
No. of Private Baths: **1**
Max. No. Sharing Bath: **4**
Double/pb: **$60**
Double/sb: **$60**
Open: **All year**
Breakfast: **Continental**
Pets: **No**
Children: **No**
Smoking: **No**
Social Drinking: **Permitted**

Robert and Mary spent seven years doing a meticulous and extensive restoration on this bed & breakfast, which includes central heat and air. The interior boasts six fireplaces—each with a unique curly pine mantel—paddle fans in every room, a grand stairwell, and elegant woodwork. Guests will have their pick of cable TV, video and audio tapes, and complimentary snacks and beverages. Furnishings are tasteful, with a blend of old and new, including a mirrored oak cabinet that graced a Wellborn store nearly a century ago. Outside, a cedar gazebo crowns the garden area, which includes a swing, fountain arbor, walkways, a goldfish pond, and the Collectibles Shoppe in the barn. Nearby attractions include Stephen Foster Folk Culture Center, Florida Sports Hall of Fame, Ichetucknee Springs, and Suwannee River and Osceola Forest state parks.

West Palm Beach Bed & Breakfast ✪

419 32ND STREET, OLD NORTHWOOD HISTORIC DISTRICT, WEST PALM BEACH, FLORIDA 33407-4809
E-mail: wpbbb@aol.com

Tel: **(800) 736-4064; (407) 848-4064; fax: (407) 848-2422**
Best Time to Call: **9 AM–10 PM**
Host: **Dennis Keimel**
No. of Rooms: **4**
No. of Private Baths: **4**
Double/pb: **$75–$115**
Open: **All year**
Reduced Rates: **May–Oct.**
Breakfast: **Continental, plus**
Credit Cards: **AMEX, DC, MC, VISA**
Pets: **No**
Children: **No**
Smoking: **No**
Social Drinking: **Permitted**
Airport/Station Pickup: **Yes**

West Palm Beach Bed & Breakfast is a cozy but deceptively large property reminiscent of a Key West guest house with poolside cottages. The main house is pastel pink with aqua striped awnings and white picket fences. Inside, bright colors, whimsical decorations and white wicker furniture make for a fun, comfortable island atmosphere. All guest rooms have air-conditioning, color cable TV and paddle fans, each with its own style. The warm hospitality and ideal location near beaches, Palm Beach, and the downtown waterfront have made this B&B extremely popular with guests, including Europeans and Canadians. Enjoy a tropical breakfast buffet each morning prior to your adventures, or just relax by the pool.

GEORGIA

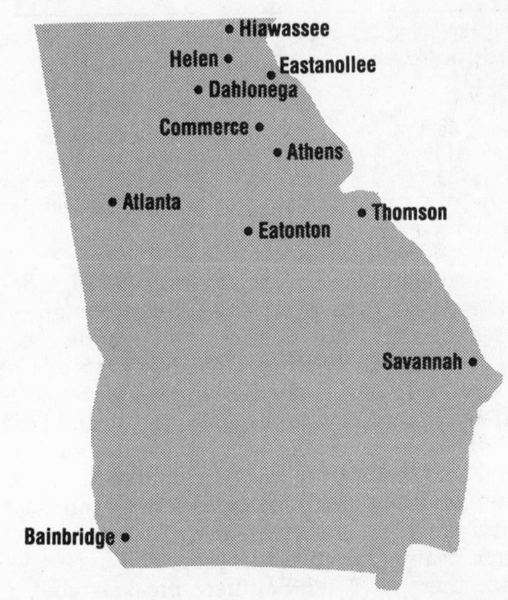

Oakwood Bed & Breakfast

4959 BARNETT SHOALS ROAD, ATHENS, GEORGIA 30605

Tel: **(706) 546-7886**
Best Time to Call: **9AM–7 PM**
Hosts: **Bob and Gerri Tate**
Location: **5 mi. SE of Athens**
No. of Rooms: **5**
No. of Private Baths: **5**
Double/pb: **$75–$120**
Suites: **$150**
Open: **All year**
Reduced Rates: **10% seniors**
Breakfast: **Full**
Credit Cards: **AMEX, DC, DISC, MC, VISA**
Pets: **No**
Children: **No**
Smoking: **No**
Social Drinking: **Permitted**
Airport Pickup: **Yes**

This 1860s Victorian property has been lovingly renovated to provide comfortable, simple elegance with a romantic aura of yesterday. Fenced and gated for privacy, the five-and-a-half-acre property nestles under a canopy of large oak trees. Many barns, a smokehouse, and a cottage add to the tranquility. Oakwood is located in an affluent neighborhood of acreage homes only minutes from downtown nightlife and the University of Georgia.

Atlanta's Woodruff Bed & Breakfast

223 PONCE DE LEON AVENUE, ATLANTA, GEORGIA 30308

Tel: **(404) 875-9449; (800) 473-9449**
Hosts: **Joan and Douglas Jones**
No. of Rooms: **12**
No. of Private Baths: **10**
Max. No. Sharing Bath: **4**
Double/pb: **$89–$149**
Single/pb: **$79–$129**
Suites: **$109–$149**
Open: **All year**
Reduced Rates: **10% seniors**
Breakfast: **Full**
Credit Cards: **AMEX, DISC, MC, VISA**
Pets: **Sometimes**
Children: **Welcome**
Smoking: **No**
Social Drinking: **Permitted**
Foreign Languages: **Spanish, French**

The moment you step into Atlanta's Woodruff Bed & Breakfast you'll experience the slower pace of times gone by. Joan and Douglas have exquisitely restored this turn-of-the-century home, keeping the old charm and character that once was. There are three Jacuzzi hot tubs, three fireplaces and several porches to insure a stay to everyone's liking. Centrally located to fine restaurants, cultural activities, and to most convention centers, yet bordering the residential area, the home was designed and built by a premier architect of the 1900s for a prominent family. In the 1950s, Bessie Woodruff purchased the home, where she and nineteen female assistants operated a licensed physiotherapy center. Many of Atlanta's finest politicians availed themselves of this needed therapy. A full Southern breakfast and true Southern hospitality will get your day started. Free pickup is provided from the MARTA, Atlanta's subway system.

Magnolia Station

1020 EDGEWOOD AVENUE NORTHEAST, ATLANTA, GEORGIA 30307

Tel: **(404) 523-2005**
Hosts: **Jim Piroli and Raymond Manci**
No. of Rooms: **3**
No. of Private Baths: **1**
Max. No. Sharing Bath: **4**
Double/pb: **$75**
Single/pb: **$65**
Double/sb: **$65**
Single/sb: **$55**
Open: **All year**
Reduced Rates: **10% after 4th night**
Breakfast: **Continental**
Credit Cards: **MC, VISA**
Pets: **No**
Children: **No**
Smoking: **No**
Social Drinking: **Permitted**

Magnolia Station is located in the Inman Park Historic District, one of the last enclaves of Atlanta's Victorian architecture. Relax by the pool or stroll the quiet streets where the city's most affluent resided,

including the inventor and founders of Coca-Cola. Beautifully restored and furnished with antiques and 18th-century reproductions, Magnolia Station stands on the site of the Civil War Battle of Atlanta and is across the street from the rapid-rail station. Walk to parks, the Carter Presidential Center, and the Little Five Points and Virginia-Highlands business districts. There is easy rail access to downtown, malls, and Atlanta's airport.

The White House B&B

320 WASHINGTON STREET, BAINBRIDGE, GEORGIA 31717

Tel: **(912) 248-1703**
Hosts: **John and Mary Patterson**
Location: **45 mi. NW of Tallahassee, Florida**
No. of Rooms: **3**
No. of Private Baths: **1**
Max. No. Sharing Bath: **4**
Double/pb: **$60**
Single/pb: **$55**
Double/sb: **$50**
Single/sb: **$45**
Open: **All year**
Reduced Rates: **Over 3 days**
Breakfast: **Continental**
Pets: **No**
Children: **Welcome, over 10**
Smoking: **No**
Social Drinking: **No**
Airport/Station Pickup: **Yes**

This antebellum dogtrot-style home (circa 1840–50) in the historic district of Bainbridge features original hand-hewn columns and rived pine floors. The decor is a blend of family antiques, heirloom fabrics, and needlework. Guests are encouraged to enjoy the swimming pool and gazebo, gallery library, and sitting room. Nearby attractions include historic homes, antique shops, Lake Seminole for fishing and water sports, May Artsfest, and local celebrations. Convenient for business and leisure travelers, it is an easy drive from Plains, Tallahassee, Florida, the Gulf beaches, and Florida theme parks.

Magnolia Inn ✪

206 CHERRY STREET, COMMERCE, GEORGIA 30529

Tel: **(706) 335-7257**
Best Time to Call: **9AM–noon; 6–9 PM**
Hosts: **Annette and Jerry Potter**
Location: **60 mi. N of Atlanta**
No. of Rooms: **4**
No. of Private Baths: **4**
Double/pb: **$60–$85**
Single/pb: **$50–$75**
Open: **All year**
Reduced Rates: **10% seniors; Dec.–Feb.**
Breakfast: **Full**
Credit Cards: **MC, VISA**
Pets: **No**
Children: **Welcome, over 10; under 10 by arrangement**
Smoking: **No**
Social Drinking: **Permitted**
Airport/Station Pickup: **Yes**

Built in 1909, this restored Queen Anne Victorian is decorated with antiques and collectibles. In historic Commerce, you can browse through an antique mall, enjoy an old-fashioned soda at the local drugstore, or visit the crafts and gift shops. Magnolia Inn is only minutes away from the outlet malls, Atlanta Dragway, and Road Atlanta. It's twenty minutes to the University of Georgia and one hour to Atlanta. Take part in a thrilling Murder Mystery Weekend or just relax in the porch swing and rockers on the front veranda.

The Pittman House ✪

81 HOMER ROAD, COMMERCE, GEORGIA 30529

Tel: **(706) 335-3823**
Best Time to Call: **7 AM–9 PM**
Hosts: **Tom and Dot Tomberlin**
Location: **60 mi. NE of Atlanta**
No. of Rooms: **4**
No. of Private Baths: **3**
Max. No. Sharing Bath: **4**
Double/pb: **$65**
Double/sb: **$55**
Single/sb: **$50**
Open: **All year**
Breakfast: **Full**
Credit Cards: **MC, VISA**
Pets: **No**
Children: **Welcome, over 12**
Smoking: **No**
Social Drinking: **No**

This gracious white Colonial, built in 1890, is decorated throughout with period pieces. If the furniture inspires you, visit Granny's Old Things, an antique shop right next door. Other points of interest include Château Elan Winery, in neighboring Braselton, and the Crawford W. Long Museum—honoring the doctor who discovered the use of ether as an anesthetic—in the town of Jefferson. Swimmers and sailors have their choice of Lake Lanier and Lake Hartwell; Hurricane Shoals is another lovely outdoor recreational area.

The Mountain Top Lodge

ROUTE 7, BOX 150, DAHLONEGA, GEORGIA 30533

Tel: **(706) 864-5257; (800) 526-9754**
Best Time to Call: **10 AM–6 PM**
Host: **Karen A. Lewan**
Location: **70 mi. N of Atlanta**
No. of Rooms: **13**
No. of Private Baths: **13**
Double/pb: **$70–$85**
Suites: **$115–$125**
Open: **All year**
Breakfast: **Full**
Pets: **No**
Children: **Welcome, over 12**
Smoking: **No**
Social Drinking: **Permitted**

Flanked by porches and decks, this gambrel-roofed, rustic cedar lodge is a secluded rural retreat on 40 acres, with a 360-degree mountain view. Decorated with art and antiques, the pine furniture and accessories made by mountain craftsmen add to the charm. Dahlonega was the site of America's first gold rush, and nature buffs will appreciate the Chattahoochee National Forest and Amicalola Falls State Park. Rafting, hiking, and horseback riding are all nearby. Don't miss the "Alpine village" of Helen, Georgia, only 30 minutes away. It now offers deluxe rooms with in-bath Jacuzzi whirlpool tubs and gas-log fireplaces.

Royal Guard Inn

203 SOUTH PARK STREET, DAHLONEGA, GEORGIA 30533

Tel: **(706) 864-1713**
Best Time to Call: **10 AM–9 PM**
Hosts: **John and Farris Vanderhoff**
Location: **50 mi. N of Atlanta**
No. of Rooms: **5**
No. of Private Baths: **5**
Double/pb: **$70–$80**
Open: **All year**
Reduced Rates: **$5 seniors, Sun.–Thurs.**
Breakfast: **Full**
Credit Cards: **AMEX, MC, VISA**
Pets: **No**
Children: **By arrangement**
Smoking: **No**
Social Drinking: **Permitted**

Located in the northeast Georgia mountains, Dahlonega is where the first major U.S. gold rush occurred in 1828. Dahlonega Gold Museum, Price Memorial Hall—on the site of one of the first U.S. branch mints—and gold-panning areas are all in the heart of the historic downtown. Royal Guard Inn, a half-block from the old town square, is a restored and enlarged old home. John and Farris serve complimentary wine and cheese on the great wraparound porch. Breakfast, served on fine china and silver on crisp white linen, includes a casserole, pastries, or hotcakes from an old family recipe, and fresh fruit and whipped cream.

Apple Orchard Country Inn ✪

ROUTE 2, BOX 353, LIBERTY HILL ROAD, EASTANOLLEE, GEORGIA 30538

Tel: **(706) 779-7292; fax: (706) 779-7705**
Hosts: **Wade M. and Lu Loraine Lambert**
Location: **90 mi. E of Atlanta**
No. of Rooms: **4**
No. of Private Baths: **4**
Double/pb: **$75–$95**
Single/pb: **$75**
Suites: **$125**
Open: **All year**
Reduced Rates: **10% weekly**
Breakfast: **Full**
Other Meals: **Available**
Credit Cards: **MC, VISA**
Pets: **No**
Children: **Welcome, over 7**
Smoking: **No**
Social Drinking: **Permitted**
Station Pickup: **Yes**

Apple Orchard Country Inn is located sixty-five miles west of Greenville and Spartanburg, and thirty minutes from scenic Alpine Helen. Cleveland, home of the Cabbage Patch Dolls, is one hour away. There's gold mining in Dahlonega as well as quaint shops and antiques. Water sports are available at Lakes Hanier and Hartwell; golf, tennis, horseback riding, and other outdoor activities are at state and federal parks. Apple Orchard Country Inn's own attractions include a producing apple orchard, a pre-Civil War cemetery, and an old baptismal. This two-story home sits on twenty acres of wooded parklike land. The interior is furnished with a mixture of Oriental and traditional antiques.

The Crockett House

671 MADISON ROAD, EATONTON, GEORGIA 31024

Tel: **(706) 485-2248**
Hosts: **Christa and Peter Crockett**
Location: **73 mi. E of Atlanta**
No. of Rooms: **6**

No. of Private Baths: **6**
Double/pb: **$65–$85**
Open: **All year**
Reduced Rates: **10% Nov.–Feb.; extended stays; seniors; families**
Breakfast: **Full**
Pets: **No**
Children: **Welcome, over 10**
Smoking: **No**
Social Drinking: **Permitted**
Airport Pickup: **Yes**

This stately and gracious turn-of-the-century home captures the history and charm of a bygone era. Guests receive a warm welcome and comfortable accommodations year-round. The home features seven bedrooms and eleven fireplaces. The large cozy bedrooms are thoughtfully decorated, some with private baths and fireplaces. Separate innkeepers' quarters insure the privacy of guests. Wander throughout the home and enjoy the principal rooms (equipped with telephones and TVs), balcony, wraparound porch, and tranquil setting of the three-acre yard.

Hilltop Haus ✪

P. O. BOX 154, CHATTAHOOCHEE STREET, HELEN, GEORGIA 30545

Tel: **(706) 878-2388**
Best Time to Call: **8 AM–10 PM**
Host: **Frankie Allen**
Location: **60 mi. from I-85**
No. of Rooms: **5**
No. of Private Baths: **3**
Max. No. Sharing Bath: **3**
Double/pb: **$60–$90**
Single/pb: **$50–$80**
Double/sb: **$50–$75**
Suites: **$80–$135**
Open: **All year**
Breakfast: **Continental, Plus**
Credit Cards: **MC, VISA**
Pets: **No**
Children: **Welcome**
Smoking: **Permitted**
Social Drinking: **Permitted**

This contemporary split-level overlooks the Alpine town of Helen and the Chattahoochee River. It is near the foothills of the Smoky Mountains, six miles from the Appalachian Trail. Rich wood paneling and fireplaces create a homey atmosphere for the traveler. Guests may choose a private room or the efficiency cottage with separate entrance. Each morning a hearty breakfast includes homemade biscuits and preserves. Your hostess will direct you to many outdoor activities and sights.

Henson Cove Place ✪

3840 CAR MILES ROAD, HIAWASSEE, GEORGIA 30546-9585

Tel: **(800) 714-5542**
Best Time to Call: **After 10 AM**
Hosts: **Bill and Nancy Leffingwell**
Location: **2 hrs. N of Atlanta**
No. of Rooms: **2**
No. of Private Baths: **2**
Double/pb: **$55**
Suites: **$55**
Open: **All year**
Breakfast: **Full**
Credit Cards: **MC, VISA**
Pets: **No**
Children: **Welcome, over 10**
Smoking: **No**
Social Drinking: **Permitted**

Henson Cove Place has a warm homey atmosphere that will envelop you as you head for your room. The furniture and decorations are from Bill and Nancy's families and have stories behind them. You can browse through the magazine collection, read any of 2000 books, watch TV in the sitting room, and relax on the front porch. Or attend a festival, country music show, hike or stop in the many small shops in the area. In the morning you'll be greeted with hot coffee and breakfast. A typical menu might be fruit cup, juice, muffins, rolled stuffed omelette, apple French toast with baby sausages, or sausage strata. Bill is a furniture maker specializing in reproductions. Nancy operates a business service above his workshop. Both like talking to guests and making their stay an enjoyable one.

R.S.V.P. Savannah—B&B Reservation Service

9489 WHITFIELD AVENUE, BOX 49, SAVANNAH, GEORGIA 31406

Tel: **(912) 232-7787; (800) 729-7787**
Best Time to Call: **9:30 AM–5:30 PM Mon.–Fri.**
Coordinator: **Sonja Lazzaro**
States/Regions Covered: **Brunswick, Savannah, St. Simons Island, Tybee Island; South Carolina—Beaufort, Charleston**
Rates (Single/Double): **$70–$225**
Credit Cards: **AMEX, DISC, MC, VISA**

Accommodations include elegantly restored inns, guest houses, private homes, and even a villa on the water. They're located in the best historic districts as well as along the coast, from South Carolina's Low Country to Georgia's Sea Islands. A special blend of cordial hospitality, comfort, and services is provided. All are air-conditioned in the summer. Facilities for children and the disabled are often available. Please note that while some hosts accept credit cards, some do not.

Joan's on Jones ✪

17 WEST JONES STREET, SAVANNAH, GEORGIA 31401

Tel: **(912) 234-3863; (800) 407-3863; fax: (912) 234-1455**
Hosts: **Joan and Gary Levy**
Location: **140 mi. N of Jacksonville, FL**
Suites: **$115–$130; sleeps 2–4**
Open: **All year**
Reduced Rates: **Weekly**
Breakfast: **Continental**
Pets: **Sometimes**
Children: **Welcome**
Smoking: **No**
Social Drinking: **Permitted**
Minimum Stay: **3 days for St. Patrick's Day week only**

Clip-clopping along the brick streets of the city's historic district, horse-drawn carriages take you back to a more serene and elegant era. This bed and breakfast maintains the old-fashioned mood, with its original heart-pine floors, antique furnishings, and Savannah gray brick walls. (Note the late nineteenth-century documents that slipped behind one of the fireplace mantels.) All the historic places of interest, including the famous squares, are a short walk away. Joan and Gary, former restaurateurs, live upstairs and invite you to tour their home if you're staying at least two nights.

Lion's Head Inn

120 EAST GASTON STREET, SAVANNAH, GEORGIA 31401

Tel: **(912) 232-4580**
Host: **Christy Dell'orco**
Location: **Downtown Savannah**
No. of Rooms: **5**
No. of Private Baths: **5**
Double/pb: **$90–$130**
Single/pb: **$85–$115**
Suites: **$125–$170**
Open: **All year**
Reduced Rates: **Available**
Breakfast: **Continental**
Credit Cards: **AMEX, MC, VISA**
Pets: **No**
Children: **Welcome**
Smoking: **No**
Social Drinking: **Permitted**

This elegant nineteenth-century mansion is tastefully adorned with pristine Empire furniture and accessories. A collection of European and American art, Italian marble, and French bronze sculptures and 19th-century lighting beautify each room. The Inn is located on Gaston Street, the prime residential street in the historic district. Stroll across the street to picturesque Forsyth Park and enjoy all the historic attractions and amenities within walking distance. The innkeeper, Christy, a retired sales manager, now is a registered Savannah tour guide and antiquarian. She'll help you enjoy gracious living at its best and experience true nineteenth-century grandeur at the Lion's Head Inn.

Four Chimneys B&B

2316 WIRE ROAD SOUTHEAST, THOMSON, GEORGIA 30824

Tel: **(706) 597-0220**
Best Time to Call: **9 AM–10 PM**
Hosts: **Maggie and Ralph Zieger**
Location: **35 mi. W of Augusta**
No. of Rooms: **4**
No. of Private Baths: **3**
Double/pb: **$50**
Single/pb: **$45**
Open: **All year**
Breakfast: **Continental, plus**
Credit Cards: **MC, VISA**
Pets: **No**
Children: **Welcome, over 12**
Smoking: **Permitted**
Social Drinking: **Permitted**
Foreign Languages: **German**

Escape from the modern world at this early 1800s country house with a rocking-chair porch. The old-fashioned landscape features a large herb garden and heirloom flowers. Antique and reproduction furniture complement the original heart-pine interior. A small library and a cozy parlor invite you to relax at your leisure. Guest rooms have four-poster beds and working fireplaces. Restaurants, golf courses, and antique shops are nearby. Fox hunts and other equestrian events take place throughout the year.

KENTUCKY

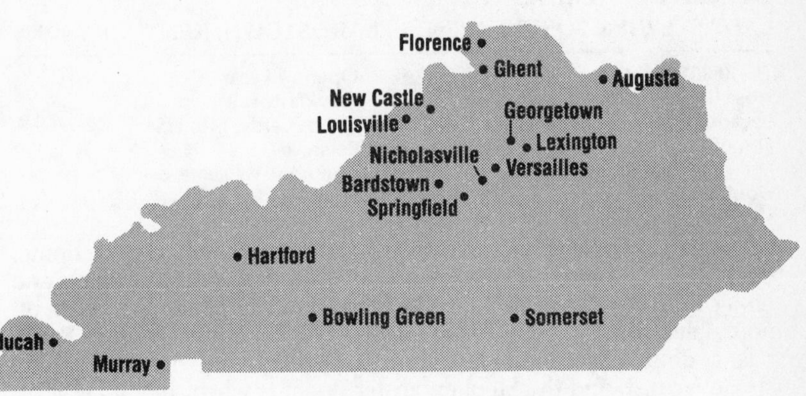

Augusta White House Inn B&B ✪

307 MAIN STREET, AUGUSTA, KENTUCKY 41002

Tel: **(606) 756-2004**	Open: **All year**
Best Time to Call: **9–11 AM**	Reduced Rates: **Available**
Host: **Rebecca Spencer**	Breakfast: **Full**
Location: **50 mi. SE of Cincinnati, Ohio**	Credit Cards: **AMEX, DISC, MC, VISA**
No. of Rooms: **5**	Pets: **No**
Max. No. Sharing Bath: **4**	Children: **No**
Double/sb: **$79**	Smoking: **No**
Single/sb: **$59**	Social Drinking: **No**
Guest Cottage: **$75**	Airport/Station Pickup: **Yes**

AWHIBB is located in the downtown section of historic Augusta, in a beautifully restored, two-story brick structure (the Buerger Tin Shop, circa 1840) that combines Victorian elegance and Southern hospitality. Comfortably sized rooms with flowered wallpaper and high, crown-molded ceilings may well remind you of your grandparents' home, albeit with all modern conveniences. In addition to their own room, guests have use of the parlor, formal dining and living rooms, and outside garden deck. Breakfast includes fresh-baked bread with an array of gourmet entrees and side dishes to please even the most discriminating palates. Antique shops and excellent restaurants are a short stroll away.

Beautiful Dreamer ✪

EAST STEPHEN FOSTER AVENUE, BARDSTOWN, KENTUCKY 40004

Tel: **(800) 811-8312**
Host: **Lynell Ginter**
Location: **30 mi. SE of Louisville**
No. of Rooms: **4**
No. of Private Baths: **4**
Double/pb: **$85**
Open: **All year**
Breakfast: **Full**
Credit Cards: **MC, VISA**
Pets: **No**
Children: **Welcome, over 8**
Smoking: **No**

Decorated with antiques and cherry furniture, this Federal-style home, circa 1995, is located in the historic district. Relax on the porch and enjoy a breathtaking view of My Old Kentucky Home, or show off your talent on the baby grand piano. The Beautiful Dreamer Room has a double Jacuzzi, the Captain's Room has a fireplace and a single Jacuzzi, and the Stephen Foster Room is wheelchair accessible, featuring a shower with rails and a double sink that can accommodate a wheelchair. All rooms are air-conditioned, have queen-size beds, and include a hearty breakfast. Music lovers will be happy to know that this B&B is within walking distance of the Stephen Foster Story.

Jailer's Inn ✪

111 WEST STEPHEN FOSTER AVENUE, BARDSTOWN, KENTUCKY 40004

Tel: **(502) 348-5551; (800) 948-5551**
Best Time to Call: **10 AM–5 PM**
Hosts: **Challen and Fran McCoy**
Location: **35 mi. S of Louisville**
No. of Rooms: **6**
No. of Private Baths: **6**
Double/pb: **$65–$100**
Open: **Mar.–Dec.**
Reduced Rates: **Available**
Breakfast: **Continental, plus**
Credit Cards: **AMEX, DISC, MC, VISA**
Pets: **No**
Children: **Welcome**
Smoking: **No**
Social Drinking: **Permitted**
Station pickup: **Yes**

For the ultimate in unusual experiences, spend the night in "jail" without having committed a crime. Built in 1819, this former jailer's residence originally housed prisoners upstairs, and has been completely remodeled and furnished with fine antiques and oriental rugs. An adjacent building, once used as the women's cell, has been transformed into a charming suite, where bunk beds are suspended from a brick wall and the decor is black-and-white checks instead of stripes. The town is famous for *The Stephen Foster Story,* an outdoor musical production. Take time to visit the Getz Museum of Whiskey History and a Civil War museum, and take a tour of My Old Kentucky Home conducted by guides in antebellum costumes. Two guest rooms have Jacuzzi tubs.

Alpine Lodge ✪

5310 MORGANTOWN ROAD, BOWLING GREEN, KENTUCKY 42101

Tel: **(502) 843-4846**
Best Time to Call: **9 AM–9 PM**
Hosts: **Dr. and Mrs. David Livingston**
Location: **60 mi. N of Nashville, Tenn.**
No. of Rooms: **5**
No. of Private Baths: **3**
Max. No. Sharing Bath: **4**
Double/pb: **$50**
Single/pb: **$40**
Double/sb: **$45**
Single/sb: **$35**
Guest Cottage: **$150, sleeps 6**
Suites: **$75**
Open: **All year**
Reduced Rates: **Weekly**
Breakfast: **Full**
Other Meals: **Available**
Pets: **Dogs welcome**
Children: **Welcome**
Smoking: **Permitted**
Social Drinking: **Permitted**
Airport/Station Pickup: **Yes**
Foreign Languages: **Spanish**

The lush Bluegrass Region of Kentucky is the setting for this spacious Swiss chalet–style home that's situated on four lovely acres and furnished with many antiques. A typical Southern breakfast of eggs, sausage, biscuits and gravy, fried apples, grits, coffee cake, and beverage starts your day. If you can manage to get up from the table, stroll the grounds complete with nature trails and gardens or take a swim in the pool. Afterwards, take in the sights and sounds of Opryland, Mammoth Cave, or the battlefields of historic Bowling Green. In the evening, relax in the living room, where Dr. Livingston, a music professor, may entertain you with selections played on the grand piano.

Twin Pines ✪

28 LACRESTA DRIVE, FLORENCE, KENTUCKY 41042

Tel: **(606) 282-0456**
Best Time to Call: **8 AM–10 PM**
Hosts: **Coleen and Mike Detzel**
Location: **10 mi. S of Cincinnati, Ohio**
No. of Rooms: **3**
No. of Private Baths: **1**
Max. No. Sharing Bath: **4**
Double/pb: **$60**
Single/pb: **$50**
Double/sb: **$50**
Single/sb: **$40**
Open: **All year**
Reduced Rates: **10% seniors**
Breakfast: **Full**
Credit Cards: **MC, VISA**
Pets: **Sometimes**
Children: **Welcome, over 10**
Smoking: **No**
Social Drinking: **Permitted**
Airport/Station Pickup: **Yes**

Twin Pines is a classic brick ranch, beautifully decorated and filled with lots of interesting collectibles and antiques. Enjoy reading or relaxing in the living room, or try the 1950s style lower level featuring TV, games, and a pinball machine. Its home-cooked Kentucky breakfast includes pancakes, homemade syrup, biscuits and gravy, fresh eggs, fried apples, and several cold cereals for those wanting lighter fare. Your hosts Coleen and Mike will tell you about the great shopping, restaurants, and excellent attractions close by.

Jordan Farm Bed & Breakfast ✪

4091 NEWTOWN PIKE, GEORGETOWN, KENTUCKY 40324

Tel: **(502) 863-1944, 868-9002**
Best Time to Call: **Anytime**
Hosts: **Harold and Becky Jordan**
Location: **8 mi. N of Lexington**
Suites: **$75, sleeps 4**
Open: **All year**
Breakfast: **Continental**
Pets: **No**
Children: **Welcome**
Smoking: **No**
Social Drinking: **Permitted**
Minimum Stay: **2 nights weekends Apr. and Oct.**
Airport/Station Pickup: **Yes**

Derby fans will want to stay on this 100-acre thoroughbred farm in the middle of Kentucky's legendary horse country. Indeed, the Kentucky Horse Park is only five minutes away. From the guest room's private deck, you can watch the Jordans' horses cavort in the fields. Or drop a line into the fishing pond and try your luck. Separate guest house with two large Jacuzzi suites and mini-kitchens.

Ghent House B&B ✪

411 MAIN STREET, U.S. 42, GHENT, KENTUCKY 41045

Tel: **(502) 347-5807 weekends; (606) 291-0168 weekdays**
Best Time to Call: **After 7 PM; weekends**
Host: **Wayne Young**
Location: **Halfway between Cincinnati and Louisville off I-71, Carrollton exit**
No. of Rooms: **3**
No. of Private Baths: **3**
Double/pb: **$60**
Single/pb: **$50**
Suites: **$75–$120**
Open: **All year**
Reduced Rates: **Available**
Breakfast: **Full**
Pets: **No**
Children: **Welcome (crib)**
Smoking: **No**
Social Drinking: **Permitted**
Airport/Station Pickup: **Yes**

Ghent House is a gracious antebellum residence, built in the usual style of the day—a central hall with rooms on either side and the kitchen and dining room in the rear. A beautiful fantail window and two English coach lights enhance the front entrance. Guests can look out over the Ohio River and imagine the time when steamboats regularly traveled the waterways. The view includes the lovely homes of the Vevay, Indiana, side of the river. Ghent House has two-person Jacuzzis and a five-person hot tub.

Ranney Porch Bed & Breakfast ✪

3810 HIGHWAY 231 NORTH, HARTFORD, KENTUCKY 42347

Tel: **(502) 298-7972**
Best time to Call: **After 4 PM**
Hosts: **Peggy Jo and Rance Ranney**
Location: **17.7 mi. S of Owensboro**
No. of Rooms: **1**
No. of Private Baths: **1**
Double/pb: **$50**
Single/pb: **$40**
Open: **All year**
Breakfast: **Full**
Pets: **No**
Children: **Welcome**
Smoking: **No**
Social Drinking: **No**

One of the unique features of this country B&B is the fifty-seven-foot porch spanning the length of the building, which is modeled after a Georgia tenant house. The exterior has blue trim, black shutters, and a candy apple red door. Inside, a Story and Clark piano sits on the foyer's red brick floor tiles, which came from the roof of a train depot. In the living room, cherry furniture complements the cherry wood floor. The bedroom's antique quilts and firm mattress assure you a good night's sleep. Numerous special events throughout the year, such as the Bar-be-que Festival, Yellow Banks Dulcimer Festival, and Bluegrass Music Festival, make this a place to visit often. Traditional and vegetarian meals are offered.

A True Inn ✪

467 WEST SECOND STREET, LEXINGTON, KENTUCKY 40507

Tel: **(800) 374-6151; (606) 252-6166**
Best Time to Call: **5–8 PM**
Hosts: **Bobby and Beverly True**
Location: **Downtown Lexington**
No. of Rooms: **5**
No. of Private Baths: **4**
Max. No. Sharing Bath: **4**
Double/pb: **$85**
Double/sb: **$65**
Suites: **$95–$125**
Open: **All year**
Breakfast: **Full**
Credit Cards: **AMEX, DC, MC, VISA**
Pets: **No**
Children: **Welcome, over 12**
Smoking: **No**
Social Drinking: **Permitted**
Airport/Station Pickup: **Yes**

Located in the heart of downtown Lexington, A True Inn is only two blocks from Rupp Arena, restaurants, antique and specialty shops, the opera house, and historic homes and churches. This large Victorian home, built in 1843, welcomes you to Lexington's past with stained and leaded glass, seven ornately carved Richardsonian and Victorian mantels, original chandeliers, and spacious formal rooms and gardens. All rooms are decorated with antiques and reproduction furnishings. Lovely quilts and afghans are in your room for afternoon naps and reading. A true Kentucky breakfast is served each morning, delightful refreshments in the afternoon. Bobby and Beverly and their families have been in Lexington for generations and are anxious to share their home and provide guests with true Southern hospitality.

The Victorian Secret Bed & Breakfast ✪

1132 SOUTH FIRST STREET, LOUISVILLE, KENTUCKY 40203

Tel: **(502) 581-1914; (800) 449-4691, Pin 0604**
Hosts: **Nan and Steve Roosa**
Location: **1 mi. S of downtown Louisville**
No. of Rooms: **3**
No. of Private Baths: **1**
Max. No. Sharing Bath: **3**
Double/pb: **$68–$89**
Double/sb: **$58–$68**
Open: **All year**
Reduced Rates: **Weekly**
Breakfast: **Continental**
Pets: **No**
Children: **Welcome**
Smoking: **Permitted**
Social Drinking: **Permitted**

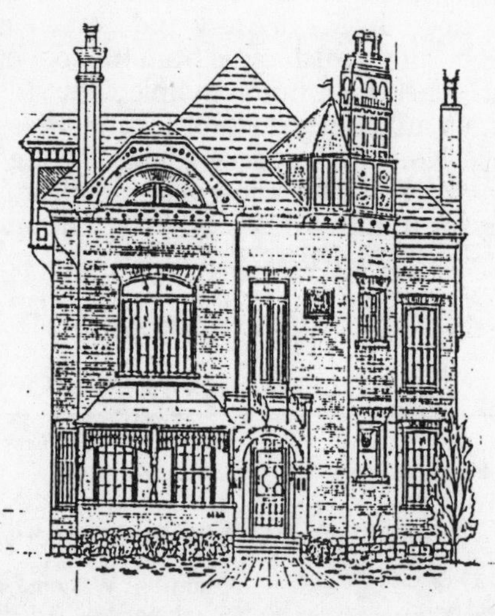

An elegant brick Victorian with lavish woodwork, this B&B has modern amenities like an exercise room with a bench press and a rowing machine, and color TVs in guest rooms. The Louisville area is rich in historic homes. Railbirds and would-be jockeys will want to make pilgrimages to the famous tracks at Churchill Downs (site of the Kentucky Derby) and Louisville Downs (home of harness races).

Diuguid House Bed & Breakfast ✪

603 MAIN STREET, MURRAY, KENTUCKY 42071

Tel: **(502) 753-5470**
Best Time to Call: **4–10 PM**
Hosts: **Karen and George Chapman**
Location: **45 mi. S of Paducah**
No. of Rooms: **3**
Max. No. Sharing Bath: **5**
Double/sb: **$40**
Open: **All year**
Reduced Rates: **Seventh night free**
Breakfast: **Full**

Credit Cards: **MC, VISA**
Pets: **No**
Children: **Welcome**
Smoking: **No**
Social Drinking: **Permitted**
Airport/Station Pickup: **Yes**

Upon walking into this 1890s Queen Anne, listed on the National Register of Historic Places, guests see an impressive sweeping oak staircase and unusual hallway fretwork. In addition to their rooms, visitors have use of the parlor, TV lounge, and dining room. Murray State University houses a local history museum, an art gallery, and the National Boy Scout Museum. The town, a top-rated retirement community, offers lots of theatrical and musical events. For outdoor activities, take the twenty-minute drive to Land Between the Lakes, where you can hike, hunt, fish, admire the resident buffalo herd, or see a working historical farm.

The Oldham House B&B and Antiques ✪

111 SOUTH MAIN STREET, P.O. BOX 628, NEW CASTLE, KENTUCKY 40050

Tel: **(502) 845-0103**
Host: **Emmy Houweling**
Location: **35 mi. NE of Louisville**
No. of Rooms: **2**
No. of Private Baths: **2**
Double/pb: **$70**
Single/pb: **$65**
Suite: **$75**
Open: **All year**
Reduced Rates: **Available**
Breakfast: **Full**
Pets: **No**
Children: **Welcome, over 12**
Smoking: **No**
Social Drinking: **Permitted**
Airport Pickup: **Yes**
Foreign Languages: **Dutch, French, German**

A Federal period structure built in 1820, Oldham House is located a short distance north of the Bluegrass Region and convenient to Louisville, Lexington, and Cincinnati. The B&B is decorated in primitive antiques and accessories, most of which are for sale at Emmy's antique shop located on the property. The kitchen had once been the slave kitchen with separate quarters above. The original smokehouse still remains on the property. Things to do include horse racing twice a year in Louisville and Lexington horse farms, visiting scenic Ohio River towns and state parks, golfing, and of course, antiquing galore.

Sandusky House & O'Neal Log Cabin Bed & Breakfast ✪

1626 DELANY FERRY ROAD, NICHOLASVILLE, KENTUCKY 40356

Tel: **(606) 223-4730**
Best Time to Call: **8 AM–10 PM**
Hosts: **Jim and Linda Humphrey**
Location: **6 mi. SW of Lexington**
No. of Rooms: **3**
No. of Private Baths: **3**
Double/pb: **$69**
Guest Cabin: **$85**
Open: **All year**
Reduced Rates: **Available**
Breakfast: **Full; Continental plus in cabin**

Credit Cards: **MC, VISA**
Pets: **No**
Children: **Welcome, over 12 in house; no age restriction in cabin**
Smoking: **No**
Social Drinking: **Permitted**
Airport/Station Pickup: **Yes**

A tree-lined drive to the Sandusky House is just a prelude to the handsome Greek Revival residence built about 1850 with bricks fired on the premises. Once the property was a 1000-acre farm owned by Revolutionary War veteran Jacob Sandusky—he acquired the site in a 1780 land grant from Patrick Henry, then the governor of Virginia. Today the B&B sits on a ten-acre estate amid horse farms, yet is close to downtown Lexington, Keeneland Race Track, Kentucky Horse Park, and many other attractions. The 180-year-old authentic log cabin has been reconstructed and has two bedrooms, kitchen, living room with a fireplace, whirlpool tub, and air-conditioning.

Ehrhardt's B&B ✪

285 SPRINGWELL LANE, PADUCAH, KENTUCKY 42001

Tel: **(502) 554-0644**
Best Time to Call: **7–9 AM; 4–6 PM**
Hosts: **Eileen and Phil Ehrhardt**
Location: **1 mi. from I-24**
No. of Rooms: **2**
Max. No. Sharing Bath: **4**
Double/sb: **$45**
Single/sb: **$40**
Open: **All year**
Reduced Rates: **10% seniors**
Breakfast: **Full**
Other Meals: **Available**
Pets: **No**
Children: **Welcome, over 12**
Smoking: **Permitted**
Social Drinking: **Permitted**
Airport/Station Pickup: **Yes**

This brick Colonial ranch home is just a mile off I-24, which is famous for its beautiful scenery. Your hosts hope to make you feel at home in antique-filled bedrooms and a den with a fireplace. Homemade biscuits and jellies, and country ham and gravy are breakfast specialties. Enjoy swimming in the Ehrhardts' pool and boating at nearby Lake Barkley, Ky Lake, and Land Between the Lakes. Paducah features quarterhorse racing from June through November, and the National Quilt Show in April.

Shadwick House ✪

411 SOUTH MAIN STREET, SOMERSET, KENTUCKY 42501

Tel: **(606) 678-4675**
Best Time to Call: **Anytime**
Host: **Ann Epperson**
Location: **84 mi. S of Lexington**
No. of Rooms: **4**
Max. No. Sharing Bath: **4**
Double/sb: **$40**
Single/sb: **$40**
Open: **All year**
Breakfast: **Full**
Credit Cards: **MC, VISA**
Pets: **No**
Children: **Welcome**
Smoking: **No**
Social Drinking: **Permitted**

Shadwick House has been known for its Southern hospitality for more than seventy years—the home was built in 1920 by Nellie Stringer Shadwick, great-grandmother of the present owner. The first floor has been converted into an antique and crafts shop. Kentucky ham and biscuits are served for breakfast in the original dining room. This B&B is tucked into the Cumberland Mountain foothills, near Lake Cumberland. Other local attractions are Renfro Valley, Cumberland Falls State Park, Tombstone Junction, and Big South Fork National Park.

Maple Hill Manor B&B ✪

2941 PERRYVILLE ROAD, SPRINGFIELD, KENTUCKY 40069

Tel: **(606) 336-3075; (800) 886-7546**
Hosts: **Bob and Kay Carroll**
No. of Rooms: **7**
No. of Private Baths: **7**
Double/pb: **$60–$85**
Single/pb: **$50**
Open: **All year**
Reduced Rates: **Available**
Breakfast: **Full**
Credit Cards: **MC, VISA**
Pets: **No**
Children: **Welcome (crib)**
Smoking: **No**
Social Drinking: **Permitted**

This hilltop manor house built in 1851 is situated on 14 tranquil acres in the scenic Bluegrass Region of Kentucky. Listed on the National Register of Historic Places, its Italianate design features 13-foot ceilings, 9-foot windows and doors, a profusion of fireplaces, and a solid cherry spiral staircase. The bedrooms are large, airy, and beautifully decorated with carefully chosen antique furnishings. The romantic honeymoon bed chamber has a canopy bed and Jacuzzi bath. In the evening, Bob and Kay graciously offer complimentary beverages and homemade dessert. Within an hour of Lexington and Louisville, you can visit Perryville Battlefield and Shaker Village and take a tour of distilleries. Murder mystery packages and gift certificates available.

Shepherd Place ✪

31 HERITAGE ROAD (U.S. 60), VERSAILLES, KENTUCKY 40383

Tel: **(606) 873-7843; (800) 278-0864**
Hosts: **Marlin and Sylvia Yawn**
Location: **10 mi. W of Lexington**
No. of Rooms: **3**
No. of Private Baths: **3**
Double/pb: **$75**
Single/pb: **$65**
Open: **All year**
Breakfast: **Full**
Pets: **No**
Children: **Welcome, over 12**
Smoking: **No**
Social Drinking: **Permitted**
Airport/Station Pickup: **Yes**

Marlin and Sylvia encourage you to make yourself comfortable in their pre–Civil War home, built around 1815. Rest in a spacious, beautifully decorated bedroom or relax in the parlor. Enjoy the lovely scenery while sitting on the patio or the porch swing. You might even want to pet the resident ewes, Abigail and Victoria. Brochures, menus, and plenty of ideas will be available to help you plan the rest of your stay.

LOUISIANA

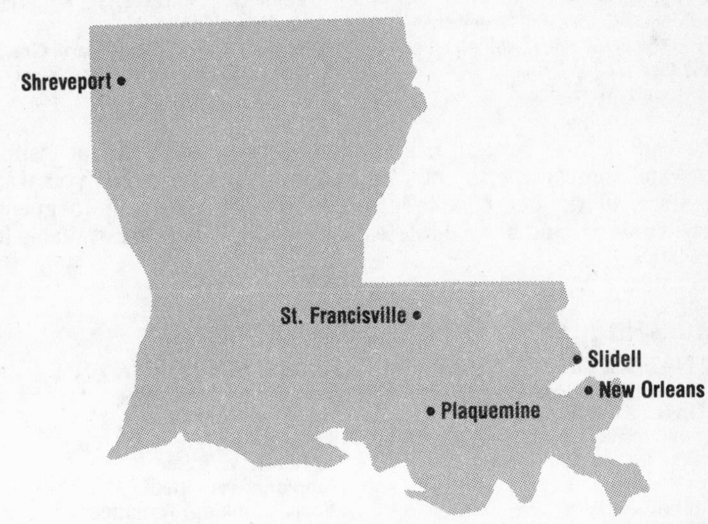

Bed & Breakfast, Inc.—New Orleans ✪

1021 MOSS STREET, BOX 52257, NEW ORLEANS, LOUISIANA 70152-2257

Tel: **(504) 488-4640; (800) 729-4640;**
fax: **(504) 488-4639**
Coordinator: **Hazell Boyce**
States/Regions Covered: **New Orleans**
Descriptive Directory: **Free**

Rates (Single/Double):
Modest: **$36–$46 / $41–$51**
Average: **$41–$76 / $41–$76**
Luxury: **$71–$86 / $76–$86**
Credit Cards: **No**

New Orleans is called The City That Care Forgot. You are certain to be carefree, visiting the French Quarter, taking Mississippi riverboat rides, taking plantation tours, as well as dining in fine restaurants and attending jazz concerts. Hazell's hosts, many with historic properties along the streetcar line and in the French Quarter, will help you get the most out of your stay.

New Orleans Bed & Breakfast and Accommodations ✪

P.O. BOX 8163, NEW ORLEANS, LOUISIANA 70182-8163

Tel: **(504) 838-0071, 838-0072; fax: (504) 838-0140**
Best Time to Call: **8:30 AM–4:30 PM**
Coordinator: **Sarah-Margaret Brown**
States/Regions Covered: **Louisiana—Covington, Jeanerette, Lafayette, Mandeville, Natchitoches, New Iberia, New Orleans, Shreveport, St. Francisville**

Rates (Single/Double):
Modest: **$30–$45 / $40–$45**
Average: **$45–$50 / $50–$55**
Luxury: **$65–$200**
Credit Cards: **AMEX, DISC, MC, VISA (for deposit only)**
Minimum Stay: **5 nights Mardi Gras, Jazz Festival; 3 nights Sugar Bowl**

Since 1979 Sarah-Margaret has arranged accommodations for visitors in private homes, apartments, and condos. Tell her what you want and she will do her best to please you. Care is given to guests' safety, comfort, and special interests. Discount tickets are available for many attractions.

Beau Séjour ✪

1930 NAPOLEON AVENUE, NEW ORLEANS, LOUISIANA 70115

Tel: **(504) 897-3746**
Best Time to Call: **10 AM–8 PM**
Hosts: **Gilles and Kim Gagnon**
No. of Rooms: **5**
No. of Private Baths: **5**
Double/pb: **$95**
Single/pb: **$90**
Suites: **$130**
Open: **All year**

Breakfast: **Continental**
Pets: **No**
Children: **Welcome**
Smoking: **Permitted**
Social Drinking: **Permitted**
Minimum Stay: **2 nights special events and holidays**
Foreign Languages: **French**

Kim and Gilles recently restored their 1906 Beau Séjour house to its original character, with beautiful detailing and wood floors. It is decorated in the best New Orleans style, blending country and European antiques with Louisiana and New Orleans touches. Located in one of the most picturesque neighborhoods of New Orleans, surrounded by lush tropical plantings, and on the Mardi Gras parade route, the mansion is convenient to convention and tourist attractions. Kim and Gilles are dedicated to New Orleans preservation and enjoy sharing their knowledge of local restaurants, excursions, and the culture of the "Big Easy."

The Chimes Bed & Breakfast

CONSTANTINOPLE AT COLISEUM, BOX 52257, NEW ORLEANS, LOUISIANA 70152-2257

Tel: **(504) 488-4640; (800) 729-4640**
Best Time to Call: **10 AM–5 PM Mon.–Fri.**
Hosts: **Jill and Charles Abbyad and Susan Smith**
Location: **In New Orleans**
No. of Rooms: **5**
No. of Private Baths: **5**
Double/pb: **$66–$79**
Suites: **$86–$126**
Open: **All year**
Reduced Rates: **Available**
Breakfast: **Continental, plus**
Pets: **Sometimes**
Children: **Welcome**
Social Drinking: **Permitted**
Minimum Stay: **Special events**
Foreign Languages: **French**

These quaint guest quarters sit behind a Victorian uptown home. Stained and leaded glass windows, French doors, cypress staircases, and a brick courtyard enhance the friendly, relaxed atmosphere here. Caring for a property of this magnitude is an ongoing commitment and truly a labor of love. Your hosts, who are coming to the end of a two-year renovation, typify Southern hospitality. Three blocks from St. Charles Avenue, the Chimes cottages are minutes away from major New Orleans attractions including the French Quarter, convention centers, Audubon Zoological Gardens with the walk-through Louisiana Swamp Exhibit, the Mississippi River, and universities. The historic St. Charles Avenue streetcar makes the famous restaurants, jazz clubs, art galleries, and antique shops accessible without an auto. Your hosts live on the second floor of the main house—their door is always open! They willingly share their vast knowledge of New Orleans, offering suggestions for tours and restaurants. For your convenience, each suite has a telephone, tea/coffeepot, television set, and stereo. Laundry facilities and use of a refrigerator are available.

The Glimmer Inn ✪

1631 SEVENTH STREET, NEW ORLEANS, LOUISIANA 70115

Tel: **(504) 897-1895**
Best Time to Call: **9 AM–9 PM**
Hosts: **Sharon Agiewich and Cathy Andros**

No. of Rooms: **6**
No. of Private Baths: **1**
Max. No. Sharing Bath: **4**
Double/pb: **$90**
Double/sb: **$70**
Single/sb: **$60**
Open: **All year**
Breakfast: **Continental, plus**
Pets: **No**
Children: **Welcome, by arrangement**
Smoking: **Permitted**
Social Drinking: **Permitted**

This restored 1891 Victorian home has wonderful period elements: twelve-foot cove ceilings, cypress woodwork, side and front galleries, a wraparound front porch, and an enclosed brick patio. Public rooms are comfortably furnished for reading, TV viewing, and musical enjoyment. The main house's guest rooms are beautifully appointed, with antiques, ceiling fans, and individually controlled air-conditioning and heat. Also offered is a private carriage house with bath, refrigerator, and central air-conditioning and heating. Glimmer Inn is across the street from the historic Garden District, a block from the trolley line and Mardi Gras parade route, and fifteen minutes from the French Quarter. Let Cathy and Sharon know your interests; they pride themselves on meeting guests' travel needs in a relaxed but attentive atmosphere.

Sully Mansion

2631 PRYTANIA STREET, NEW ORLEANS, LOUISIANA 70130

Tel: **(504) 891-0457**
Best Time to Call: **7 AM–10 PM**
Host: **Maralee Prigmore**
No. of Rooms: **5**
No. of Private Baths: **5**
Double/pb: **$85–$150**
Suites: **$175**
Open: **All year**
Reduced Rates: **June 15–Sept. 1**
Breakfast: **Continental**
Credit Cards: **MC, VISA**
Pets: **Sometimes**
Children: **No**
Smoking: **No**
Social Drinking: **Permitted**
Minimum Stay: **2 nights weekends, 5 nights special events**

A Queen Anne named to honor its architect, Sully Mansion shows his discerning eye in its 12-foot ceilings, 10-foot doors, grand staircase, and stained glass. The house is furnished with a blend of yesterday's antiques and today's comfortable pieces, and most of the bedrooms have fireplaces. Other architectural jewels fill the surrounding historic Garden District; board the St. Charles streetcar for a 15-minute ride to New Orleans's main attractions.

Old Turnerville B&B ✪

23230 NADLER STREET, PLAQUEMINE, LOUISIANA 70764

Tel: **(504) 687-5337**
Best Time to Call: **10 AM–4 PM**
Host: **Brenda Bourgoyne Blanchard**
Location: **20 mi. S of Baton Rouge**
No. of Rooms: **1**
No. of Private Baths: **1**
Double/pb: **$65**
Single/pb: **$60**

Cottage: **$75**
Open: **All year**
Reduced Rates: **10% seniors**
Breakfast: **Continental**
Pets: **No**
Children: **Welcome**
Smoking: **Permitted**
Social Drinking: **Permitted**

Old Turnerville is an 1800s village on the Mississippi in the heart of plantation country. Bed and breakfast accommodations are available at Miss Louise's House, built more than a century ago. The antique-furnished home includes a guest bedroom with private bath, TV, air-conditioning, and ceiling fan. Guests can enjoy the swing and rockers on the wide front gallery and stroll along the top of the Mississippi River levee. A separate guest cottage sleeps up to four. Restaurants and historic attractions are close by. Tariff includes guided tour of Miss Louise's House and Marietta's House, an 1800s cottage across the street.

Barrow House B&B ✪

P.O. BOX 700, 9779 ROYAL STREET, ST. FRANCISVILLE, LOUISIANA 70775-0700

Tel: **(504) 635-4791**
Host: **Shirley Dittloff**
Location: **25 mi. N of Baton Rouge**
No. of Rooms: **8**
No. of Private Baths: **8**
Double/pb: **$85–$95**
Single/pb: **$75**
Suites: **$115–$135**
Open: **All year, except Dec. 21–25**
Breakfast: **Continental**
Pets: **No**
Children: **Welcome**
Smoking: **Permitted**
Social Drinking: **Permitted**

A saltbox erected in 1809, with a Greek Revival wing that was added some four decades later, Barrow House is listed on the National Register of Historic Places. Appropriately enough, Shirley furnished her B&B with 19th-century pieces from the American South. Other notable homes are in the area; Shirley likes to send guests on a cassette walking tour of the neighborhood. Afterward, sit on the screened front porch and sip a glass of wine or iced tea. Breakfast options range from a simple Continental meal to a full-course New Orleans spread. Shirley is a fabulous cook, and private candlelight dinners, featuring Cajun and Creole specialties, can also be arranged.

Butler Greenwood ✪

8345 U.S. HIGHWAY 61, ST. FRANCISVILLE, LOUISIANA 70775

Tel: **(504) 635-6312**
Best Time to Call: **Anytime**
Host: **Anne Butler**
Location: **25 mi. N of Baton Rouge**
Guest Cottages: **$80–$100, sleeps 2–6**
Open: **All year**
Reduced Rates: **Families**
Breakfast: **Continental, plus**
Credit Cards: **AMEX, MC, VISA**
Pets: **Sometimes**
Children: **Welcome**
Smoking: **Permitted**
Social Drinking: **Permitted**

Butler Greenwood offers six cottages on picturesque plantation grounds. Choose from the 1796 kitchen, with exposed beams and skylights; the nineteenth-century cook's cottage, with a fireplace and porch swing; the romantic gazebo with antique stained glass windows; the treehouse at the edge of a steep wooded ravine, with a wonderful 3-level deck and fireplace; the dovecote, three stories, sleeps six, with a fireplace and Jacuzzi; or the pond house on its own pond. All sites have private baths, partial kitchens, and cable TV. Rates include a tour of the main house—listed on the National Register of Historic Places—and the extensive grounds. A tour book is available, describing the area's history and attractions. Continental-plus breakfast is served; other amenities include a pool, nature walks, and ballooning.

2439 Fairfield "A Bed and Breakfast Inn" ✪

2439 FAIRFIELD AVENUE, SHREVEPORT, LOUISIANA 71104

Tel: **(318) 424-2424**
Best Time to Call: **8 AM–10 PM**
Host: **Jimmy Harris**
Location: **½ mi from I-20**
No. of Rooms: **4**
No. of Private Baths: **4**
Double/pb: **$95–$150**
Single/pb: **$95–$150**
Open: **All year**
Reduced Rates: **Available**
Breakfast: **Full**
Credit Cards: **AMEX, DC, MC, VISA**
Pets: **No**
Children: **No**
Smoking: **No**
Social Drinking: **Permitted**

2439 Fairfield is a meticulously restored three-story Victorian mansion located in the Highland historic district and was featured on the front cover of the 1992 edition of *Bed & Breakfast U.S.A.* This home is surrounded by century-old oaks, rose gardens, and azaleas—you can enjoy the scenic view from your own private balcony complete with porch swings and rocking chairs. The gracious guest rooms are furnished with antiques, Amish quilts, quality linens, feather beds, and down pillows and comforters. Each guest bath has a whirlpool tub. Hearty English breakfasts are served in the morning room. Then it's off to the races at nearby Louisiana Downs. The Strand Theatre, art galleries, and fine restaurants are all within reasonable driving distances.

Salmen-Fritchie House Circa 1895 ✪

127 CLEVELAND AVENUE, SLIDELL, LOUISIANA 70458

Tel: **(504) 643-1405; (800) 235-4168, for reservations**
Best Time to Call: **8 AM–9 PM**
Hosts: **Homer and Sharon Fritchie**
Location: **30 mi. N of New Orleans**
No. of Rooms: **5**
No. of Private Baths: **5**
Double/pb: **$75–$85**
Single/pb: **$75–$85**
Cottage: **$150 for 2**
Suites: **$115–$150**
Open: **All year**
Reduced Rates: **Available**
Breakfast: **Full**
Credit Cards: **AMEX, MC, VISA**
Pets: **No**
Children: **Welcome, over 12**
Smoking: **No**
Social Drinking: **Permitted**
Station Pickup: **Yes**

You'll feel the sense of history as you step inside this magnificent sixteen-room house listed on the National Register of Historic Places. From the front door to the back, the great hall measures twenty feet wide and eighty-five feet long! All the rooms are filled with beautiful antiques, reminiscent of days gone by. Hospitality is a way of life here. Arrive by 4 PM and you can join your hosts for tea in the parlor and afterward, a tour of the house and grounds. In the morning, you'll receive fresh hot coffee in your room. Then you'll enjoy a full Southern breakfast in the bright, cheery breakfast room. A cottage has been added, with a screened-in porch, living room, kitchen, and marble tub Jacuzzi.

MARYLAND

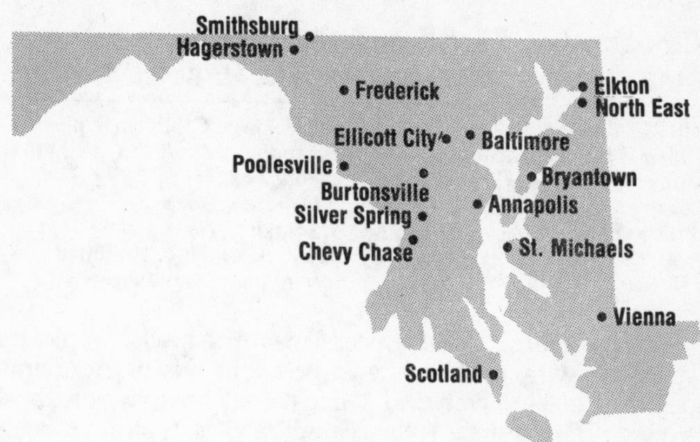

Bed & Breakfast of Maryland/The Traveller in Maryland, Inc. ✪

P.O. BOX 2277, ANNAPOLIS, MARYLAND 21404-2277

Tel: **(410) 269-6232; (800) 736-4667;**
fax: (410) 263-4841
Best Time to Call: **9 AM–5 PM**
Coordinator: **Greg Page**
States/Regions Covered: **Annapolis, Baltimore, Central Maryland, Eastern and Southern Shore, Western Maryland; London, England, United Kingdom**

Descriptive Directory of B&Bs: **$5**
Rates (Single/Double):
Modest: **$55 / $60**
Average: **$60 / $70**
Luxury: **$80 / $100**
Credit Cards: **AMEX, MC, VISA**

This reservation service is one of Maryland's oldest, representing fine-quality, inspected accommodations throughout Maryland and the United Kingdom. Greg will lead you to hosted and unhosted accommodations in interesting and exciting B&B homes, inns, yachts, apartments, and guest cottages. Bed & Breakfast of Maryland offers you a variety of urban and rural locations. Professional staff will help you find just the right location for business, family vacation, relocation, interim housing, romantic getaway, and special occasions. All listings are held to a strict set of standards to ensure your comfort and enjoyment. Greg and his staff look forward to helping you with your travel requests.

Chesapeake Bay Lighthouse B&B ✪

1423 SHARPS POINT ROAD, ANNAPOLIS, MARYLAND 21401

Tel: **(410) 757-0248**
Hosts: **Bill and Janice Costello**
Location: **6 mi. from historic Annapolis**
No. of Rooms: **3**
No. of Private Baths: **3**
Double/pb: **$95**
Open: **All year**
Breakfast: **Continental, plus**
Credit Cards: **AMEX, MC, VISA**
Pets: **No**
Children: **No**
Smoking: **No**
Social Drinking: **Permitted**
Minimum Stay: **2 nights**

For the vacation of a lifetime, come to Annapolis, a picturesque Colonial town with cobblestone streets, the Naval Academy, the Chesapeake, and blue crab and sailboats galore. Join your hosts on the breezy bay shore in a full-size replica of a typical cottage-style lighthouse. On this three-acre setting you'll enjoy panoramic views from every room: you'll see osprey and blue heron feeding, plus spectacular vistas of the Bay Bridge, Thomas Point Lighthouse, and the entrance to the Annapolis harbor. For closer views, you can borrow binoculars from Bill and Janice. Other amenities include individually controlled air-conditioning units in all guest rooms, and an upstairs common room with a well-stocked refrigerator.

College House Suites ✪

ONE COLLEGE AVENUE, ANNAPOLIS, MARYLAND 21401

Tel: **(410) 263-6124**
Best Time to Call: **10 AM–4 PM**
Hosts: **Jo Anne and Don Wolfrey**
Suites: **$170**
Open: **All year**
Breakfast: **Continental**
Credit Cards: **MC, VISA**
Pets: **No**
Children: **No**
Smoking: **No**
Social Drinking: **Permitted**
Minimum Stay: **2 nights**

This brick town house is nestled between the U.S. Naval Academy and St. John's College. The Annapolitan suite has a fireplace, light Victorian decor, and a private entrance through the ivy-covered courtyard. The Colonial suite has superb oriental rugs, antiques, and views of the Academy. The hosts pay close attention to details such as fresh flowers, fruit baskets, and chocolates. College House Suites is a short walk to the city dock, Paca House and Gardens, fine restaurants, fascinating shops and boutiques, art and antique galleries, museums, historic buildings, churches, and theater. A "breakfast-out" option is available.

Amanda's B&B Reservation Service ✪

1428 PARK AVENUE, BALTIMORE, MARYLAND 21217

Tel: **(410) 225-0001; fax (410) 728-8957**
Best Time to Call: **8:30 AM–5:30 PM Mon.–Fri.; 8:30 AM–noon Sat.**
Coordinator: **Betsy Grater**
States/Regions Covered: **Delaware, District of Columbia, Maryland, New Jersey, Pennsylvania, Virginia, West Virginia**
Descriptive Directory of B&Bs: **$5**
Rates (Single/Double):
Modest: **$60**
Luxury: **$75–$125**
Credit Cards: **AMEX, DISC, MC, VISA**

Amanda's is a regional reservation service for private homes, small inns and yachts. This service represents almost 200 properties throughout Maryland and the six surrounding states. Accommodations include everything from economical to luxury rooms with Jacuzzis and private baths.

Betsy's Bed and Breakfast ✪

1428 PARK AVENUE, BALTIMORE, MARYLAND 21217

Tel: **(410) 383-1274**
Best Time to Call: **9:30 AM–10 PM**
Host: **Betsy Grater**
No. of Rooms: **3**
No. of Private Baths: **3**
Double/pb: **$85**
Single/pb: **$65**
Open: **All year**
Breakfast: **Full**
Credit Cards: **AMEX, MC, VISA**
Pets: **No**
Children: **Welcome**
Smoking: **No**
Social Drinking: **Permitted**

A petite estate, this four-story row house is in Bolton Hill, a historic Baltimore neighborhood listed on the National Registry. The interior features 12-foot ceilings with center medallions, a hall floor inlaid with oak and walnut, crown moldings, and carved marble fireplaces. This charming old house is uniquely decorated with a large collection of original brass rubbings, heirloom quilts, and interesting wall groupings. Modern amenities include a hot tub. Betsy's B&B is just a few blocks from a new light-rail stop at "Cultural Station," and steps away from Meyerhoff Symphony Hall, the Lyric Opera House, Antique Row, and the Maryland Institute of Art. The Inner Harbor is seven minutes away by car.

Shady Oaks of Serenity ✪

P.O. BOX 842, BRYANTOWN, MARYLAND 20617-0842

Tel: **(800) 597-0924**
Best Time to Call: **4–11 PM**
Hosts: **Kathy and Gene Kazimer**
Location: **35 mi. from Washington, D.C.**
Suites: **$65**
Open: **All year**

Breakfast: **Continental**
Pets: **No**
Children: **Welcome, over 14**
Smoking: **No**
Social Drinking: **Permitted**

Shady Oaks of Serenity is a new Georgia Victorian situated on three acres and surrounded by trees. This secluded home is off the beaten path, yet within a 45-minute drive of the nation's capital and Annapolis, home of the U.S. Naval Academy. Just down the road is Amish country with antiques and unique shops, historic churches, the renowned Dr. Mudd Home, and Gilbert Run Park, a favorite county stop. Also, this retreat may be of interest to those visiting patients at the Charlotte Hall Veterans Home, only minutes away. Decorated with the Amish theme, the suite has a private bath. Visitors are welcome to gather in the sitting room, the front porch or enjoy an evening on the deck. This room has a king-size bed for a peaceful night's rest. Kathy and Gene cordially invite you to be a guest in their home and visit historic Charles County. The morning brings fresh coffee, homemade muffins or breads and a variety of fresh fruits.

The Taylors' B&B ✪

P.O. BOX 238, BURTONSVILLE, MARYLAND 20866-0238

Tel: **(301) 236-4318**
Best Time to Call: **9–11 AM; 7–9 PM**
Hosts: **Ruth and Fred Taylor**
Location: **30 min. from Washington, D.C., and the Inner Harbor**
No. of Rooms: **1**
No. of Private Baths: **1**
Double/pb: **$60**
Open: **All year**
Breakfast: **Continental**
Pets: **No**
Children: **No**
Smoking: **No**
Social Drinking: **Permitted**
Foreign Languages: **French**

This gracious two-story Colonial home offers a breath of fresh country air just 30 minutes from Washington, D.C., and Baltimore's Inner Harbor district. Guests can enjoy the grand piano, the extensive collection of books in the library, and Ruth's paintings. In warm weather, cool drinks are served in the gazebo; in winter, guests gather by the fireplace in the family room. Both of your hosts are retired. Ruth likes to read, sew, paint, and cook; Fred enjoys reading, writing, history, and music. They've traveled extensively and know how to make guests feel welcome. Tennis courts, horseback riding, and nature trails are nearby.

Chevy Chase Bed & Breakfast

6815 CONNECTICUT AVENUE, CHEVY CHASE, MARYLAND 20815

Tel: **(301) 656-5867; fax (301) 656-5867**
Best Time to Call: **Anytime**
Host: **S. C. Gotbaum**
Location: **1 mi. N of Washington**
No. of rooms: **2**
No. of Private Baths: **2**
Double/pb: **$70**

Single/pb: **$60**
Open: **All year**
Reduced Rates: **Families**
Breakfast: **Continental, plus**
Pets: **No**
Children: **Welcome**
Smoking: **No**
Social Drinking: **Permitted**

Enjoy the convenience of being close to the transportation and sights of Washington, D.C., and Maryland's Montgomery County while staying at a relaxing, turn-of-the century, country-style house. Rooms have beamed ceilings and are filled with rare tapestries, oriental rugs, baskets, copperware, and native crafts from Mexico to the Mideast. The garden room has a cathedral ceiling and private deck. The gabled skylight room has a king-size bed. Your host is a sociologist with a private consulting business. Breakfast items include homemade breads, jams, pancakes, French toast, and a special blend of Louisiana coffee. When you want to take a break from touring, the lovely garden is there for you. There is a $5 surcharge for one-night stays.

The Garden Cottage at Sinking Springs Herb Farm ✪

234 BLAIR SHORE ROAD, ELKTON, MARYLAND 21921

Tel: **(410) 398-5566**
Best Time to Call: **9 AM–9 PM**
Hosts: **Ann and Bill Stubbs**
Location: **4½ mi. from Rte. 40**
No. of Rooms: **1**
No. of Private Baths: **1**
Guest Cottage: **$88 for 2; sleeps 3**
Open: **All year**
Reduced Rates: **5% seniors**
Breakfast: **Full**
Credit Cards: **MC, VISA**
Other Meals: **Available**
Pets: **No**
Children: **Welcome**
Smoking: **No**
Social Drinking: **Permitted**
Airport/Station Pickup: **Yes**

Guests frequently comment on the peaceful beauty of this 128-acre historic farm. The garden cottage has a sitting room and fireplace adjoining the bedroom. Breakfast features coffee ground from organically grown beans, herbal teas, homemade buns, fruit, and juice. A full country breakfast prepared with unprocessed food fresh from the farm is available at no extra charge. Lectures on herbs and craft classes are available, and a gift shop is on the premises. Longwood Gardens and the famed Winterthur Museum are close by. Historic Chesapeake City is five minutes away, with excellent restaurants.

Hayland Farm

5000 SHEPPARD LANE, ELLICOTT CITY, MARYLAND 21042

Tel: **(410) 531-5593**
Host: **Dorothy Mobley**
Location: **Bet. Baltimore and D.C.**
No. of Rooms: **3**
No. of Private Baths: **1**
Max. No. Sharing Bath: **4**
Double/pb: **$60**
Single/pb: **$40**
Double/sb: **$40**
Single/sb: **$25**
Open: **All year**
Breakfast: **Full**

Pets: **No**
Children: **No**
Smoking: **No**
Social Drinking: **Permitted**

When you breathe the country-fresh air, it may surprise you that Baltimore and Washington, D.C., are only a short drive away. At Hayland Farm you will find gracious living in a large manor house furnished in a handsome, yet comfortable, style. Dorothy is retired and has traveled extensively. She enjoys sharing conversation with her guests. In warm weather, the 20- by 50-foot swimming pool is a joy.

Middle Plantation Inn ✪

9549 LIBERTY ROAD, FREDERICK, MARYLAND 21701

Tel: **(301) 898-7128**
Best Time to Call: **6–10 PM**
Hosts: **Shirley and Dwight Mullican**
Location: **5 mi. E of Frederick**
No. of Rooms: **4**
No. of Private Baths: **4**
Double/pb: **$95–$110**
Open: **All year**
Breakfast: **Continental**
Credit Cards: **MC, VISA**
Pets: **No**
Children: **Welcome, over 15**
Smoking: **No**
Social Drinking: **Permitted**

Dwight and Shirley have furnished their handsome stone and log home with antiques collected on their travels. Their rustic B&B will appeal to Civil War buffs, since Gettysburg, Pennsylvania, Sharpsburg, Maryland, and Harpers Ferry, West Virginia, are all 40 minutes away by car. Closer to home, Frederick's 33-block historic district boasts a fascinating mix of museums, galleries, antique shops, and eateries. And for more antiquing, guests should head to nearby New Market.

Beaver Creek House Bed and Breakfast ✪

20432 BEAVER CREEK ROAD, HAGERSTOWN, MARYLAND 21740

Tel: **(301) 797-4764**
Best Time to Call: **Anytime**
Hosts: **Don and Shirley Day**
Location: **4 mi. E of Hagerstown**
No. of Rooms: **5**
No. of Private Baths: **5**
Double/pb: **$90**
Single/pb: **$80**
Open: **All year**
Reduced Rates: **$10 less Mon.–Thurs.**
Breakfast: **Full**
Credit Cards: **AMEX, DISC, MC, VISA**
Pets: **No**
Children: **Welcome, over 10**
Smoking: **No**
Social Drinking: **Permitted**
Airport/Station Pickup: **Yes**

This turn-of-the-century country home enjoys a wonderful view of South Mountain. Start your day with a bountiful country breakfast served on the wraparound screened porch. Then it's off to South Mountain for a hike along the Appalachian Trail. Or perhaps you'd rather bicycle along the scenic country roads. Civil War buffs will want to visit nearby historic parks like Antietam Battlefield and Harpers Ferry, while duffers can choose between two professional courses. Whatever your pleasure, save time to explore the beautifully maintained B&B grounds, with their gardens, fish pond, and patio.

Lewrene Farm B&B ✪

9738 DOWNSVILLE PIKE, HAGERSTOWN, MARYLAND 21740

Tel: **(301) 582-1735**
Hosts: **Lewis and Irene Lehman**
Location: **3½ mi. from I-70 and I-81**
No. of Rooms: **5**
No. of Private Baths: **3**
Max. No. Sharing Bath: **4**
Double/pb: **$75–$90**
Double/sb: **$50–$65**
Suites: **$90**
Open: **All year**
Breakfast: **Full**
Children: **Welcome**
Smoking: **No**
Social Drinking: **No**
Foreign Languages: **Spanish**

Lewis and Irene will help you discover the peaceful beauty of their 125-acre farm located in a historic area near the Antietam Battlefield. Guests are treated like old friends and are welcome to lounge in front of the fireplace or to play the piano in the Colonial-style living room. You're invited to enjoy snacks and a video in the evening. Harpers Ferry, Fort Frederick, the C&O Canal, and Gettysburg are nearby. Irene sells antiques and collectibles on the premises.

Sunday's Bed & Breakfast ✪

39 BROADWAY, HAGERSTOWN, MARYLAND 21740

Tel: **(800) 221-4828; (301) 797-4331**
Best Time to Call: **Anytime**
Host: **Bob Ferrino**
Location: **70 mi. NW of Washington, D.C.**
No. of Rooms: **4**

No. of Private Baths: **4**
Double/pb: **$75–$125**
Single/pb: **$55–$95**
Open: **All year**
Reduced Rates: **Available**
Breakfast: **Full**
Other Meals: **Available**
Pets: **Sometimes**
Children: **Welcome, over 10**
Smoking: **No**
Social Drinking: **Permitted**
Airport Pickup: **Yes**

Built in 1890, this elegant Queen Anne Victorian is located in Hagerstown's historic north end, on a street lined with other grand old homes. Relax in your room or in the many public areas and porches. You may want to visit the area's numerous attractions, such as the National Historical Parks of Antietam, Harpers Ferry, Whitetails Ski Resort, and the C&O Canal. Or choose among the myriad other historic sites, antique shops, fishing areas, golf courses, museums, shopping outlets, and theaters.

The Wingrove Manor Inn ✪

635 OAK HILL AVENUE, HAGERSTOWN, MARYLAND 21740
Internet: http://www.interaccess.com/wingrove manor/index.html

Tel: **(301) 797-7769; fax (301) 797-8659**
Host: **Winnie Price**
Location: **70 mi. NW of Washington, D.C.**
Suites: **$85–$125**
Open: **All year**
Reduced Rates: **Available**
Breakfast: **Continental**
Credit Cards: **MC, VISA**
Pets: **No**
Children: **Welcome, off-season**
Smoking: **No**
Social Drinking: **Permitted**
Minimum Stay: **2 nights peak season**
Airport Pickup: **Yes**

The Wingrove Manor is a beautifully restored bed and breakfast on a street lined with Victorian mansions. Relax in the wicker rockers stretched across a large Southern porch surrounded by 23 white columns, ceramic tiled floors, and breathtaking beauty. Inside you will find magnificent turn-of-the-century craftsmanship, marble fireplaces, a winding staircase, oriental rugs, crystal chandeliers, and towering white columns—all reflecting the home's lineage. The common rooms are elegant. Featured on the first floor is the Canopy Suite with a queen-size bed, marble fireplace, private entrance, TV, VCR, and a full bath with a Jacuzzi, ideally suited for honeymooners. On the second floor are three spacious rooms all with TV, VCR, telephone, double-thick towels, fragrant sprays, sweet soaps, and queen beds that bid travelers welcome and promise a good night's sleep.

The Mill House B&B ✪

102 MILL LANE, NORTH EAST, MARYLAND 21901

Tel: **(410) 287-3532**
Best Time to Call: **Before 9 AM; after 4 PM**
Hosts: **Lucia and Nick Demond**
Location: **40 mi. NE of Baltimore**
No. of Rooms: **2**
Max. No. Sharing Bath: **4**
Double/sb: **$65–$75**
Single/sb: **$60–$70**
Open: **March 1–Dec. 1**
Breakfast: **Full**
Credit Cards: **MC, VISA**
Pets: **No**
Children: **Welcome, over 12**
Smoking: **No**
Social Drinking: **Permitted**

A genuine mill house that dates to the early 18th century, this B&B is furnished entirely in antiques. You'll see picturesque mill ruins and wildflowers on the grounds, but you won't see the parlor's original Queen Anne paneling; that was purchased by Henry Francis Du Pont and installed in his Winterthur estate bedroom. The Winterthur Museum and the Brandywine River Museum are less than an hour's drive away, as is Baltimore's Inner Harbor. Sightseers will be sustained with a full breakfast, including homemade breads fresh from the oven.

Rocker Inn ✪

17924 ELGIN ROAD, POOLESVILLE, MARYLAND 20837

Tel: **(301) 972-8543**
Best Time to Call: **After 5:30 PM**
Host: **Nancy Hopkinson**
Location: **25 mi. NW of Washington, D.C.**
No. of Rooms: **2**
No. of Private Baths: **1**
Double/pb: **$45**
Single/pb: **$40**
Open: **All year**
Breakfast: **Continental**
Pets: **Sometimes**
Children: **Welcome**
Smoking: **No**
Social Drinking: **Permitted**

Built in 1915 as a local telephone house, Rocker Inn takes its name from the rocking chairs and two swings that fill its 48-foot front porch.

Inside, the home is decorated in an informal country mode. Walking tours of Poolesville and Frederick, along with a hike on the C&O Canal, are minutes away. For more ambitious excursions, Harpers Ferry, Gettysburg Battlefield, and historic Leesburg are within an hour's drive.

Parsonage Inn ✪

210 NORTH TALBOT STREET, ST. MICHAELS, MARYLAND 21663

Tel: **(800) 394-5519**
Hosts: **Anthony and Jodie Deyesu**
Location: **11 mi. off Rte. 50**
No. of Rooms: **8**
No. of Private Baths: **8**
Double/pb: **$100–$145**
Open: **All year**
Reduced Rates: **10% seniors; $20 less midweek**
Breakfast: **Full**
Credit Cards: **MC, VISA**
Pets: **No**
Children: **Welcome**
Smoking: **No**
Social Drinking: **Permitted**

Built in the 1880s with bricks fired in the St. Michaels brickyard, the Parsonage Inn was completely restored in 1985. This striking Victorian B&B is part of the town's historic district, and it's an easy stroll to shops, restaurants, and the Chesapeake Bay Maritime Museum. More ambitious guests may borrow the Inn's 12-speed bicycles and venture farther afield.

St. Michael's Manor B&B

ST. MICHAEL'S MANOR, SCOTLAND, MARYLAND 20687

Tel: **(301) 872-4025**
Hosts: **Joe and Nancy Dick**
Location: **9 mi. S of St. Marys City**
No. of Rooms: **4**

Max. No. Sharing Bath: **4**
Double/sb: **$70**
Single/sb: **$50**
Open: **All year**
Breakfast: **Full**
Pets: **No**
Children: **By arrangement**
Smoking: **Downstairs**
Social Drinking: **Permitted**

St. Michael's Manor was built in 1805 on land patented to Leonard Calvert during the seventeenth century. Today, the white stucco manor home on picturesqure Long Neck Creek is included in the state's Pilgrimage Tour. The beautiful handcrafted woodwork has been preserved and is complemented by antiques and handcrafts. Your hosts offer you the use of a canoe, paddleboat, bikes, spa, and swimming pool. Estate wine tasting is also available. The manor house is near Point Lookout State Park, the Chesapeake Bay, and historic St. Marys City.

Park Crest House Bed and Breakfast ✪

8101 PARK CREST DRIVE, SILVER SPRING, MARYLAND 20910

Tel: **(301) 588-2845**
Hosts: **Lowell and Rosemary Peterson**
Location: **7 mi. N of Washington, D.C.**
No. of Rooms: **3**
No. of Private Baths: **2**
Max. No. Sharing Bath: **4**
Double/sb: **$60**
Single/sb: **$50**
Suites: **$75**
Open: **All year**
Reduced Rates: **10% seniors**
Breakfast: **Continental, plus**
Pets: **Welcome**
Children: **Welcome**
Smoking: **No**
Social Drinking: **Permitted**
Minimum Stay: **2 nights**
Foreign Languages: **French, German**

The English nationality of the hostess is reflected in the beautiful decor of this bed & breakfast. Chintzes, oriental carpets, and European antiques create an atmosphere of elegance. Park Crest is located one-and-a-half miles from the Silver Spring and Takoma stations and three minutes from the bus stop. Breakfast is served in the gardens, weather permitting.

Blue Bear Bed & Breakfast ✪

13810 FRANK'S RUN ROAD, SMITHSBURG, MARYLAND 21783

Tel: **(800) 381-2292**
Best Time to Call: **After 4 PM**
Hosts: **Ellen Panchula and Marilyn Motter**
Location: **6 mi. from I-70, exit 35**
No. of Rooms: **2**
No. of Private Baths: **2**
Double/pb: **$60–$65**
Single/pb: **$50–$55**
Open: **All year**
Breakfast: **Continental**
Pets: **No**
Children: **Welcome, over 12**
Smoking: **No**
Social Drinking: **Permitted**

Ellen, a full-time schoolteacher, and her sister Marilyn, a professional dog groomer, have joined together at the Blue Bear B&B to offer guests year-round hospitality. Their home is decorated in an informal country mode, with several antiques and a charming collection of friendly-faced teddy bears throughout the house. Guests can relax and enjoy beautiful views from the front porch or tour nearby battlefields. Breakfast consists of fresh fruits, homemade breads, pastries and coffee cake. Snacks are offered in the evening.

The Tavern House ✪

111 WATER STREET, P.O. BOX 98, VIENNA, MARYLAND 21869

Tel: **(410) 376-3347**
Hosts: **Harvey and Elise Altergott**
Location: **15 mi. NW of Salisbury**
No. of Rooms: **4**
Max. No. Sharing Bath: **4**
Double/sb: **$65–$75**
Single/sb: **$60–$70**
Open: **All year**
Breakfast: **Full**
Credit Cards: **MC, VISA**
Pets: **No**
Children: **Welcome, over 12**
Smoking: **Permitted**
Social Drinking: **Permitted**

Vienna is a quiet little town on the Nanticoke River, where one can escape the stress of the 20th century. Careful restoration has brought back the simple purity of this Colonial tavern. The stark white "lime, sand, and hair" plaster accents the authentic furnishings. This is a place for those who enjoy looking at the river and marshes, watching an osprey in flight, or taking a leisurely walk. Days begin with a special full breakfast that is always a social event. For the sports minded, there's tennis, boating, and flat roads for bicycling, all within easy reach. This is an excellent base for exploring the Eastern Shore, interesting small towns, and Blackwater National Wildlife Refuge.

MISSISSIPPI

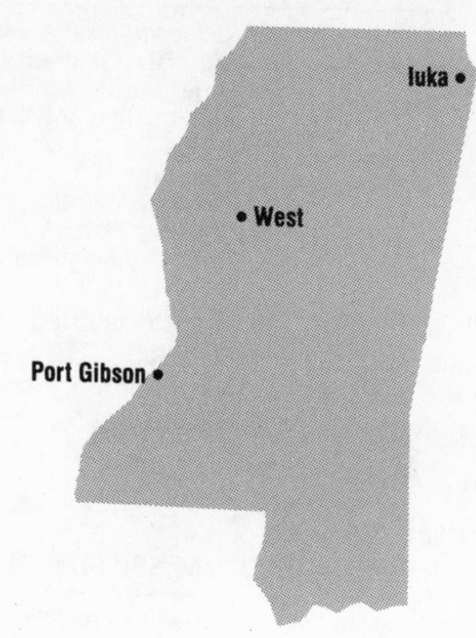

Lincoln, Ltd. Bed & Breakfast—Mississippi Reservation Service

P.O. BOX 3479, 2303 23RD AVENUE, MERIDIAN, MISSISSIPPI 39303

Tel: **(601) 482-5483; resv. only: (800) 633-MISS [6477]; fax: (601) 693-7447**
Best Time to Call: **9 AM–5 PM**
Coordinator: **Barbara Lincoln Hall**
States/Regions Covered:
Mississippi—Natchez to Memphis, Alabama

Descriptive Directory: **$3.50**
Rates (Single/Double):
Average: **$65–$75 / $75–$85**
Luxury: **$85–$125 / $95–$165**
Credit Cards: **AMEX, MC, VISA**

For the traveling businessperson or for the vacationer, a stay with one of Barbara's hosts offers a personal taste of the finest Southern hospitality. All rooms have private baths. Mississippi abounds with historic-house tours, called "pilgrimages," in March and April, and Natchez and Vicksburg have similar pilgrimages in autumn. In May,

Meridian is host to the Jimmie Rodgers Festival. Accommodations range from a cozy, historic log cabin to an elegant antebellum mansion.

Eastport Inn Bed & Breakfast ✪

100 SOUTH PEARL STREET, IUKA, MISSISSIPPI 38852

Tel: **(601) 423-2511**
Best Time to Call: **8 AM–5 PM**
Host: **Betty Watson**
No. of Rooms: **7**
No. of Private Baths: **7**
Double/pb: **$50**
Single/pb: **$40**
Suites: **$50**
Open: **All year**
Reduced Rates: **Available**
Breakfast: **Continental**
Other Meals: **Available**
Credit Cards: **AMEX, DC, DISC, MC, VISA**
Pets: **No**
Children: **Welcome**
Smoking: **No**
Social Drinking: **Permitted**

This gracious home was built in 1864 and is decorated in period style, with four-poster beds and floral bedspreads. For swimming and boating, Pickwick Lake is six miles away; Shiloh National Park, Tishomingo State Park, Coleman State Park, and the Natchez Trace Drive are also nearby.

Oak Square Plantation ✪

1207 CHURCH STREET, PORT GIBSON, MISSISSIPPI 39150

Tel: **(601) 437-4350; (800) 729-0240**
Best Time to Call: **Anytime**
Hosts: **Mr. and Mrs. William D. Lum**
Location: **On Hwy. 61 between Natchez and Vicksburg**
No. of Rooms: **12**
No. of Private Baths: **12**
Double/pb: **$85–$95**
Single/pb: **$70–$75**
Open: **All year**
Breakfast: **Full**
Credit Cards: **AMEX, DISC, MC, VISA**
Pets: **No**
Children: **Welcome**
Smoking: **No**
Social Drinking: **Permitted**

Port Gibson is the town that Union General Ulysses S. Grant said was "too beautiful to burn." Oak Square is the largest and most palatial antebellum mansion, circa 1850, in Port Gibson, and is listed on the National Register of Historic Places. The guest rooms are all furnished with family heirlooms, and all have canopied beds. Guests will enjoy the courtyard, gazebo, and beautiful grounds. A chairlift for upstairs rooms is available. You will enjoy the delightful Southern breakfast and tour of the mansion. Your hosts offer complimentary wine, tea, or coffee, and will enlighten you on the many historic attractions in the area.

The Alexander House ✪

210 GREEN STREET, P.O. BOX 187, WEST, MISSISSIPPI 39192

Tel: **(800) 350-8034**
Hosts: **Ruth Ray and Woody Dinstel**
Location: **70 mi. N of Jackson**
No. of Rooms: **5**
No. of Private Baths: **3**
Max. No. Sharing Bath: **4**
Double/pb: **$65**
Double/sb: **$65**
Suites: **$110**
Open: **All year**
Breakfast: **Full**
Other Meals: **Available**
Pets: **Sometimes**
Children: **Welcome, over 10**
Smoking: **No**
Social Drinking: **Permitted**
Station Pickup: **Yes**

The Alexander House, which has been dated to the 1880s, opened as a bed and breakfast in March 1994. Located in the town historic district, the house has been carefully restored with authentic decor, but with added conveniences. A full breakfast is served each morning and may include hot biscuits, fruit compote, grits, eggs, or casseroles. The two-story home has three bedrooms and a suite.

NORTH CAROLINA

Abbington Green Bed and Breakfast Inn

46 CUMBERLAND CIRCLE, ASHEVILLE, NORTH CAROLINA 28801

Tel: **(704) 251-2454**
Best Time to Call: **10 AM–9 PM**
Hosts: **Valerie, Gabrielle and Julie Larrea**
Location: **¾ mi from I-240 Exit 4C**
No. of Rooms: **6**
No. of Private Baths: **6**
Double/pb: **$85–$120**
Suites: **$150**
Open: **All year**
Breakfast: **Full**
Credit Cards: **AMEX, MC, VISA**
Pets: **No**
Children: **Welcome, over 10**
Smoking: **No**
Social Drinking: **Permitted**
Minimum Stay: **2 nights weekends**

Enjoy elegance with a romantic English flavor. This sunlit 1908 Colonial Revival home in the Montford Historic District is a delight to behold inside and out. Stylishly appointed guest rooms are named after parks and gardens around London; each has a canopy-draped queen-size bed, antiques, fine rugs, and air-conditioning. Three guest rooms have fireplaces. Play piano or chess, daydream, or relax with a good book beside the parlor or living room fireplaces. Start each morning with a homemade breakfast featuring crepes or quiche. Abbington Green is located minutes from Biltmore House, Blue Ridge Parkway, University of North Carolina, and fine restaurants and shops.

A Bed of Roses ✪

135 CUMBERLAND AVENUE, ASHEVILLE, NORTH CAROLINA 28801

Tel: **(704) 258-8700; (800) 471-4182**
Best Time to Call: **10 AM–9 PM**
Host: **Caroline Logie**
Location: **½ mi. N of Asheville**
No. of Rooms: **4**
No. of Private Baths: **4**
Double/pb: **$85–$95**
Suites: **$115 for 2**
Open: **All year**
Reduced Rates: **10% seniors, Jan.–Mar.**
Breakfast: **Full**
Credit Cards: **MC, VISA**
Pets: **No**
Children: **Welcome, over 8**
Smoking: **No**
Social Drinking: **Permitted**
Minimum Stay: **3 nights holidays; 2 nights in-season weekends**

Styled after an English country cottage, this inn is a cheery Queen Anne Victorian, circa 1897, listed on the Register of Historic Homes. Each guest room is uniquely decorated, some with antique bath fixtures and claw-footed tubs. Guests are invited to enjoy a cool glass of lemonade or iced tea and cookies on the front porch rockers. There are a couple of bicycles available for you to use. Breakfast consists of homemade granola, muffins, seasonal fruit, waffles and crepes. Gourmet coffees and English teas are always available. Biltmore House and Gardens, the Thomas Wolfe Memorial, botanical gardens, and the Blue Ridge Parkway are just minutes from the inn.

Acorn Cottage

25 SAINT DUNSTANS CIRCLE, ASHEVILLE, NORTH CAROLINA 28803

Tel: **(704) 253-0609; (800) 699-0609**
Best Time to Call: **10 AM–9 PM**
Host: **Sharon Tabor**
Location: **1¼ mi. from Route I-40, exit 50/50B**
No. of Rooms: **4**
No. of Private Baths: **4**
Double/pb: **$80–$95**
Single/pb: **$75**
Open: **All year**
Breakfast: **Full**
Credit Cards: **DISC, MC, VISA**
Pets: **No**
Children: **Welcome (crib)**
Smoking: **No**
Social Drinking: **Permitted**
Minimum Stay: **2 nights weekends, March 15–Dec. 31**

An English country cottage in the woodsy heart of Asheville, Acorn is built of local granite; the interior boasts maple floors and a granite fireplace. The guest rooms feature queen-size beds, fine linens, air-conditioning, TV, and baths stocked with special soaps. A delicious full breakfast is served each morning with fresh fruit, varied entrees, juice, coffee or tea, and an assortment of breads. Then you're ready for the quarter-mile trip to the Biltmore Estate.

Cairn Brae

217 PATTON MOUNTAIN ROAD, ASHEVILLE, NORTH CAROLINA 28804

Tel: **(704) 252-9219**
Hosts: **Milli and Ed Adams**
No. of Rooms: **3**
No. of Private Baths: **3**
Double/pb: **$90**
Suites: **$105–$140**
Open: **Apr. 1–Nov. 30**
Breakfast: **Full**
Credit Cards: **DISC, MC, VISA**
Pets: **No**
Children: **Welcome, over 10**
Smoking: **No**
Social Drinking: **Permitted**
Airport/Station Pickup: **Yes**

Cairn Brae is a secluded mountain retreat on wooded acreage, just minutes from downtown Asheville. Enjoy the beautiful mountain views and walking trails, or relax by the fireplace in the cozy guest living room. Afternoon refreshments are served on the terrace, and a full homemade breakfast is offered in the morning.

Carolina Bed & Breakfast ✪

177 CUMBERLAND AVENUE, ASHEVILLE, NORTH CAROLINA 28801

Tel: **(704) 254-3608**
Best Time to Call: **10 AM–9 PM**
Hosts: **Sam and Karin Fain**
Location: **½ mi. from Route 240, Exit 4C**
No. of Rooms: **5**
No. of Private Baths: **5**
Double/pb: **$85–$100**
Open: **All year**
Breakfast: **Full**
Credit Cards: **MC, VISA**
Pets: **No**
Children: **Welcome, over 12**
Smoking: **No**
Social Drinking: **Permitted**
Minimum Stay: **2 nights holidays, in-season weekends**

This turn-of-the-century Colonial Revival home has been painstakingly restored; feel free to relax on the front and back porches, or just take in the view from the second-floor guest rooms, with their distinctive, twelve-over-one panes. In springtime, the grounds bloom with dogwoods and rhododendrons. On cooler days, you can curl up in front of one of the house's seven fireplaces. Your hosts serve a different full breakfast each day; the usual fare includes eggs or quiche and fresh bread and muffins.

The Colby House

230 PEARSON DRIVE, ASHEVILLE, NORTH CAROLINA 28801

Tel: **(704) 253-5644; (800) 982-2118**
Hosts: **Everett and Ann Colby**
No. of Rooms: **4**
No. of Private Baths: **4**
Double/pb: **$80–$110**
Open: **All year**

Breakfast: **Full**
Credit Cards: **MC, VISA**
Pets: **No**
Children: **Welcome, over 12**
Smoking: **Restricted**
Social Drinking: **Permitted**

This elegant Dutch-Tudor house in the Montford Historic District is a special place, thanks to its porch, beautiful gardens, and inviting fireplaces. Each guest room has its own individual decor and queen-size beds. Refreshments are available at all times, and wine and cheese are served in the evening. Breakfasts vary daily, but are always served on fine china, with heirloom crystal and silver. Southern hospitality abounds in your hosts' personal attention to every guest's needs.

Corner Oak Manor ✪

53 ST. DUNSTANS ROAD, ASHEVILLE, NORTH CAROLINA 28803

Tel: **(704) 253-3525**
Best Time to Call: **9 AM–9 PM**
Hosts: **Karen and Andy Spradley**
Location: **1¼ mi. from Rte. 40, Exit 50**
No. of Rooms: **4**
No. of Private Baths: **4**
Double/pb: **$90–$115**
Single/pb: **$75–$85**
Cottage: **$130–$145**
Open: **All year**
Breakfast: **Full**
Credit Cards: **AMEX, DISC, MC, VISA**
Pets: **No**
Children: **Welcome, over 12**
Smoking: **No**
Social Drinking: **Permitted**

Surrounded by maple, oak, and evergreen trees, this lovely English Tudor home is located minutes away from the famed Biltmore Estate and Gardens. The rooms have queen-size beds beautifully covered in fine linen. The window treatments and coordinated wall coverings could easily grace the pages of a decorating magazine. Handmade wreaths, weavings, and stitchery complement the furnishings. Breakfast specialties include orange French toast, blueberry-ricotta pancakes, or four-cheese-herb quiche. A living room fireplace, baby grand piano, outdoor deck, and Jacuzzi are among the gracious amenities.

Flint Street Inns

100 & 116 FLINT STREET, ASHEVILLE, NORTH CAROLINA 28801

Tel: **(704) 253-6723**
Hosts: **Rick, Lynne, and Marion Vogel**
Location: **¼ mi. from Rte. 240**
No. of Rooms: **8**
No. of Private Baths: **8**
Double/pb: **$85**
Single/pb: **$70**
Open: **All year**
Breakfast: **Full**
Credit Cards: **AMEX, DISC, MC, VISA**
Pets: **No**
Children: **No**
Smoking: **Permitted**
Social Drinking: **Permitted**

These turn-of-the-century homes on an acre with century-old trees are listed in the National Register of Historic Places. Stained glass, pine floors, and a claw-footed bathtub are part of the Victorian decor. The Inns are air-conditioned for summer comfort; some have fireplaces for winter coziness. Guests are served coffee and soft drinks. The Blue Ridge Parkway is close by.

The Banner Elk Inn Bed & Breakfast ✪

ROUTE 3, BOX 1134, HIGHWAY 194 NORTH, BANNER ELK, NORTH CAROLINA 28604

Tel: **(704) 898-6223**
Best Time to Call: **9 AM–10 PM**
Host: **Beverly Lait**
Location: **17 mi. W of Boone**
No. of Rooms: **5**
No. of Private Baths: **4**
Double/pb: **$75–$100**
Single/pb: **$65–$90**
Suites: **$100–$150; sleeps 4**
Open: **All year**
Reduced Rates: **Available**
Breakfast: **Full**
Credit Cards: **MC, VISA**
Pets: **Yes**
Children: **Welcome, Sun.–Thurs.; over 6, weekends**
Smoking: **No**
Social Drinking: **Permitted**
Minimum Stay: **Mid-July; first 2 weeks of Oct.; ski season Dec. 25–Mar. 30; 2 nights weekends**
Foreign Languages: **Spanish, German**

Your host, Beverly, spent years with the Foreign Service, and original tapestries, artwork, and antiques from around the world fill her stunningly renovated historic home. The Inn is located halfway between the Sugar Resort and Beech Mountain ski slopes, near such major tourist attractions as Grandfather Mountain and Natural Habitat, Linville Falls, Valle Crucis, and the Blue Ridge Parkway. You'll have energy to visit all these places after Beverly's full breakfasts of homemade breads, eggs, fruit, juice, and coffee or tea.

Delamar Inn ✪

217 TURNER STREET, BEAUFORT, NORTH CAROLINA 28516

Tel: **(919) 728-4300; (800) 349-5823**
Best Time to Call: **Anytime**
Hosts: **Tom and Mabel Steepy**
Location: **140 mi. SE of Raleigh**
No. of Rooms: **4**
No. of Private Baths: **4**
Double/pb: **$94**
Single/pb: **$94**
Open: **All year**
Breakfast: **Continental, plus**
Credit Cards: **MC, VISA**
Pets: **No**
Children: **Welcome, over 10**
Smoking: **Restricted**
Social Drinking: **Permitted**
Airport/Station Pickup: **Yes**

The Delamar Inn, built in 1866, is located in historic Beaufort, North Carolina's third oldest town. The Inn offers three guest rooms furnished with antiques, each room with a private bath. After a delightful breakfast, stroll down to the historic restoration grounds, maritime museum, or the open-air bus, or browse in the waterfront specialty shops. Tom and Mabel, your hosts, can offer directions to local beaches for shell collecting, sunbathing, or fishing. Try a short ride to Fort Macon, Tryon Palace, or the ferry to the Outer Banks. Selected for the '95 historic homes tour.

Maple Lodge ✪

P. O. BOX 1236, 152 SUNSET DRIVE, BLOWING ROCK, NORTH CAROLINA 28605

Tel: **(704) 295-3331**
Best Time to Call: **10 AM–9 PM**
Hosts: **Marilyn and David Bateman**
No. of Rooms: **11**
No. of Private Baths: **11**
Double/pb: **$73.39–$110.09**
Single/pb: **$64.22–$100.92**
Suites: **$110.09**
Open: **April 1–Jan. 1**
Reduced Rates: **Available**
Breakfast: **Full**
Credit Cards: **DISC, MC, VISA**
Pets: **No**
Children: **Welcome, over 12**
Smoking: **No**
Social Drinking: **Permitted**
Minimum Stay: **2 nights weekends and special occasions**

This charming inn reflects the simplicity and grace of the 30s and 40s. Guest rooms are furnished with antiques, handmade quilts, and goose-down comforters. Two parlors offer guests a homey atmosphere, complete thanks to the stone fireplace, old-timey pump organ, books, and games. Breakfast features fruits, cereals, home-baked breads and muffins, and a different main dish each day. Maple Lodge is within a short stroll to craft shops, art galleries, antiques, fine restaurants, and the Blowing Rock Stage Company, which performs during the summer. Outside town is the Blue Ridge Parkway and the Moses Cone Park; nearby is Grandfather Mountain, golf, canoeing, and white-water rafting.

Estes Mountain Retreat ✪

ROUTE 1, BOX 1316A (OFF BAKER'S CREEK ROAD), BURNSVILLE, NORTH CAROLINA 28714

Tel: **(704) 682-7264**
Best Time to Call: **After 7 PM**
Hosts: **Bruce and Maryallen Estes**
Location: **37 mi. NE of Asheville**
No. of Rooms: **2**
No. of Private Baths: **2**
Double/pb: **$65**
Open: **All year**
Reduced Rates: **15% weekly; 10% seniors**
Breakfast: **Full**
Pets: **No**
Children: **Welcome, over 3**
Smoking: **No**
Social Drinking: **Permitted**
Foreign Languages: **French**

Breathtaking mountain views await you at this three-level cedar log home with a rock chimney, fireplace, and porches. Because Burnsville is in Pisgah National Forest, you won't have to travel far to go rafting, fishing, hiking, and rock and gem hunting, and there's golfing next door at Mountain Air Country Club. Mt. Mitchell, Linville Caverns, outdoor theater, the Biltmore Mansion, and the Carl Sandburg Home are all within an hour's drive.

Hamrick Inn ✪

7787 HIGHWAY 80 SOUTH, BURNSVILLE, NORTH CAROLINA 28714

Tel: **(704) 675-5251**
Best Time to Call: **Mornings**
Hosts: **Neal and June Jerome**
Location: **55 mi. NE of Asheville; 16 mi. from I-40, Exit 72**
No. of Rooms: **4**
No. of Private Baths: **4**
Double/pb: **$60–$70**
Single/pb: **$55–$65**
Open: **Apr. 2–Oct. 31**
Reduced Rates: **Weekly**
Breakfast: **Full**
Pets: **No**
Children: **Welcome**
Smoking: **Permitted**
Social Drinking: **Permitted**

This charming three-story Colonial-style stone inn is nestled at the foot of Mt. Mitchell, the highest mountain east of the Mississippi River. Much of the lovely furniture was built by Neal and June. The den has a fine selection of books as well as a TV set for your enjoyment. There is a private porch off each bedroom, where you may take in the view and the cool mountain breezes. Golfing, hiking, fishing, rock hounding, crafts shopping, and fall foliage wandering are local activities. Pisgah National Park, Linville Caverns, Crabtree Meadows, and the Parkway Playhouse are area diversions.

The Morse's Little South-Toe-Hold ✪

873 SOUTH TOE RIVER ROAD, BURNSVILLE, NORTH CAROLINA 28714

Tel: **(704) 675-5036**
Best Time to Call: **10 AM–9 PM**
Hosts: **Ursala and Jay Morse**
Location: **55 mi. NE of Asheville**

No. of Rooms: **1**
No. of Private Baths: **1**
Double/pb: **$75**
Single/pb: **$70**
Suites: **$90**
Open: **May 1–Nov. 15**
Reduced Rates: **Weekly, 10% seniors**
Breakfast: **Full**
Pets: **No**
Children: **No**
Smoking: **No**
Social Drinking: **Permitted**
Foreign Languages: **German, Spanish, French**

Set among rhododendrons and eighty-foot pines, this lovely chalet home features a Great Room with a cathedral ceiling, antiques, objets d'art and paintings, and a library of books for your enjoyment. South-Toe-Hold is surrounded by two national parks, scenic South Toe River, and the Blue Ridge Parkway. You are invited to hike, swim, fish, water-tube, or gem-mine at Little Switzerland. Mt. Mitchell Golf Course is within walking distance. Nearby attractions include the Biltmore Estate, Penland Art School, Mt. Mitchell, and Grandfather Mountain with its Biosphere and bear habitat.

The Elizabeth Bed & Breakfast ✪

2145 EAST 5TH STREET, CHARLOTTE, NORTH CAROLINA 28204

Tel: **(704) 358-1368**
Best Time to Call: **Evening**
Host: **Joan Mastny**
Location: **3 mi. from Rte I-77, Exit 10B**

No. of Rooms: **3**
No. of Private Baths: **3**
Double/pb: **$58–$78**
Single/pb: **$55–$70**
Guest cottage: **$80–$88**
Open: **All year**
Breakfast: **Full, Continental**
Credit Cards: **MC, VISA**
Pets: **No**
Children: **Welcome, over 12**
Smoking: **No**
Social Drinking: **Permitted**

This 1927 lavender "lady" is in historic Elizabeth, Charlotte's second oldest neighborhood. Rooms are decorated in European country style and are beautifully appointed with antiques, ceiling fans, decorator linens, and unique collections. For privacy a guest cottage is available, furnished in an elegant Southwestern style. All rooms have central air-conditioning; some have TV and phone. Enjoy a full breakfast on weekends and Continental on weekdays. Guests may relax in the garden courtyard complete with a charming gazebo or stroll beneath giant oak trees to convenient restaurants and shopping.

The Homeplace

5901 SARDIS ROAD, CHARLOTTE, NORTH CAROLINA 28270

Tel: **(704) 365-1936; fax: (704) 366-2729**
Hosts: **Peggy and Frank Dearien**
Location: **10 mi. from I-77; I-85**
No. of Rooms: **3**
No. of Private Baths: **3**
Double/pb: **$93**
Single/pb: **$80**
Suite: **$115**
Open: **All year**
Breakfast: **Full**
Credit Cards: **AMEX, MC, VISA**
Pets: **No**
Children: **Welcome, over 10**
Smoking: **No**
Social Drinking: **No**

The warm and friendly atmosphere hasn't changed since 1902. The minute you arrive at this country Victorian and walk up to the wraparound porch with its rockers, you'll feel you've "come home." The handcrafted staircase, 10-foot beaded ceilings, and heart-pine floors add to the interior's beauty. It's convenient to malls, furniture and textile outlets, and treasure-filled antique shops.

Still Waters ✪

6221 AMOS SMITH ROAD, CHARLOTTE, NORTH CAROLINA 28214

Tel: **(704) 399-6299**
Best Time to Call: **Evenings**
Hosts: **Janet and Rob Dyer**
Location: **3 mi. W of Charlotte**
No. of Rooms: **3**
No. of Private Baths: **3**
Double/pb: **$65–$85**
Open: **All year**
Reduced Rates: **Available**
Breakfast: **Full**
Credit Cards: **MC, VISA**
Pets: **No**
Children: **Welcome**
Smoking: **No**
Social Drinking: **Permitted**

Relax on the river just outside Charlotte city limits—only minutes away from downtown, the airport, or the interstates, but a world away from the bustle of everyday life. Visit this lakefront log home on two wooded acres. Enjoy the deck, garden, dock, and boat ramp, or play on the sport court. Guests stay in either of two large rooms or in a suite. Full breakfasts always feature homemade sourdough rolls and fresh-ground coffee.

Windsong: A Mountain Inn ✪

120 FERGUSON RIDGE, CLYDE, NORTH CAROLINA 28721

Tel: **(704) 627-6111**
Best Time to Call: **8 AM–9 PM**
Hosts: **Donna and Gale Livengood**
Location: **36 mi. W of Asheville**
No. of Rooms: **5**
No. of Private Baths: **5**
Double/pb: **$99–$140**
Single/pb: **$89–$103**
Open: **All year**
Reduced Rates: **10%, singles and weekly bookings**
Breakfast: **Full**
Credit Cards: **DISC, MC, VISA**
Pets: **No**
Children: **Welcome, over 8**
Smoking: **No**
Social Drinking: **Permitted**

From its mountainside perch near Waynesville, this immense contemporary log home affords spectacular views of the surrounding countryside. Inside, the house is bright and airy, thanks to the large windows and skylights and the high exposed-beam ceilings. Each oversized room boasts its own patio, fireplace, and deep tubs for two. There is a tennis court and in-ground pool, plus a billiard table and an extensive video library with in-room VCRs. You'll love their llama herd with group pack trips going into the national forests. Nearby attractions include horseback riding, white-water rafting, Cherokee Indian Reservation, Great Smoky Mountain National Park, Biltmore House, and the Appalachian Trail. You'll relish home-baked breakfast goods. Typical entrees are buckwheat banana pancakes and egg-sausage strata with mushrooms.

The Blooming Garden Inn ✪

513 HOLLOWAY STREET, DURHAM, NORTH CAROLINA 27701

Tel: **(919) 687-0801; fax: (919) 688-1401**
Best Time to Call: **Evenings**
Hosts: **Frank and Dolly Pokrass**
Location: **Downtown Durham**
No. of Rooms: **5**
No. of Private Baths: **5**
Double/pb: **$85–$105**
Suites: **$145–$160**
Open: **All year**
Reduced Rates: **Corporate**
Breakfast: **Full**
Credit Cards: **AMEX, DC, DISC, MC, VISA**
Pets: **No**
Children: **Welcome**
Smoking: **No**
Social Drinking: **Permitted**

If you appreciate flowers—and who doesn't?—you'll love staying at this restored 1892 Victorian with glorious gardens at every turn. The house is handsome, too, with its gabled roof, beveled and stained glass windows, and wraparound porch supported by Tuscan columns. What's more, you're right in the center of Durham's historic Holloway District, just moments from shops, galleries, theaters, Duke Univer-

sity, and the University of North Carolina. For the ultimate in pampering, luxury suites with Jacuzzis are available. A big feature at Blooming Garden Inn is the gourmet breakfast. Guests are given a brief local tour by hosts.

Old North Durham Inn ✪

922 NORTH MANGUM STREET, DURHAM, NORTH CAROLINA 27701

Tel: **(919) 683-1885**
Best Time to Call: **Afternoons, evenings**
Hosts: **Debbie and Jim Vickery**
Location: **½ mi. N of Durham**
No. of Rooms: **4**
No. of Private Baths: **4**
Double/pb: **$85**
Single/pb: **$80**
Suites: **$130**
Open: **All year**
Reduced Rates: **10% after 5th night**
Breakfast: **Full**
Credit Cards: **AMEX, MC, VISA**
Pets: **No**
Children: **Welcome**
Smoking: **No**
Social Drinking: **Permitted**

Built in the early 1900s, this Colonial Revival home is a recipient of the Durham Historic Preservation Society's "Architectural Conservation Citation" and is located in one of the city's oldest residential neighborhoods. Guest rooms are decorated in turn-of-the-century fashion, featuring queen-size beds, 10-foot coffered ceilings, fireplaces, ceiling fans, floral wallpaper, and beautiful oak and pine floors. One favorite is the Lavender Room, featuring nine lace-covered windows, a painted iron bed, and a whirlpool tub. A wraparound porch is a favorite spot for enjoying early-morning coffee or an afternoon snack of homemade cookies. Debbie and Jim are only five minutes from the Durham Bulls' ballpark and offer complimentary tickets to all home games. Warm hospitality and personal service are the key elements of the Inn's success. As one guest wrote, "It truly seems like another world that you have created. Everything about your inn speaks welcome, weary traveler, enter and find rest."

Blaine House ✪

661 HARRISON AVENUE, HIGHWAY 28 NORTH, FRANKLIN, NORTH CAROLINA 28734
E-mail: blainebb@dnet.net

Tel: **(704) 349-4230**
Best Time to Call: **10 AM–8 PM**
Hosts: **Suzy Chandler and Karin Gorboff**
Location: **65 mi. SW of Asheville**
No. of Rooms: **3**
No. of Private Baths: **3**
Double/pb: **$70–$75**
Single/pb: **$65–$70**
Suites: **$85**
Open: **All year**
Reduced Rates: **10% Nov. 15–March 15**
Breakfast: **Full**
Credit Cards: **MC, VISA**
Pets: **No**
Children: **Welcome, over 13**
Smoking: **No**
Social Drinking: **Permitted**
Minimum Stay: **2 nights in Oct.**
Foreign Languages: **French**

Blaine House reflects the grace and serenity reminiscent of days gone by. Built in 1910 by Charles Blaine, this house was transformed to a bed & breakfast in 1995 and furnished with period antiques, heirlooms, silk trees, and chandeliers. Gaze outside for gorgeous views of the Smokey Mountains. Guest rooms have been distinctively decorated to enhance their individuality. Awake to the aroma of a gourmet breakfast served by candlelight. Within minutes of the Blaine House you will find gem mines, shops, restaurants, a Cherokee casino, the Smokey Mountain Railway, and the Biltmore Estate.

Buttonwood Inn ✪

190 GEORGIA ROAD, FRANKLIN, NORTH CAROLINA 28734

Tel: **(704) 369-8985**
Best Time to Call: **After 5 PM**
Host: **Liz Oehser**
Location: **75 mi. SW of Asheville**
No. of Rooms: **4**
No. of Private Baths: **2**
Max. No. Sharing Bath: **4**
Double/pb: **$60–$75**
Single/pb: **$50**
Double/sb: **$55**
Single/sb: **$45**
Suites: **$95**
Open: **Apr. 15–Nov. 15**
Breakfast: **Full**
Pets: **No**
Children: **Welcome, over 10**
Smoking: **Permitted**
Social Drinking: **Permitted**

The Buttonwood is a small country inn surrounded by towering pines, a spacious lawn, and mountain views. The original residence was a small cottage built in the late 1920s adjacent to the greens of the Franklin golf course. Years later, a new wing was added with rustic, charming rooms. Guests may choose from comfortable bedrooms decorated with antiques, cozy quilts, and handcrafts, many of which are offered for sale. Breakfast selections include sausage-apple ring, eggs Benedict, or cheese frittata, with coffee cake and plenty of hot coffee or tea. Golfers will be glad to be so close to the beautiful fairways and Bermuda grass greens right next door. Nearby there are also crafts shops, hiking trails, the Blue Ridge Parkway, gem mines, and plenty of places to swim and ride.

Heritage Inn ✪

101 HERITAGE HOLLOW, FRANKLIN, NORTH CAROLINA 28734

Tel: **(704) 524-4150**
Best Time to Call: **3-9 PM**
Host: **Sally Wade**
Location: **135 mi. NE Atlanta, Georgia**
No. of Rooms: **6**
No. of Private Baths: **6**
Double/pb: **$55–$75**
Single/pb: **$48–$65**
Cottage: **$95–$110, sleeps 4**
Open: **April–Nov.**
Breakfast: **Full, Continental**
Pets: **No**
Children: **Welcome, over 14**
Smoking: **No**
Social Drinking: **Permitted**
Minimum Stay: **2 nights, holiday and October weekends**
Airport Pickup: **Yes**

Rocking on the veranda over a cascading waterfall is one of the favorite pastimes at this tin-roofed, in-town country inn. Nestled in the Smoky Mountains tall pines, it is close to gem mining, white-water rafting, hiking trails, and country auctions, within walking distance of museums, mountain crafts and antique shops. On the premises is a gallery of tribal art and artifacts that Sally collected in her world travels. Each immaculate, tastefully furnished room has its own entrance and porch for added privacy. Kitchenettes are available. A full breakfast and evening dessert are served. Complimentary beverages are offered throughout the day and evening at the lovely, creekside gazebo.

MeadowHaven Bed & Breakfast ✪

NC HIGHWAY 8, P.O. BOX 222, GERMANTON, NORTH CAROLINA 27019

Tel: **(910) 593-3996**
Best Time to Call: **9 AM–9 PM**
Hosts: **Samuel and Darlene Fain**
Location: **16 mi. N of Winston-Salem**
No. of Rooms: **3**
No. of Private Baths: **3**
Double/pb: **$70–$99**
Cabins: **$125–$175**
Open: **All year**
Breakfast: **Full, Continental, plus**
Pets: **No**
Children: **No**
Smoking: **No**
Social Drinking: **Permitted, in guest rooms**
Minimum Stay: **3 nights weekends; holidays and special event weeks**

MeadowHaven is a chalet-style retreat on 25 acres, with stunning mountain views from the B&B's large deck. Immerse yourself in the hot tub or the heated indoor pool, grab some snacks from the pantry, and test your skills in the game room, at the fishing pond, or on the archery ranges. For honeymooners, the Lovebirds' Retreat, with its whirlpool tub and steam shower, is ideal. You won't have to travel far for horseback riding, canoeing, and golf; other local attractions include a winery, an art gallery, and Sauratown Mountain. Darlene, a former controller for the Marriott Corporation, runs her family's construction business, and Sam is a retail manager interested in greenhouse gardening, magic, and birds.

The Waverly Inn ✪

783 NORTH MAIN STREET, HENDERSONVILLE, NORTH CAROLINA 28792
E-mail: jsheiry@aol.com

Tel: **(800) 537-8195; (704) 693-9193; fax: (704) 692-1010**
Best Time to Call: **9:30 AM–10 PM**
Hosts: **John and Diane Sheiry**
Location: **20 mi. S of Asheville**
No. of Rooms: **14**
No. of Private Baths: **14**
Double/pb: **$79–$149**
Single/pb: **$79**
Open: **All year**
Reduced Rates: **Off-season**
Breakfast: **Full**
Credit Cards: **AMEX, DISC, MC, VISA**
Pets: **No**
Children: **Welcome**
Smoking: **Restricted**
Social Drinking: **Permitted**

Built as a boardinghouse in 1898, the Waverly is distinguished by its handsome Eastlake staircase—a factor that earned the Inn a listing on the National Register of Historic Places. Furnishings like four-poster canopy beds and claw-footed tubs combine Victorian stateliness and Colonial Revival charm. You'll walk away sated from all-you-can-eat breakfasts of pancakes and French toast. Noteworthy local sites include the Biltmore Estate, the Carl Sandburg house, the Blue Ridge Parkway, and the Flat Rock Playhouse.

Colonial Pines Inn ✪

ROUTE 1, BOX 22B, HICKORY STREET, HIGHLANDS, NORTH CAROLINA 28741

Tel: **(704) 526-2060**
Best Time to Call: **Afternoons**
Hosts: **Chris and Donna Alley**
Location: **80 mi. SW of Asheville**
No. of Rooms: **7**
No. of Private Baths: **7**
Double/pb: **$65–$95**
Single/pb: **$60–$80**
Suites: **$105–$130**
Guest Cottages: **$85–$200; sleep 4–6**
Open: **All year**
Reduced Rates: **Winter**
Breakfast: **Full**
Credit Cards: **MC, VISA**
Pets: **No**
Children: **Welcome, in cottage only**
Smoking: **No**
Social Drinking: **Permitted**

Located in a charming, uncommercial mountain resort town, this white Colonial is flanked by tall columns and is surrounded by two acres. The scenic view may be enjoyed from comfortable rocking chairs on the wide veranda. Donna, a former interior decorator, has furnished the Inn with antiques, art, and interesting accessories. Chris is a classical guitarist, woodworker, and great cook. The hearty breakfast includes a variety of homemade breads.

The Guest House ✪

RT. 2, BOX 649E (HWY E 64), HIGHLANDS, NORTH CAROLINA 28741

Tel: **(704) 526-4536**
Best Time to Call: **9 AM–9 PM**
Host: **Juanita Hernandez**
Location: **100 mi. NE of Atlanta**
No. of Rooms: **4**
No. of Private Baths: **4**
Double/pb: **$68–$85**
Single/pb: **$60–$70**
Open: **All year**
Reduced Rates: **Available**
Breakfast: **Full**
Credit Cards: **MC, VISA**
Pets: **No**
Children: **Welcome**
Smoking: **No**
Social Drinking: **Permitted**
Minimum Stay: **Weekends July–Sept., holidays, and October**
Foreign Languages: **Spanish, German**

A charming Alpine-style mountain chalet nestled among stately trees, this B&B is more ample than its compact looks suggest. Inside you'll admire the plush, cream-colored carpeting, chestnut paneling, light wallcoverings, teakwood furniture, and native stone fireplace. Deep contemporary seats invite guests to slip off their shoes and relax. Partake of the spectacular view from the open deck, with its sun umbrella and rocking chairs. After a restful night in your tastefully decorated room—accented with Juanita's artistic touches—you'll wake up to one of her superb breakfasts.

Lakeside Inn ✪

1921 FRANKLIN ROAD, HIGHLANDS, NORTH CAROLINA 28741

Tel: **(704) 526-4498**
Best Time to Call: **After 6 PM**
Hosts: **Cathy and Hank Ross**
Location: **120 mi. NE of Atlanta**
No. of Rooms: **4**
No. of Private Baths: **4**
Double/pb: **$70–$85**
Single/pb: **$65–$80**
Open: **All year**
Breakfast: **Full, Continental**
Credit Cards: **MC, VISA**
Pets: **No**
Children: **Welcome**
Smoking: **No**
Social Drinking: **Permitted**
Minimum Stay: **June–Oct. 2 nights, weekends**

Nestled among the oaks and hemlocks, Lakeside Inn has a lovely view of Lake Sequoyah and borders the Nantahala National Forest. You can enjoy the scenery from the patio of this restored 1930s lodge or use the canoe that is provided by your hosts for a leisurely ride. Lakeside Inn offers cozy rooms and has a common area with a fireplace, cable TV, books and games. Breakfast entrees include French toast, burritos, fresh fruits, and freshly baked muffins. Area activities range from hiking, horseback riding, mountain biking, fishing, rappelling, and white-water rafting to enjoying the quaint town of Highlands.

Ye Olde Stone House ✪

ROUTE 2, BOX 7, HIGHLANDS, NORTH CAROLINA 28741

Tel: **(704) 526-5911**
Best Time to Call: **Afternoons; evenings**
Hosts: **Jim and Rene Ramsdell**
Location: **80 mi. SW of Asheville**
No. of Rooms: **4**
No. of Private Baths: **4**
Double/pb: **$70–$85**
Single/pb: **$65–$70**
Chalet: **$95–$115, sleeps 4**
Guest cabin: **$130–180, sleeps 7**
Open: **All year**
Reduced Rates: **Available**
Breakfast: **Full**
Credit Cards: **MC, VISA**
Pets: **No**
Children: **Welcome**
Smoking: **No**
Social Drinking: **Permitted**
Minimum Stay: **2 nights holiday weekends**

Built of stones taken from a local river by mule and wagon, the house is less than a mile from the center of town, where you will find a nature center, museum, galleries, tennis courts, swimming pool, and shops offering antiques or mountain crafts. The rooms are bright, cheerful, and comfortably furnished. The sunroom and porch are perfect spots to catch up on that book you've wanted to read. On cool evenings, the Ramsdells invite you to gather round the fireplace for snacks and conversation.

Cherokee Inn Bed & Breakfast ✪

500 NORTH VIRGINIA DARE TRAIL, KILL DEVIL HILLS, NORTH CAROLINA 27948

Tel: **(919) 441-6127; (800) 554-2764**
Best Time to Call: **Evenings**
Hosts: **Bob and Kaye Combs**
Location: **75 mi. S of Norfolk**
No. of Rooms: **6**
No. of Private Baths: **6**
Double/pb: **$65–$95**
Open: **Apr. 1–Oct. 30**
Reduced Rates: **$5 less per night, seniors**
Breakfast: **Continental**
Credit Cards: **AMEX, MC, VISA**
Pets: **No**
Children: **No**
Smoking: **No**
Social Drinking: **Permitted**
Minimum Stay: **2 nights July–Aug.; 3 nights holidays**

Only 500 feet from the Atlantic Ocean you'll find this beach house with wraparound porches, soft cypress interiors, and white ruffled curtains. Cherokee Inn is near the historic Roanoke Island settlement, Cape Hatteras, and the Wright Brothers Memorial at Kitty Hawk. Of course, you may just want to spend the day at the beach. In the evening, curl up with a book or watch TV. You'll start the next day with coffee and pastries.

The Laurels ✪

P.O. BOX 1354, LAKE JUNALUSKA, NORTH CAROLINA 28745

Tel: **(704) 456-7186**
Hosts: **Mary and Roger Kayler**
Location: **20 mi. W of Asheville**
No. of Rooms: **3**
No. of Private Baths: **1**
Max. No. Sharing Bath: **4**
Double/pb: **$75**
Single/pb: **$70**
Double/sb: **$65**
Single/sb: **$60**
Open: **All year**
Breakfast: **Full**
Pets: **No**
Children: **Welcome, over 10**
Smoking: **No**
Social Drinking: **Permitted**
Airport/Station Pickup: **Yes**

This two-story, four-square house sits on 1.5 acres, shaded by lovely old hemlocks and stately white oaks, and surrounded by rhododendrons and laurels. Recently restored, The Laurels is furnished with treasured family antiques, many crafted with wood from local forests. It maintains the warmth and charm of a stately mountain home. Rock on the expansive side porch or relax in the parlor with a glass of sherry. Fine linens, down comforters and pillows, terry robes, flowers, and gourmet chocolates pamper guests. A full breakfast, casual in atmosphere, is served on fine china, crystal, and old family silver. The Laurels lies in the heart of the Blue Ridge Mountains near Waynesville, Maggie Valley, and adjacent to the Methodist Assembly at Lake Junaluska. This area offers many outdoor activities and shopping opportunities. Inquire about mystery weekends.

The Boxley Bed & Breakfast

117 EAST HUNTER STREET, MADISON, NORTH CAROLINA 27025

Tel: **(800) 429-3516**
Best Time to Call: **8 AM–8 PM**
Hosts: **JoAnn and Monte McIntosh**
Location: **22 mi. N of Greensboro**
No. of Rooms: **4**
No. of Private Baths: **4**
Double/pb: **$65**
Single/pb: **$55**
Open: **All year**
Reduced Rates: **10% seniors, weekly**
Breakfast: **Full**
Credit Cards: **AMEX, MC, VISA**
Pets: **No**
Children: **Welcome**
Smoking: **No**
Social Drinking: **Permitted**

This Greek Federal-style home was built in 1825 on over an acre, located in the historic district of Madison. Furnished with oriental rugs, antiques, fine linens and china, the house possesses an aura of simple elegance, charm, and grace. Guests will enjoy the peacefulness and serenity of this 19th-century setting. A gourmet breakfast is served in the country kitchen, dining room or on the porch. JoAnn and Monte are full-time hosts; their interests are gardening and refinishing furniture. The Boxley is your home away from home.

Kimball Oaks ✪

ROUTE 1, BOX 158, MANSON, NORTH CAROLINA 27553

Tel: **(919) 456-2004**
Best Time to Call: **8 AM–6 PM**
Hosts: **Allen and Jeanette Kimball**
Location: **50 mi. N of Raleigh, Durham**
No. of Rooms: **3**
No. of Private Baths: **2**
Max. No. Sharing Bath: **4**
Double/pb: **$80–$100**
Double/sb: **$70**
Open: **All year**
Reduced Rates: **10% after 1st night**
Breakfast: **Full**
Other Meals: **Available**
Pets: **No**
Children: **Welcome, over 12**
Smoking: **No**
Social Drinking: **Permitted**
Foreign Languages: **Italian, French**

Allen and Jeanette invite you to their two-story home in a grove of 200-year-old oaks surrounded by lawns, flower/herb beds and a vegetable garden, set in the middle of a farm community. Portions of their Colonial home date back to the 1840s. Rooms are decorated in light airy colors and tastefully furnished in traditional style with many antiques. Guests are greeted with iced tea and lemonade, with fresh fruit and flowers in the rooms. Participate in a lawn game—horseshoes, badminton, croquet, bocce or volleyball/basketball for the young at heart—or take a good book down to the shade-covered beaver pond for relaxed reading. Your hosts are a retired Army officer and his wife, whose entertaining skills have been honed by years of military and diplomatic living in Brussels, Geneva, Verona, Rome, and Washington. Come for a real treat!

New Berne House Bed and Breakfast Inn ✪

709 BROAD STREET, NEW BERN, NORTH CAROLINA 28560

Tel: **(919) 636-2250; (800) 842-7688**
Hosts: **Marcia Drum and Howard Bronson**
Location: **1 mi. from Hwy. 70**
No. of Rooms: **7**
No. of Private Baths: **7**
Double/pb: **$80**
Single/pb: **$60**
Open: **All year**
Reduced Rates: **AAA, AARP**
Breakfast: **Full**
Credit Cards: **AMEX, MC, VISA**
Pets: **No**
Children: **Welcome, over 12**
Smoking: **No**
Social Drinking: **Permitted**
Airport/Station Pickup: **Yes**

Located in the heart of New Bern's historic district, this brick Colonial is furnished in the style of an English country manor with a mixture of antiques, traditional pieces, and attic treasures. Guests are pampered with afternoon tea or coffee served in the parlor. A sweeping stairway leads upstairs to romantic bedchambers, one with a brass bed reportedly rescued in 1897 from a burning brothel. Breakfast specialties such as praline and cream waffles, honey-glazed ham, and homemade breads and muffins are served in the dining room. New Berne House is within walking distance of Tryon Palace, North Carolina's Colonial capitol, and the governor's mansion. Ask about the exciting Mystery Weekends.

Key Falls Inn ✪

151 EVERETT ROAD, PISGAH FOREST, NORTH CAROLINA 28768

Tel: **(704) 884-7559**
Best Time to Call: **9 AM–9 PM**
Hosts: **Clark and Patricia Grosvenor, and Janet Fogleman**
No. of Rooms: **4**
No. of Private Baths: **4**
Double/pb: **$60–$75**
Single/pb: **$50–$65**
Suites: **$90**
Open: **All year**
Breakfast: **Full**
Credit Cards: **AMEX, DC, MC, VISA**
Pets: **No**
Children: **Welcome, over 6**
Smoking: **No**
Social Drinking: **Permitted**

Visitors to this B&B will be able to make the most of western North Carolina's natural and cultural attractions. Key Falls Inn is situated on a 28-acre estate with its own tennis court, pond, and outdoor barbecue. For quieter moments, sit on one of the porches and enjoy the mountain views. Music lovers will want to get tickets to the acclaimed Brevard Festival, an annual summer event.

Breakfast Creek ✪

4361 OCEAN BREEZE AVENUE SW, SHALLOTTE, NORTH CAROLINA 28470

Tel: **(910) 754-3614**
Best Time to Call: **Mornings**
Hosts: **Tim Tryon and Diana Turtle**
Location: **35 mi. S of Wilmington**
No. of Rooms: **3**
No. of Private Baths: **2**
Max. No. Sharing Bath: **4**
Double/pb: **$60**
Suite: **$75**
Open: **All year**
Breakfast: **Full**
Pets: **No**
Children: **Welcome**
Smoking: **No**
Social Drinking: **Permitted**

Breakfast Creek is a modest white brick house filled with sunlight and antiques. It overlooks the Atlantic Ocean, Shallotte Inlet, Intracoastal Waterway, and acres of living wetlands. Diana is a devoted gardener, Tim is a musician and woodworker; both love sailing and the beach. The B&B is located fifteen minutes from Ocean Isle, and twenty minutes from Holden Beach, Calabash, Southport, Fort Fisher, Wilmington, and the Grand Strand. None of these are reachable without passing at least one golf course. During his first visit, a guest said, "It's like staying with friends at the beach without the sand."

Bed and Breakfast at Laurel Ridge

3188 SILER CITY–SNOW CAMP ROAD, SILER CITY, NORTH CAROLINA 27344

Tel: **(800) 742-6049; (919) 742-6049**
Best Time to Call: **9 AM–9 PM**
Hosts: **David Simmons and Lisa Reynolds**
Location: **35 mi. SE of Greensboro**
No. of Rooms: **3**
No. of Private Baths: **4**
Double/pb: **$59–$69**
Single/pb: **$59**
Suites: **$99**
Cottage: **$125**
Open: **All year**
Reduced Rates: **6th night free**
Breakfast: **Full**
Credit Cards: **AMEX, MC, VISA**
Pets: **No**
Children: **Welcome, over 10**
Smoking: **No**
Social Drinking: **Permitted**

Bed and Breakfast at Laurel Ridge is a contemporary rustic post and beam home situated on 26 forested acres that border the Rocky River. Centrally located in the heart of North Carolina, between the Triad furniture markets, Research Triangle Park, North Carolina Zoo, and Seagrove Pottery, this guest house provides visitors with many choices of things to do. Some say David, a professional chef for over 25 years, prepares the best breakfast in North Carolina using locally grown, organic products. The menu may include soufflés, specialty pancakes, and stuffed French toast.

Turby Villa B&B ✪

STAR ROUTE 1, BOX 48, SPARTA, NORTH CAROLINA 28675

Tel: **(910) 372-8490**
Host: **Mrs. Maybelline Turbiville**
No. of Rooms: **3**
No. of Private Baths: **3**
Double/pb: **$60**
Single/pb: **$45**
Open: **All year**
Breakfast: **Full**
Pets: **No**
Children: **Welcome**
Smoking: **Permitted**
Social Drinking: **Permitted**

At an altitude of 3000 feet, this contemporary two-story brick home is the centerpiece of a 20-acre farm. The house is surrounded by an acre of trees and manicured lawns, and the lovely views are of the scenic Blue Ridge Mountains. Breakfast is served either on the enclosed porch with its white wicker furnishings or in the more formal dining room with its Early American–style furnishings. Mrs. Turbiville takes justifiable pride in her attractive, well-maintained B&B.

Cedar Hill Farm B&B ✪

778 ELMWOOD ROAD, STATESVILLE, NORTH CAROLINA 28677

Tel: **(704) 873-4332; (800) 948-4423**
Best Time to Call: **Before 2 PM; after 5 PM**
Hosts: **Brenda and Jim Vernon**
Location: **45 mi. N of Charlotte**
No. of Rooms: **2**

No. of Private Baths: **2**
Double/pb: **$60**
Guest Cottage: **$75**
Open: **All year**
Breakfast: **Full**
Credit Cards: **MC, VISA**
Pets: **Sometimes**
Children: **Welcome**
Smoking: **No**
Social Drinking: **Permitted**

A three-story Federal farmhouse furnished with antique and country pieces, Cedar Hill is surrounded by 32 acres of rolling green, the better to feed the Vernons' sheep. Brenda and Jim sell fleece coverlets and crafts from their own hand-spun wool; they also make furniture and cure turkey and ham in a smokehouse on site. Stay in the farmhouse or in a private cottage. Either way you'll have an air-conditioned room with a telephone and cable TV. The country breakfasts will leave you full, thanks to servings of ham, sausage, fruit, potatoes, and buttermilk biscuits with homemade preserves. You can work off calories swimming in your hosts' pool or playing badminton, but you might want to relax in a porch rocker or hammock first. The cottage now has a working fireplace.

Scott's Keep ✪

308 WALNUT STREET, SWANSBORO, NORTH CAROLINA 28584

Tel: **(910) 326-1257; (800) 348-1257**
Best Time to Call: **Anytime**
Hosts: **Frank and Norma Scott**
Location: **150 mi. SE of Raleigh**
No. of Rooms: **3**
Max. No. Sharing Bath: **4**
Double/pb: **$60**
Double/sb: **$50**
Open: **All year**
Reduced Rates: **15% weekly**
Breakfast: **Full**
Credit Cards: **AMEX, DISC, MC, VISA**
Pets: **No**
Children: **Welcome, over 6**
Smoking: **No**
Social Drinking: **Permitted**
Minimum Stay: **2 nights, May 15–Sept. 15**

This simple contemporary is located on a quiet street two blocks from the waterfront. Your hosts want you to feel right at home in the bright, spacious living room and comfortable guest rooms. The larger bedroom is decorated with wicker and features an antique trunk, queen-size bed, and colorful quilts. The smaller bedroom is furnished in classic maple with twin beds and grandmother's quilts. For breakfast, Norma serves blueberry or apple spice muffins with fruit and homemade jellies. This historic seaside village is filled with inviting shops and waterside seafood restaurants. Your hosts will point the way to beautiful beaches, waterskiing, sailing, and windsurfing.

Four Rooster Inn ✪

403 PIREWAY ROAD, ROUTE 904, TABOR CITY, NORTH CAROLINA 28463

Tel: **(910) 653-3878**
Hosts: **Gloria and Bob Rogers**
Location: **24 mi. NW of Myrtle Beach, South Carolina; 45 min. from I-95**

No. of Rooms: **4**
No. of Private Baths: **2**
Max. No. Sharing Bath: **4**
Double/pb: **$65–$75**
Single/pb: **$55–$65**
Double/sb: **$55–$65**
Single/sb: **$45–$55**
Open: **All year**
Reduced Rates: **Fifth night free**
Breakfast: **Full**
Credit Cards: **MC, VISA**
Pets: **No**
Children: **Welcome, by arrangement**
Smoking: **No**
Social Drinking: **Permitted**
Airport/Station Pickup: **Yes**

Experience the warm, gracious hospitality of the old South in the charm of a country setting. The Inn has been restored to a comfortable elegance with china, crystal, antiques, beautiful fabrics and fine linens. Amenities include afternoon tea, evening turn-down service accented with chocolates, and coffee or tea at your door when you awake. A full breakfast is served in the dining room and may include yam bread, French toast, or eggs Benedict. The Four Rooster Inn is located forty-five minutes from Interstate 95 and a short drive from Myrtle Beach golf courses, Waccamaw Pottery shopping, Brookgreen Gardens, and historic Wilmington. The Inn provides a comfortable haven whether you are traveling for business or pleasure. Gloria and Bob are dedicated to the art of service for their guests.

Little Warren ✪

304 EAST PARK AVENUE, TARBORO, NORTH CAROLINA 27886

Tel: **(919) 823-1314; (800) 309-1314**
Hosts: **Patsy and Tom Miller**
Location: **Easy access from I-95**
No. of Rooms: **3**
No. of Private Baths: **3**
Double/pb: **$65**
Single/pb: **$58**
Open: **All year**
Reduced Rates: **Corporate, upon request**
Breakfast: **Full**
Credit Cards: **AMEX, DISC, MC, VISA**

Pets: **No**
Children: **Welcome, over 6**
Smoking: **Permitted**
Social Drinking: **Permitted**
Foreign Languages: **Spanish**

Little Warren is actually a large and gracious family home built in 1913. It is located along the Albemarle Trail in Tarboro's historic district. The deeply set, wraparound porch overlooks one of the last originally chartered town commons still in existence. Inside, you'll find rooms of beautiful antiques from England and America. In the morning, choose from a full English, Southern, or expanded Continental breakfast.

Barkley House Bed & Breakfast ✪

ROUTE 6, BOX 12, TAYLORSVILLE, NORTH CAROLINA 28681

Tel: **(704) 632-9060**
Best Time to Call: **Mornings**
Host: **Phyllis Barkley**
Location: **60 mi. NW of Charlotte**
No. of Rooms: **4**
No. of Private Baths: **3**
Double/pb: **$59**
Single/pb: **$48**
Open: **All year**
Breakfast: **Full**
Credit Cards: **AMEX, DISC, MC, VISA**
Pets: **Sometimes**
Children: **Welcome**
Smoking: **Permitted**
Social Drinking: **Permitted**
Airport/Station Pickup: **Yes**

After staying in European B&Bs, Phyllis opened the first one in Taylorsville, a small town surrounded by mountains. Barkley House is a white Colonial with yellow shutters and a gracious front porch with four columns. The furnishings are homey, combining antiques and pieces from the '50s. Haystack eggs and fruity banana splits are two of Phyllis's breakfast specialties; she'll be happy to cater to guests on restricted diets.

Mill Farm Inn ✪

P.O. BOX 1251, TRYON, NORTH CAROLINA 28782

Tel: **(704) 859-6992; (800) 545-6992**
Best Time to Call: **9 AM**
Hosts: **Chip and Penny Kessler**
Location: **45 mi. SE of Asheville**
No. of Rooms: **8**
No. of Private Baths: **8**
Double/pb: **$65**
Single/pb: **$49**
Suites: **$80–$140**
Open: **All year**
Reduced Rates: **10% seniors**
Breakfast: **Continental, plus**
Pets: **No**
Children: **Welcome**
Smoking: **No**
Social Drinking: **Permitted**
Foreign Languages: **French**

The Pacolet River flows past the edge of this three-and-one-half-acre property in the foothills of the Blue Ridge Mountains. Sitting porches, a gazebo, and the living room with fireplace are fine spots to relax. A hearty breakfast of fresh fruit, cereal, French toast, Belgian waffles, soft-boiled eggs, preserves, and coffee is served. Crafts shops, galleries, and antiquing will keep you busy.

Acadian House Bed & Breakfast ✪

129 VAN NORDEN STREET, WASHINGTON, NORTH CAROLINA 27889

Tel: **(919) 975-3967**
Best Time to Call: **Mornings and evenings**
Hosts: **Johanna and Leonard Huber**
Location: **105 mi. E of Raleigh**
No. of Rooms: **4**
No. of Private Baths: **4**
Double/pb: **$55–$65**
Suites: **$95**
Open: **Feb. 1–Dec. 14**
Breakfast: **Full**
Credit Cards: **AMEX, DISC, MC, VISA**
Pets: **No**
Children: **Welcome, over 12**
Smoking: **No**
Social Drinking: **Permitted**

Acadian House Bed & Breakfast, a 1900 home located in Colonial Washington, features a unique herringbone-patterned brick porch. It is decorated throughout with antiques and local crafts. A Victorian staircase leads to guest rooms and the library, where books and games are provided. Johanna and Leonard, transplanted New Orleanians, serve a full breakfast featuring southern Louisiana Acadian specialties such as beignets and café au lait along with traditional breakfast foods. Acadian House is one block from the scenic Pamlico River; museums and antique shops are nearby. The business traveler will find a writing table and telephone available. Fax and copying facilities are also nearby.

Pamlico House ✪

400 EAST MAIN STREET, WASHINGTON, NORTH CAROLINA 27889

Tel: **(919) 946-7184; (800) 948-8507**
Best Time to Call: **9 AM–8 PM**
Hosts: **Lawrence and Jeanne Hervey**
Location: **20 mi. E of Greenville**
No. of Rooms: **4**
No. of Private Baths: **4**
Double/pb: **$65–$75**
Single/pb: **$55–$65**
Open: **All year**
Breakfast: **Full**
Credit Cards: **AMEX, DISC, MC, VISA**
Pets: **No**
Children: **Welcome, over 6**
Smoking: **No**
Social Drinking: **Permitted**
Airport/Station Pickup: **Yes**

Located in the center of a small, historic town, this stately Colonial Revival home's large rooms are a perfect foil for the carefully chosen antique furnishings. Guests are drawn to the classic Victorian parlor or to the spacious wraparound porch for relaxing conversation. Take a self-guided walking tour of the historic district or a stroll along the quaint waterfront. Recreational pleasures abound. Nature enthusiasts

enjoy the wildlife and exotic plants in nearby Goose Creek State Park. Should you get homesick for your favorite pet, Lawrence and Jeanne will share theirs.

Belle Meade Inn ✪

5170 SOUTH MAIN STREET, WAYNESVILLE, NORTH CAROLINA 28786

Tel: **(704) 456-3234**
Hosts: **Gloria and Al DiNofa**
Location: **27 mi. W of Asheville**
No. of Rooms: **4**
No. of Private Baths: **4**
Double/pb: **$65–$70**
Single/pb: **$55–$60**
Open: **All year**
Reduced Rates: **10% AARP; weekly**
Breakfast: **Full**
Credit Cards: **DISC, MC, VISA**
Pets: **No**
Children: **Welcome, over 6**
Smoking: **No**
Social Drinking: **Permitted**

Nestled in the mountains, and within easy reach of the Great Smoky National Park, this elegant home is a frame dwelling built in the craftsman style popular in the early 1900s. The warm richness of the chestnut woodwork in the formal rooms and the large stone fireplace in the living room complement the appealing blend of antique and traditional furnishings. The friendly attention to guests' needs is exemplified in such thoughtful touches as "early bird" coffee brought to your door, complimentary refreshments on the veranda, and fresh flowers and mints in your room. Nearby attractions include Biltmore House, Cataloochee Ski Slope, mountain art and crafts festivals, and white-water rafting and tubing.

Weldon Place Inn ✪

500 WASHINGON AVENUE, WELDON, NORTH CAROLINA 27890

Tel: **(919) 536-4582; (800) 831-4470**
Best Time to Call: **Anytime**
Hosts: **Angel and Andy Whitby**
Location: **2 mi. E of I-95, exit 173**
No. of Rooms: **4**
No. of Private Baths: **4**
Double/pb: **$60–$89**
Single/pb: **$55–$60**
Open: **All year**
Reduced Rates: **Available**
Breakfast: **Full**
Credit Cards: **AMEX, MC, VISA**
Pets: **No**
Children: **Welcome, over 12**
Smoking: **Restricted**
Social Drinking: **No**

If you love antiques and country elegance, step back in time as you cross the threshold of Weldon Place Inn. Sleep in a canopy bed, wake to singing sparrows, and savor a gourmet breakfast. Then explore this historic neighborhood: the Inn, built in 1913, stands amid homes that date to the mid 1800s, and nearby, there is a canal system aqueduct that is two decades older. Breakfast specialties like sausage-and-cheese-stuffed French toast and strawberry bread will help to fuel your excursions.

Anderson Guest House ✪

520 ORANGE STREET, WILMINGTON, NORTH CAROLINA 28401

Tel: **(910) 343-8128**
Best Time to Call: **8 AM–5 PM**
Hosts: **Landon and Connie Anderson**
No. of Rooms: **2**
No. of Private Baths: **2**
Double/pb: **$85**
Single/pb: **$65**
Open: **All year**
Breakfast: **Full**
Pets: **Sometimes**
Children: **Welcome**
Smoking: **No**
Social Drinking: **Permitted**
Airport/Station Pickup: **Yes**

This 19th-century town house has a private guest house overlooking a garden. The bedrooms have ceiling fans, fireplaces, and air-conditioning. Enjoy cool drinks upon arrival and a liqueur before bed. Breakfast specialties are eggs Mornay, blueberry cobbler, and crepes. Your hosts can point out the sights of this historic town and direct you to the beaches.

Catherine's Inn ✪

410 SOUTH FRONT STREET, WILMINGTON, NORTH CAROLINA 28401

Tel: **(910) 251-0863; (800) 476-0723**
Best Time to Call: **8 AM–10 PM**
Hosts: **Walter and Catherine Ackiss**
Location: **Wilmington's historical district**
No. of Rooms: **3**
No. of Private Baths: **3**
Double/pb: **$85–$90**
Single/pb: **$70–$75**
Suite: **$170**
Open: **All year**
Reduced Rates: **Available**
Breakfast: **Full**
Credit Cards: **MC, VISA**
Pets: **No**
Children: **Welcome, by arrangement**

Smoking: **No**
Social Drinking: **Permitted**
Airport Pickup: **Yes**

Located in Wilmington's historic district, this Italianate home features wrought-iron fences, a gate, a Colonial Revival wraparound front porch and a two-story screened rear porch. The 300-foot lawn overlooks a sunken garden and the picturesque Cape Fear River. Inside, furnishing includes antiques and tasteful reproductions, high ceilings and an heirloom baby grand piano. Start your day with coffee delivered to your door, followed by an appetizing homemade breakfast served in the dining room on silver, china, and crystal. An evening turn-down service is provided, and a nightcap, too.

Taylor House Inn ✪

14 NORTH SEVENTH STREET, WILMINGTON, NORTH CAROLINA 28401

Tel: **(910) 763-7581; (800) 382-9982**
Best Time to Call: **After 11 AM**
Host: **Glenda Moreadith**
Location: **120 mi. SE of Raleigh**
No. of Rooms: **4**
No. of Private Baths: **4**
Double/pb: **$95–$100**
Single/pb: **$80–$90**
Suites: **$80–$140**
Open: **All year**
Breakfast: **Full**
Credit Cards: **AMEX, MC, VISA**
Pets: **No**
Children: **Welcome, over 12**
Smoking: **No**
Social Drinking: **Permitted**
Minimum Stay: **2 nights weekends May–Aug.**
Airport/Station Pickup: **Yes**

Upon entering the foyer of the Taylor House Inn, one is in awe of its stately elegance and warmth. The golden oak staircase with two stained glass windows, high ceilings, and parquet floors provide a dramatic expression of a long-lost art. Guest rooms include a bridal suite with an off-white color scheme and a king-size bed with a huge canopy, and a Garden Room with a gas fireplace, brass bed and a melon color scheme. A gourmet breakfast is served in the formal dining room, with bone china, crystal and candlelight. Taylor House is located in the historic district, within walking distance to the riverfront, antique shops, and museums. Walking tours and horse-drawn tours are also available. Wonderful beaches are a 15-minute drive.

Miss Betty's Bed & Breakfast Inn

600 WEST NASH STREET, WILSON, NORTH CAROLINA 27893-3045

Tel: **(919) 243-4447; (800) 258-2058 (for reservations only)**
Best Time to Call: **9 AM–9 PM**
Hosts: **Betty and Fred Spitz**
Location: **50 mi. E of Raleigh**
No. of Rooms: **10**
No. of Private Baths: **10**
Double/pb: **$60–$70**
Single/pb: **$50–$60**
Suites: **$75**

Open: **All year**
Breakfast: **Full**
Credit Cards: **AMEX, CB, DC, DISC, MC, VISA**
Pets: **No**
Children: **No**
Smoking: **No**
Social Drinking: **Permitted**

One of the best places to stay in the South, Miss Betty's is located in the downtown historic section of Wilson. The B&B comprises three beautifully restored homes—the Davis-Whitehead-Harris House (circa 1858), the adjacent Riley House, and Rosebud (circa 1943)—that recapture bygone elegance and style. Guests can browse for antiques in any of the numerous shops that have given Wilson the title of "Antique Capital of North Carolina." The town is also renowned for its tasty barbecue, gorgeous golf courses, and numerous tennis courts.

Mickle House

927 WEST FIFTH STREET, WINSTON-SALEM, NORTH CAROLINA 27101

Tel: **(910) 722-9045**
Best Time to Call: **9 AM–10 PM**
Host: **Barbara Garrison**
Location: **1 mi. from Rte. 40, Broad St. exit**
No. of Rooms: **2**
No. of Private Baths: **2**
Double/pb: **$75–$85**
Single/pb: **$75–$85**
Open: **All year**
Breakfast: **Full**
Credit Cards: **MC, VISA**
Pets: **No**
Children: **No**
Smoking: **No**
Social Drinking: **Permitted**

Step back in time to visit a quaint Victorian cottage painted a soft yellow, with dark green shutters and gingerbread trim. The fully restored home, located in the National Historic District of West End, is furnished with lovely antiques, such as the canopy and poster beds in the guest rooms. Dessert is served in the afternoon or evening, and a full breakfast, with fresh fruit and freshly-baked breads and muffins, awaits you in the morning. Old Salem, the Medical Center, and the Convention Center are five minutes away; fine restaurants, parks, shops, and the library are within walking distance.

OKLAHOMA

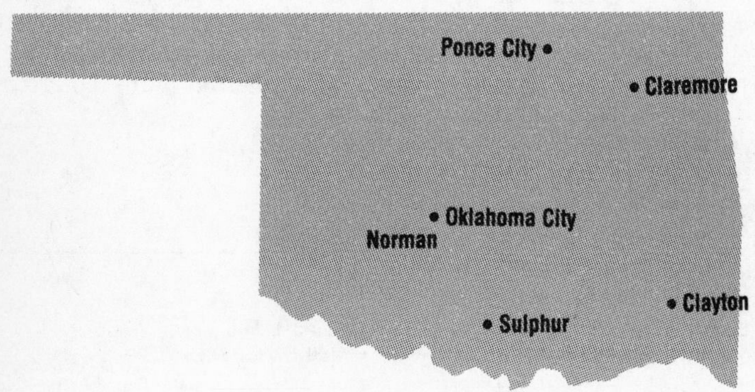

Country Inn

ROUTE 3, BOX 1925, CLAREMORE, OKLAHOMA 74017

Tel: **(918) 342-1894**
Best Time to Call: **8 AM–8 PM**
Hosts: **Leland and Kay Jenkins**
Location: **25 mi. NE of Tulsa**
No. of Rooms: **3**
No. of Private Baths: **3**
Double/pb: **$52**
Single/pb: **$35**
Suite: **$65**
Open: **All year**
Reduced Rates: **10% seniors**
Breakfast: **Full**
Children: **No**
Smoking: **No**
Social Drinking: **Permitted**

Leland and Kay look forward to making you feel right at home in the charming barn-style guest quarters, separate from the main house. They invite you to enjoy the swimming pool, improve your suntan, or just sit back in the shade and enjoy a cool drink. The Will Rogers Memorial, the J. M. Davis Gun Museum, the 29,500-acre Oologah Lake, and Oral Roberts University are close by.

Clayton Country Inn

ROUTE 1, BOX 8, HIGHWAY 271, CLAYTON, OKLAHOMA 74536

Tel: **(918) 569-4165, 747-1990**
Best Time to Call: **8 AM–9 PM**
Hosts: **Betty Lundgren, Eula and Al Taylor**
Location: **140 mi. SE of Tulsa**
No. of Rooms: **11**
No. of Private Baths: **11**
Double/pb: **$39**
Single/pb: **$33**
Guest Cottage: **$42; for 2**
Open: **All year**
Breakfast: **Continental**
Other Meals: **Available, dinner only**
Credit Cards: **AMEX, DISC, MC, VISA**
Pets: **No**
Children: **Welcome**
Smoking: **Permitted**
Social Drinking: **Permitted**

Perched on a hill amid 140 acres and surrounded by the Kiamichi Mountains is this 50-year-old, two-story, stone and wood inn. It's furnished in a simple, traditional style with a beamed ceiling and fireplace. The on-premises restaurant is noted for its fine cooking. Bass fishing at Lake Sardis is two miles away, and an 18,000-acre game preserve is just across the highway. Feel free to bring your horse and enjoy trail rides under the vast Western skies.

Holmberg House Bed & Breakfast ✪

766 DEBARR, NORMAN, OKLAHOMA 73069

Tel: **(405) 321-6221; (800) 646-6221**
Hosts: **Jo Meacham and Richard Divelbiss**
Location: **17 mi. S of Oklahoma City**
No. of Rooms: **4**
No. of Private Baths: **4**
Double/pb: **$65–$85**
Single/pb: **$55–$75**
Open: **All year**
Reduced Rates: **$10 less Sun.–Thurs.**
Breakfast: **Full**
Credit Cards: **AMEX, DISC, MC, VISA**
Pets: **No**
Children: **Welcome, over 12**
Smoking: **No**
Social Drinking: **Permitted**

Located in Norman's National Register Historic District and across the street from the University of Oklahoma's campus, this handsome 1914 Craftsman house was built by Professor Frederick Holmberg and his wife Signy. Jo and Richard bought the house in 1993 and it now accommodates many of the university's visiting scholars and parents. Guest rooms are individually decorated with antiques, private baths with claw-footed tubs, and color cable TVs. A parlor with a fireplace, porches with rockers, and gardens are for your pleasure. A hearty breakfast is served in the dining room.

Country House ✪

10101 OAKVIEW ROAD, OKLAHOMA CITY, OKLAHOMA 73165

Tel: **(405) 794-4008**
Best Time to Call: **8 AM–10 PM**
Hosts: **Dee and Nancy Ann Curnutt**
Location: **10 mi. SE of center of Oklahoma City**
No. of Rooms: **2**
No. of Private Baths: **2**
Double/pb: **$70–$90**
Single/pb: **$60–$80**
Open: **All year**
Breakfast: **Full**
Pets: **Sometimes**
Children: **Welcome**
Smoking: **Restricted**
Social Drinking: **Permitted**

At Country House you will find genuine, old-fashioned hospitality in a warm romantic setting. The house rests on five beautiful acres; the interior is tastefully furnished with 19th-century antiques and country collectibles. Nancy offers in-room color TV on request, as well as a scrumptious breakfast served on the balcony if you wish. For fishing, water sports, and horseback riding go to nearby Lake Draper, where

Captain Dee, Nancy's husband, runs a charter boat service. Ask about the large red heart-shaped whirlpool suite.

The Grandison ✪

1841 NORTHWEST FIFTEENTH STREET, OKLAHOMA CITY, OKLAHOMA 73106

Tel: **(405) 521-0011; (800) 240-INNS [4667]**
Hosts: **Claudia and Bob Wright**
Location: **2 mi. off I-44, Tenth St. exit**
No. of Rooms: **5**
No. of Private Baths: **5**
Double/pb: **$45–$85**
Suites: **$90–$125**
Open: **All year**
Breakfast: **Continental, plus**
Other Meals: **Available**
Credit Cards: **AMEX, DISC, MC, VISA**
Pets: **Sometimes**
Children: **Welcome, over 12**
Smoking: **Permitted**
Social Drinking: **Permitted**
Airport/Station Pickup: **Yes**

Named for its first owner and resident, Grandison Crawford, this turn-of-the-century brick Colonial was expanded in 1914, and again in the 1930s. It is furnished with antiques from many eras, so each bedroom has a distinctive look. The closest attractions—Civic Center Music Hall, the Convention Center, and Oklahoma City's fairgrounds—are just five minutes away. Breakfast consists of a meat and egg dish, fresh fruit, home-baked pastries, and beverage. For snacking, you'll find fruit, nuts, cookies, and mints in your bedroom.

Davarnathey Inn ✪

1001 WEST GRAND, PONCA CITY, OKLAHOMA 74601

Tel: **(405) 765-9922; (800) 763-9922**
Hosts: **David and Shirley Zimmerman**
Location: **80 mi. S of Wichita, Kans.**
No. of Rooms: **3**
No. of Private Baths: **3**
Double/pb: **$69**
Single/pb: **$59**
Open: **All year**
Breakfast: **Full**
Credit Cards: **AMEX, CB, DC, DISC, MC, VISA**
Pets: **No**
Children: **Welcome**
Smoking: **No**
Social Drinking: **Permitted**
Airport/Station Pickup: **Yes**

Built in 1906 by an Oklahoma oilman, Davarnathey Inn has its original fretwork stairway, ornate mirrored mantel, and stained glass windows. Period furnishings and floral wallpapers sustain the Victorian mood. Guests are encouraged to browse in the library; the musically inclined have both a piano and an organ to play. Other amenities include a hot tub. Snacks are served, but after a full breakfast of fresh baked Scandinavian breads, fruit crepes, soufflés, and quiche, it may be a while before you're hungry again.

Artesian Bed and Breakfast

1022 WEST 12TH STREET, SULPHUR, OKLAHOMA 73086

Tel: **(405) 622-5254**
Hosts: **Karen and Tom Byrd**
Location: **71 mi. S of Oklahoma City**
No. of Rooms: **2**
No. of Private Baths: **2**
Double/pb: **$60**
Single/pb: **$50**
Suites: **$70**
Open: **All year**
Reduced Rates: **15% Dec.–Mar.**
Breakfast: **Full**
Pets: **No**
Children: **Welcome, over 10**
Smoking: **No**
Social Drinking: **No**

A quiet, homey atmosphere prevails at this 1904 Sears, Roebuck Victorian, where the L-shaped front porch is furnished with swing and willow chairs. Inside, you'll admire the wooden staircase, the tiled parlor fireplace, and the bay windows overlooking the backyard. There's natural beauty at every turn. For hiking, swimming, or just picnicking, Chickasaw Recreation Area is only half a mile away. For fishing, boating, and water skiing, take the ten-mile drive to Arbuckle Lake. Your hosts, a retired veterinarian and a homemaker, can help you make the most of your stay.

SOUTH CAROLINA

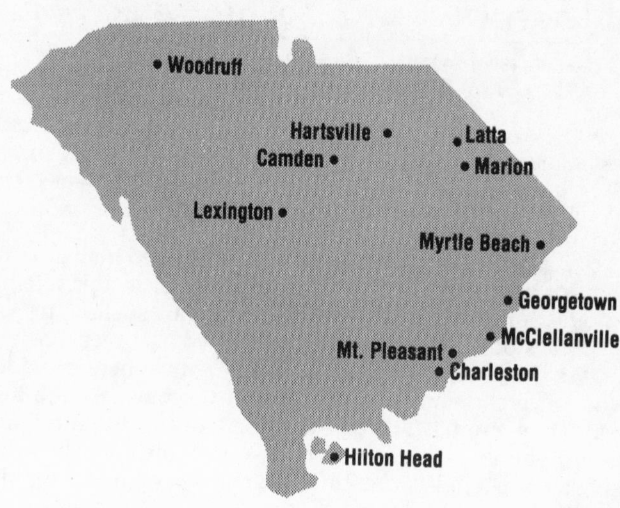

Candlelight Inn

1904 BROAD STREET, CAMDEN, SOUTH CAROLINA 29020

Tel: **(803) 424-1057**
Hosts: **George and JoAnn Celani**
Location: **30 mi. N of Columbia**
No. of Rooms: **3**
No. of Private Baths: **3**
Double/pb: **$65**
Open: **All year**
Breakfast: **Full**
Credit Cards: **MC, VISA**
Pets: **No**
Children: **Welcome, over 12**
Smoking: **No**
Social Drinking: **Permitted**
Minimum Stay: **2 nights Carolina and Colonial Cup Steeplechase**

Located in Camden's Historic District, Candlelight Inn stands on two acres, surrounded by azaleas and camellias and shaded by a canopy of grand old oaks. A brick drive will guide you to the Inn where the glow of candles illuminates the windows. The warm and inviting interior reflects George and JoAnn's interest in needlework, quilts, and antiques. Nearby, guests can enjoy antique shops, Steeplechase facilities, golf courses and fine restaurants. One description by a guest says it all: "Candlelight, comfort, camellias, charm, cookies, conversation, and cooking all add up to the Candlelight Inn."

Historic Charleston Bed & Breakfast

60 BROAD STREET, CHARLESTON, SOUTH CAROLINA 29401

Tel: **(803) 722-6606; (800) 743-3583**
Best Time to Call: **9:30 AM–6 PM Mon.–Fri.**
Coordinator: **Douglas B. Lee**
States/Regions Covered: **South Carolina**
Descriptive Directory: **Free**
Rates (Single/Double):
Modest: **$65 / $75**
Average: **$80 / $95**
Luxury: **$120 / $225**
Credit Cards: **AMEX, MC, VISA**
Minimum Stay: **2 nights Mar. 15–June 15, Oct.**

This port city is one of the most historic in the United States. Through the auspices of this service, you will enjoy your stay in a private home, carriage house, or mansion in a neighborhood of enchanting walled gardens, cobblestoned streets, and moss-draped oak trees. Each home is unique, yet each has a warm and friendly atmosphere provided by a host who sincerely enjoys making guests welcome. All are historic properties dating from 1720 to 1890, yet all are up to date with air-conditioning, phones, and television. Reduced rates may be available for weekly stays. There is a one-time $15 reservation fee charged with each reservation.

Ann Harper's Bed & Breakfast

56 SMITH STREET, CHARLESTON, SOUTH CAROLINA 29401

Tel: **(803) 723-3947**
Best Time to Call: **Before 10 AM; after 6 PM**
Host: **Ann D. Harper**
Location: **1 mi. from I-26**
No. of Rooms: **2**
Max. No. Sharing Bath: **3**
Double/pb: **$70–$80**
Single/pb: **$60–$65**
Open: **All year**
Breakfast: **Full**
Pets: **No**
Children: **Welcome, over 10**
Smoking: **Restricted**
Social Drinking: **Permitted**

This attractive home, circa 1870, is located in Charleston's historic district. The rooms, ideally suited for two friends traveling together, are decorated with wicker pieces and family treasures. Take a moment to relax on the porch or in the intimate walled garden out back. Ann serves a hot, Southern-style breakfast each morning featuring homemade bread and hominy grits. She will gladly direct you to the interesting sights of this historic area. There is a $5 surcharge for one-night stays; no single rates March 15 to June 15.

Country Victorian Bed and Breakfast ✪

105 TRADD STREET, CHARLESTON, SOUTH CAROLINA 29401

Tel: **(803) 577-0682**
Host: **Diane Deardurff Weed**
Location: **96 mi. S of Myrtle Beach**
No. of Rooms: **2**
No. of Private Baths: **2**
Double/pb: **$75–$100**
Single/pb: **$75–$100**
Suites: **$100–$140**
Open: **All year**
Breakfast: **Continental**
Pets: **No**
Children: **Welcome, over 8**
Smoking: **No**
Social Drinking: **Permitted**

As tourists pass in horse-drawn carriages, their eyes are drawn to the beautiful screen doors of this Victorianized house, built in 1820. Rooms have private entrances and are comfortably decorated with antique iron and brass beds, old quilts, and antique oak and wicker furniture. You'll find homemade cookies waiting for you when you arrive. Coffee and tea can be prepared in your room at any time, and snacks are served in the afternoon. Restaurants, churches, antique shops, museums, and art galleries are all within walking distance.

Johnson's Six Orange Street B&B

6 ORANGE STREET, CHARLESTON, SOUTH CAROLINA 29401

Tel: **(803) 722-6122**
Hosts: **Becky and Bill Johnson**
Location: **Located in historic district of Charleston**
No. of Rooms: **1**
No. of Private Baths: **1**
Apartment: **$90**
Open: **All year**
Breakfast: **Continental**
Credit Cards: **No**
Pets: **No**
Children: **Welcome (crib)**
Smoking: **No**
Social Drinking: **Permitted**
Foreign Languages: **French, German**

Within Charleston's historical district, Becky and Bill maintain an attached guest house complete with sitting room, efficiency kitchen, upstairs bedroom, and private bath and entrance. The bedroom sleeps three and features an antique sleigh bed plus an iron and brass single bed. A crib is also available for families with an infant. Enjoy scrumptious home-baked coffee cakes, pastries, and breads before you explore the numerous sights and attractions this city has to offer.

1790 House ✪

630 HIGHMARKET STREET, GEORGETOWN, SOUTH CAROLINA 29440

Tel: **(803) 546-4821; (800) 890-7432**
Best Time to Call: **9 AM–9 PM**
Hosts: **Patricia and John Wiley**
Location: **60 mi. N of Charleston**
No. of Rooms: **6**
No. of Private Baths: **6**
Double/pb: **$75–$90**
Guest Cottage: **$125**
Suites: **$95**
Open: **All year**

Reduced Rates: **Nov.–Feb. $10 less Sun.–Thurs., 10% seniors**
Breakfast: **Full**
Credit Cards: **AMEX, DISC, MC, VISA**
Pets: **No**
Children: **Welcome**
Smoking: **No**
Social Drinking: **Permitted**
Minimum Stay: **Holiday weekends**

This meticulously restored, 200-year-old Colonial plantation-style inn in Georgetown's historic district has spacious, luxurious rooms, 11-foot ceilings, and seven fireplaces. Slaves once slept in the Slave Quarters, while the elegant Rice Planters and Indigo Rooms have four-poster beds, sitting areas, and fireplaces. Your other options include the Prince George Suite, a hideaway under the eaves; Gabriella's Library, with built-in bookcases and a fireplace; and the Dependency Cottage, with its private entrance, patio, and spacious bath with a Jacuzzi. Whichever you pick, you can walk to shops, restaurants, and historic sites. Or take a short drive to Myrtle Beach, golfing at the Grand Strand, the Brookgreen Gardens, Pawleys Island, and downtown Charleston.

Missouri Inn B&B ✪

314 EAST HOME AVENUE, HARTSVILLE, SOUTH CAROLINA 29550

Tel: **(803) 383-9553**
Best Time to Call: **Noon–9 PM**
Hosts: **Kyle and Kenny Segars, and Lucy Brown**
Location: **28 mi. NW of Florence**
No. of Rooms: **5**
No. of Private Baths: **5**
Double/pb: **$85**
Single/pb: **$75**
Open: **All year**
Reduced Rates: **Corporate**
Breakfast: **Full**
Credit Cards: **AMEX, MC, VISA**
Pets: **No**
Children: **Welcome, over 10**
Smoking: **Permitted**
Social Drinking: **Permitted**

An elegant Southern mansion built around the turn of the century and completely renovated in 1990, the Missouri Inn offers discriminating guests exceptional peace, quiet, and privacy in a small, luxurious setting. Located in Hartsville's official historic district, the Inn stands opposite the lovely Coker College campus, on about five acres landscaped with stately trees and flowering shrubs. The distinctively furnished rooms not only have telephones and TVs, but terry robes, bath sheets, towel warmers, hair dryers, and fresh floral arrangements. Amenities include afternoon tea and complimentary beverages at all times.

Ambiance Bed & Breakfast

8 WREN DRIVE, HILTON HEAD, SOUTH CAROLINA 29928

Tel: **(803) 671-4981**
Host: **Marny Kridel Daubenspeck**
Location: **40 mi. from I-95, Exit 28**
No. of Rooms: **2**
No. of Private Baths: **2**
Double/pb: **$75**

Single/pb: **$70**
Open: **All year**
Breakfast: **Continental**
Pets: **No**
Children: **Welcome, over 12**
Smoking: **No**
Social Drinking: **Permitted**

Marny welcomes guests to sunny Hilton Head Island. This cypress home, nestled in subtropical surroundings, is in Sea Pines Plantation. Ambiance reflects the hostess's interior decorating business by the same name. All the amenities of Hilton Head are offered in a contemporary, congenial atmosphere. The climate is favorable year-round for all sports. Ambiance is across the street from a beautiful beach and the Atlantic Ocean.

Abingdon Manor ✪

307 CHURCH STREET, LATTA, SOUTH CAROLINA 29565

Tel: **(803) 752-5090**
Best Time to Call: **9 AM–9 PM**
Hosts: **Michael and Patty Griffey**
Location: **25 mi. N of Florence**
No. of Rooms: **5**
No. of Private Baths: **5**
Double/pb: **$95**
Suites: **$120**
Open: **All year**
Reduced Rates: **10–15% after 3 days**
Breakfast: **Full**
Credit Cards: **MC, VISA**
Pets: **No**
Children: **Welcome, over 12**
Smoking: **No**
Social Drinking: **Permitted**

This 8,000-square-foot Greek Revival mansion is located on three acres in Latta's historic district and is listed on the National Register. Abingdon Manor is filled with unique architectural detail and Old World craftmanship and is furnished with antiques and collectibles. Michael and Patty offer many amenities, including featherbeds, robes, and bikes. Things to do include golf, antiquing, and visiting historical sites. Or you may want to attend one of the monthly festivals that are available throughout the area.

Southern Hospitality B&B Reservations ✪

110 AMELIA DRIVE, LEXINGTON, SOUTH CAROLINA 29072

Tel: **(803) 356-6238; fax: (800) 799-8249**
Best Time to Call: **9 AM–5 PM Mon.–Fri.**
Coordinator: **Mesa Foard**
States/Regions Covered: **North Carolina Mountains, South Carolina—Statewide**
Descriptive Directory of B&Bs: **Free**
Rates (Single/Double):
Modest: **$45 / $55**
Average: **$65 / $75**
Luxury: **$100 / $125–$195**
Credit Cards: **MC, VISA**

Southern Hospitality is your window to quality B&B accommodations. These B&Bs are inspected for cleanliness, comfort, and host congeniality. Many can host weddings, honeymoons, and small meetings; some can provide candlelight dinners as well as catering. All homes lie within easy driving distance of major cities, colleges, and interstates.

Montgomery's Grove ✪

408 HARLEE STREET, MARION, SOUTH CAROLINA 29571

Tel: **(803) 423-5220**
Hosts: **Coreen and Rick Roberts**
Location: **20 mi. E of Florence**
No. of Rooms: **4**
No. of Private Baths: **2**
Max. No. Sharing Bath: **4**
Double/pb: **$70**
Single/pb: **$60**
Double/sb: **$70**
Single/sb: **$60**
Open: **All year**
Reduced Rates: **10% weekly; 10% seniors**
Breakfast: **Full**
Other Meals: **Available**
Pets: **No**
Children: **Welcome**
Smoking: **No**
Social Drinking: **Permitted**

Nestled among five acres of century-old trees and gardens, Montgomery's Grove is a beautiful Victorian mansion known for its exceptional architectural features. Dramatic fourteen-foot archways and elaborate woodwork greet all guests. Yet it is easy to relax in the five beautifully decorated rooms, on the wraparound porches, or with a stroll through the woods. Walk beneath the Spanish moss to historic downtown Marion, or travel just thirty minutes to Myrtle Beach. Only 15 minutes from I-95, Montgomery's Grove is the perfect midway stopping point to and from Florida. Visit Marion, the pretty little town on the way to the beach. It'll be a visit you won't forget.

Laurel Hill Plantation ✪

8913 NORTH HIGHWAY 17, P.O. BOX 190, McCLELLANVILLE, SOUTH CAROLINA 29458

Tel: **(803) 887-3708**
Best Time to Call: **Before 9 PM**
Hosts: **Jackie and Lee Morrison**
Location: **30 mi. N of Charleston**
No. of Rooms: **4**
No. of Private Baths: **4**
Double/pb: **$65–$95**
Single/pb: **$75**
Open: **All year**
Breakfast: **Full**
Pets: **No**
Children: **Welcome, over 6**
Smoking: **No**
Social Drinking: **Permitted**

The original Laurel Hill, an 1850s plantation house listed on the National Register of Historic Places, was destroyed by Hurricane Hugo in 1989. Nestled in a nook by a picturesque tidal creek, the spacious reconstruction retains the romance of the past while affording the convenience of the contemporary. Wraparound porches provide a sweeping panorama of the Atlantic Ocean and Cape Romain's salt marshes, islands, and waterways. Four charming guest rooms feature fascinating views of the landscape and are furnished with carefully chosen primitives and antiques reflecting the renowned hospitality of South Carolina's low country.

Sunny Meadows ✪

1459 VENNING ROAD, MT. PLEASANT, SOUTH CAROLINA 29464

Tel: **(803) 884-7062**
Best Time to Call: **11 AM–10 PM**
Hosts: **Charles and Agnes Houston**
Location: **5 mi. E of Charleston**
No. of Rooms: **2**
No. of Private Baths: **2**
Double/pb: **$65–$75**
Open: **All year**
Breakfast: **Full**
Pets: **No**
Children: **Welcome, over 8**
Smoking: **No**
Social Drinking: **Permitted**

Enjoy Southern hospitality at its best, where elegance blends with the charm of country living. This two-story Southern Colonial, situated on three acres of beautifully landscaped grounds, is located fifteen minutes from Historic Charleston and five minutes from Charleston's finest beaches. Guest rooms are located away from the family living area, ensuring full privacy. Each room is decorated with eighteenth-century antiques and reproductions. One room has a king and a double bed. The other has a four-poster bed, TV, and telephone. Weather permitting, you can enjoy breakfast on the back porch and read the paper on the swing. Breakfast specialties include stratta and cheese-stuffed French toast.

Brustman House

400 25TH AVENUE SOUTH, MYRTLE BEACH, SOUTH CAROLINA 29577

Tel: (803) 448-7699; (800) 448-7699; fax: (803) 626-2478
Best Time to Call: **Early evening**
Host: **Dr. Wendell C. Brustman**
Location: **90 mi. N of Charleston**
No. of Rooms: **5**
No. of Private Baths: **5**
Double/pb: **$55–$85**
Single/pb: **$50–$80**
Suites: **$80–$120**
Open: **All year**
Reduced Rates: **Extended stay; Oct. 1–Mar. 31**
Breakfast: **Full**
Pets: **No**
Children: **Welcome, over 10**
Smoking: **No**
Social Drinking: **Permitted**
Airport/Station Pickup: **Yes**

Maybe you can't have it all, but Brustman House comes close. This Georgian-style home is two short blocks from the beach, and without leaving the almost two-acre, tree-studded property you can admire the fresh herb garden or have a tête-à-tête on the glider in the rose garden gazebo. Located nearby are golf courses, seafront restaurants, discount shops, and country music theaters. Afternoon tea includes wines, waters, and sweets served on exquisite Scandinavian dinnerware. Sleep late in your quiet room, its snug bed warmed by a down comforter. The Rosewood Room has a Jacuzzi tub for two. The breakfast menu includes healthful specialties, such as ten-grain buttermilk pancakes.

Serendipity, An Inn

407 71ST AVENUE NORTH, MYRTLE BEACH, SOUTH CAROLINA 29572

Tel: **(803) 449-5268; (800) 762-3229**
Best Time to Call: **8 AM–10 PM**
Hosts: **Terry and Sheila Johnson**
Location: **60 mi. from Rte. 95**
No. of Rooms: **14**
No. of Private Baths: **14**
Double/pb: **$67–$92**
Suites: **$78–$110**
Open: **Jan.–Nov.**
Breakfast: **Continental**
Credit Cards: **MC, VISA**
Pets: **No**
Children: **Welcome**
Smoking: **Permitted**
Social Drinking: **Permitted**

Serendipity is a Spanish Mission–style inn surrounded by lush tropical plants and flowers. The setting is peaceful, the street is quiet, and the ocean is less than 300 yards away. Bedrooms are highlighted with antiques drawing from Art Deco, Oriental, wicker, and pine motifs. The Garden Room is the place for a generous breakfast of homemade breads, fresh fruit, eggs, and cereal. Your hosts invite you to use the heated pool and spa, play shuffleboard, Ping-Pong, or just share a quiet moment beside the patio fountain. Myrtle Beach is known for its fine restaurants, but the Johnsons have a gas grill if you want to do your own cooking. Terry and Sheila will gladly direct you to nearby shops, fishing villages, golf courses, miles of beaches, and music theaters.

Nicholls-Crook Plantation House ✪

120 PLANTATION DRIVE, WOODRUFF, SOUTH CAROLINA 29388

Tel: **(864) 476-8820**
Best Time to Call: **9 AM–9 PM**
Host: **Suzanne Brown**
Location: **12 mi. S of Spartanburg**
No. of Rooms: **2**
No. of Private Baths: **2**
Max. No. Sharing Bath: **4**
Double/pb: **$85–$95**
Single/pb: **$75**
Suites: **$150**
Open: **All year**
Reduced Rates: **Available**
Breakfast: **Continental**
Other Meals: **Available**
Credit Cards: **AMEX**
Pets: **Sometimes**
Children: **Welcome, over 8**
Smoking: **No**
Social Drinking: **Permitted**
Airport Pickup: **Yes**
Foreign Languages: **French, Spanish**

Surround yourself with the atmosphere of times gone by in this Georgian-style plantation house built in 1793, and listed on the National Register of Historic Places. Delight in the historical ambiance enhanced by antique period furnishings, charming gardens, and the white rock courtyard. A bountiful breakfast will add to the pleasures of your visit. Guest rooms are cozy and inviting. Relax in the parlor, play an old-fashioned board game in the tavern room, or spend your time exploring the many interesting attractions while in the area.

TENNESSEE

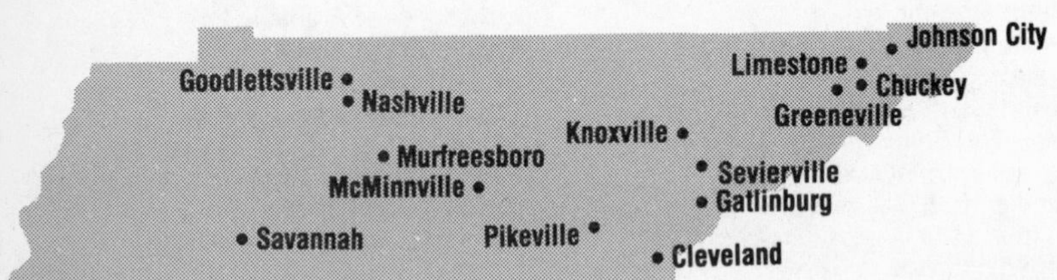

Bed & Breakfast—About Tennessee ✪

P.O. BOX 110227, NASHVILLE, TENNESSEE 37222-0227

Tel: **(615) 331-5244 for information; fax: (615) 833-7701; (800) 458-2421 for reservations**
Coordinator: **Fredda Odom**
States/Regions Covered: **Statewide**

Descriptive Directory of B&Bs: **$5**
Rates (Single/Double):
Average: **$40–$50 / $65**
Luxury: **$80–$100 / $80–$150**
Credit Cards: **AMEX, DISC, MC, VISA**

From the Great Smoky Mountains to the Mississippi, here are diverse attractions that include fabulous scenery, Tennessee's Grand Ole Opry and Opryland, universities, Civil War sites, horse farms, and much more. Fredda will arrange sightseeing tours, car rentals, tickets to events, and everything she can to assure you a pleasant stay. There is a $5 booking fee.

Harmony Hill Inn ✪

85 PLEASANT HILL ROAD, CHUCKEY, TENNESSEE 37641

Tel: **(423) 257-3893**
Best Time to Call: **8 AM–10 PM**
Host: **Dodie Melton**
Location: **8 mi. NE of Greeneville, and 20 mi. from Jonesborough**
No. of Rooms: **2**
No. of Private Baths: **2**
Double/pb: **$55**
Single/pb: **$45**
Open: **All year**
Breakfast: **Full**
Pets: **Sometimes**
Children: **Welcome**
Smoking: **No**
Social Drinking: **No**

Located on Horse Creek in the foothills of the Appalachian Mountains, this two-story 1850 farmhouse has a soothing, country atmosphere. Dodie, a registered nurse, is also a skilled woodworker and has renovated much of the house herself. After a full breakfast featuring her homemade sourdough bread—special diets considered upon request—take an easy drive to some of the area's attractions, such as Davy Crockett's birthplace, historic Jonesborough, Andrew Johnson's home and tailor shop, Bristol Caverns, Roan Mountain's rhododendron gardens, Smoky Mountain National Park, Dollywood, and North Carolina's Hot Springs Spa. For your greater relaxation, therapeutic massage is available by appointment.

Chadwick House ✪

2766 MICHIGAN AVENUE, RD NORTH EAST, CLEVELAND, TENNESSEE 37323

Tel: **(423) 339-2407**
Host: **Winnie A. Chadwick**
Location: **35 mi. N of Chattanooga**
No. of Rooms: **3**
No. of Private Baths: **1**
Max. No. Sharing Bath: **4**

Double/pb: **$52**
Double/sb: **$47**
Single/sb: **$35**
Open: **All year**
Reduced Rates: **10% seniors**
Breakfast: **Full**
Other Meals: **Available**
Pets: **No**
Children: **Welcome**
Smoking: **Permitted**
Social Drinking: **Permitted**
Airport/Station Pickup: **Yes**

White shutters and trim accent the multicolored bricks of this handsome ranch home just a half hour from Chattanooga. White-water rafting, Red Clay's historic Indian meeting grounds, and Cherokee National Forest are close by, and golfing and tennis are available right in Cleveland. In their spare moments B&B guests can watch the squirrels and birds in the back garden or relax by the fireplace with a glass of locally made wine. Winnie's full country breakfasts include homemade rolls and muffins.

Butcher House in the Mountains ✪

1520 GARRETT LANE, GATLINBURG, TENNESSEE 37738

Tel: **(423) 436-9457**
Best Time to Call: **10 AM–9 PM**
Hosts: **Hugh and Gloria Butcher**
Location: **50 mi. SE of Knoxville**
No. of Rooms: **5**
No. of Private Baths: **5**
Double/pb: **$79–$119**
Open: **All year**
Reduced Rates: **$10 less after 2nd night, Mon.–Thurs.**
Breakfast: **Full**
Credit Cards: **AMEX, MC, VISA**
Pets: **No**
Children: **Welcome, over 12**
Smoking: **No**
Social Drinking: **Permitted**
Minimum Stay: **Weekends**
Foreign Languages: **Italian**

The ambiance at Butcher House is one of elegance, warmth, and beauty. Hugh and Gloria's years of collecting have resulted in a home filled with one-of-a-kind antique treasures. Guest rooms are decorated with unique linens and furniture from various eras. Nearby attractions include Pigeon Forge, Dollywood, and Smoky Mountains National Park. Guests can enjoy hiking, fishing, skiing, golfing, or visiting the many crafts shops. Your hosts will send you on your way after a gourmet breakfast that may consist of eggs Sebastian, Italian crepes, or eggs cardamom.

Olde English Tudor Inn ✪

135 WEST HOLLY RIDGE ROAD, GATLINBURG, TENNESSEE 37738

Tel: **(423) 436-7760; (800) 541-3798**
Best Time to Call: **11 AM–9 PM**
Hosts: **Kathy and Larry Schuh**
Location: **45 mi. SE of Knoxville**
No. of Rooms: **7**
No. of Private Baths: **7**
Double/pb: **$75–$85**
Single/pb: **$65**
Suites: **$95–$105**
Open: **All year**
Reduced Rates: **10% seniors**
Breakfast: **Full**
Credit Cards: **MC, VISA**
Pets: **No**

Children: **Welcome**
Smoking: **No**
Social Drinking: **Permitted**
Airport Pickup: **Yes**

From the Olde English Tudor Inn's ideal downtown location, it's just a few minutes' walk to the attractions of Gatlinburg, and only a brief drive to Dollywood, Craft Community, outlet malls, and Great Smoky National Park. Handsomely decorated bedrooms have cable TV with HBO. Guests are invited to relax in the large, comfortably furnished community room with a TV/VCR and free-standing wood burning stove, or enjoy the peaceful seclusion of the rear patio. Generous breakfasts typically include fresh fruit, pancakes or French toast, and eggs, bacon, sausage, or ham. Make sure to save room for freshly baked breads with jams and jellies. Kathy and Larry want your visit to be memorable and will be happy to assist you with your touring, dining, and shopping questions.

Woodshire B&B ✪

600 WOODSHIRE DRIVE, GOODLETTSVILLE, TENNESSEE 37072

Tel: **(615) 859-7369**
Best Time to Call: **Before 9 AM; after 6 PM**
Hosts: **Beverly and John Grayson**
Location: **11 mi. N of Nashville**
No. of Rooms: **2**
No. of Private Baths: **2**
Double/pb: **$60**
Single/pb: **$50**
Guest Cabin: **$55–$65**
Open: **Feb. 1–Dec. 31**
Breakfast: **Continental**
Pets: **No**
Children: **Welcome**
Smoking: **No**
Social Drinking: **No**
Airport/Station Pickup: **Yes**

A blue clapboard house inspired by New England saltboxes, Woodshire B&B is 20 minutes from downtown Nashville and its attractions—Opryland Park, Andrew Jackson's Hermitage, and the homes and museums of country music stars. Beverly will gladly tell you the stories behind the antique family furniture. She's a retired art teacher, and as you look around you'll see her paintings and weavings, and John's woodcrafts. Continental breakfast features homemade preserves, breads, and waffles.

Hilltop House Bed and Breakfast Inn ✪

6 SANFORD CIRCLE, GREENEVILLE, TENNESSEE 37743

Tel: **(423) 639-8202**
Best Time to Call: **5 PM–7 PM**
Host: **Denise M. Ashworth**
Location: **7 mi. S. of Greeneville**
No. of Rooms: **3**
No. of Private Baths: **3**
Double/pb: **$75**
Single/pb: **$70**
Open: **All year**
Reduced Rates: **Available**
Breakfast: **Full**
Other Meals: **Available**
Credit Cards: **AMEX, MC, VISA**
Pets: **No**
Children: **Welcome, over 3 years**
Smoking: **No**
Social Drinking: **Permitted**
Airport/Station Pickup: **Yes**

Hilltop House is a 1920s manor house on a hillside above the Nolichucky River Valley, with the Appalachian Mountains in the background. All the guest rooms, which are furnished in eighteenth-century English antiques and period reproductions, have mountain views; two have verandas. In keeping with her British birth, the innkeeper sets out a proper English tea every afternoon. The family-style breakfast consists of fruit, cereal, egg dishes, and homemade biscuits or muffins. Then it's time to explore the great outdoors: white-water rafting, hiking, biking, trout fishing, golfing, hunting, and bird-watching are among your options. Cherokee National Forest is within striking distance, as are the Great Smoky Mountains and the Blue Ridge Parkway.

Natchez Trace B&B Reservation Service

P.O. BOX 193, HAMPSHIRE, TENNESSEE 38461

Tel: **(800) 377-2770; (615) 285-2777**
Best Time to Call: **Evening; weekends**
Coordinator: **Kay Jones**
States/Regions Covered:
Alabama—Florence, Cherokee; Mississippi—Church Hill, Corinth, French Camp, Jackson, Kosciusko, Lorman, Natchez, Port Gibson, Vicksburg; Tennessee—Columbia, Mt. Pleasant, Culleoka, Fairview, Franklin, Hohenwald, Leiper's Fork, Nashville
Descriptive Directory of B&Bs: **Free**
Rates (Single/Double):
Modest: **$55 / $65**
Average: **$70 / $80**
Luxury: **$90 / $175**
Credit Cards: **MC, VISA**

Kay's reservation service is unique in that the homes are all convenient to the Natchez Trace National Parkway, the historic Nashville-to-Natchez route that was first designated by President Thomas Jefferson. The parkway is known for both its natural beauty and the charming Southern towns along the way. Kay can help you plan your trip and give you access to homes ranging from rustic, woodsy sites to fine antebellum mansions. Call her for a free list of homes, as well as literature about the Natchez Trace.

Hart House Bed and Breakfast ✪

207 EAST HOLSTON AVENUE, JOHNSON CITY, TENNESSEE 37601

Tel: **(423) 926-3147**
Hosts: **Francis and Vanessa Gingras**
Location: **90 mi. NE of Knoxville**
No. of Rooms: **3**
No. of Private Baths: **3**
Double/pb: **$60**
Single/pb: **$50**
Open: **All year**
Reduced Rates: **10% seniors**
Breakfast: **Full**
Credit Cards: **AMEX, DISC, MC, VISA**
Pets: **Sometimes**
Children: **Welcome**
Smoking: **No**
Social Drinking: **Permitted**

Hart House is named after the original owner of this 1910 Dutch Colonial, which Francis and Vanessa have filled with antiques and collectibles. Johnson City is located in the heart of upper northeast Tennessee, an area brimming with both notable sites and scenic beauty. For history buffs, Jonesborough, the oldest town in the state, is five miles away, and those who love the great outdoors—camping, hiking, fishing, white-water rafting—will find plenty to do here. Each morning, guests wake up to an elegant breakfast of fresh fruit, homemade muffins, eggs, and fresh brewed coffee.

Windy Hill B&B ✪

1031 WEST PARK DRIVE, KNOXVILLE, TENNESSEE 37909

Tel: **(423) 690-1488**
Host: **Mary M. Mitchell**
Location: **1.6 mi. from I-75-40, Exit 380**
No. of Rooms: **1**
No. of Private Baths: **1**
Double/pb: **$40**
Single/pb: **$35**
Open: **All year**
Breakfast: **Continental**
Pets: **Sometimes**
Children: **Welcome**
Smoking: **Permitted**
Social Drinking: **Permitted**
Airport/Station Pickup: **Yes**

Located in a pleasant, quiet neighborhood with numerous shade trees, Mary's B&B is air-conditioned and has a private entrance with no steps to climb. There's a double bed and a rollaway is available. Breakfast features homemade muffins or cinnamon rolls with coffee. Windy Hill is convenient to the University of Tennessee; Oak Ridge is only a 15-minute drive while Great Smoky Mountains National Park is an hour away.

Snapp Inn B&B ✪

1990 DAVY CROCKETT PARK ROAD, LIMESTONE, TENNESSEE 37681

Tel: **(423) 257-2482**
Best Time to Call: **Before 10 AM; after 7 PM**
Hosts: **Dan and Ruth Dorgan**
Location: **4 mi. from Rte. 11 E**
No. of Rooms: **2**
No. of Private Baths: **2**
Double/pb: **$50**
Single/pb: **$40**
Open: **All year**
Breakfast: **Full**
Pets: **Welcome**
Children: **Welcome (one at a time)**
Smoking: **No**
Social Drinking: **Permitted**
Airport/Station Pickup: **Yes**

Built in 1815 and situated in farm country, this Federal brick home has lovely mountain views. The house is decorated with antiques, including a Victorian reed organ. Now retired, Ruth and Dan have the time to pursue their interests in antiques restoration, history, needlework, and bluegrass music. It is an easy walk to Davy Crockett Birthplace State Park, and 15 minutes to historic Jonesboro or the Andrew Johnson Home in Greeneville. A swimming pool, golf, and fishing are close by. You are welcome to use the laundry facilities, television, and pool table.

Falcon Manor Bed and Breakfast ✪

2645 FAULKNER SPRINGS ROAD, McMINNVILLE, TENNESSEE 37110

Tel: **(615) 668-4444**
Best Time to Call: **Anytime**
Hosts: **George and Charlien McGlothin**
Location: **72 mi. SE of Nashville**
No. of Rooms: **6**
No. of Private Baths: **2**
Max. No. Sharing Bath: **4**
Double/pb: **$85**
Single/pb: **$85**
Double/sb: **$75**
Single/sb: **$75**
Open: **All year**
Reduced Rates: **$5 off per day, 3 days or more**
Breakfast: **Full**
Credit Cards: **MC, VISA**
Pets: **No**
Children: **Welcome, over 12**
Smoking: **No**
Social Drinking: **Permitted**

This historic Victorian mansion re-creates the romance of the 1890s. Relax in the friendly warmth of this fine old house and savor the luxury of its museum-quality antiques. The huge gingerbread veranda is well stocked with rocking chairs and shaded by giant trees. Falcon Manor is a favorite for couples celebrating anniversaries. It's also the ideal base for a middle Tennessee vacation—halfway between Nashville and Chattanooga and just thirty minutes from four state parks. McMinnville is "the nursery capital of the world" and the home of America's second largest cave. George left a career in retail management to spend four years restoring the house, while Charlien pitched in during time off from her job as a NASA public affairs writer. They love sharing stories about Falcon Manor's history and their adventures bringing it back to life.

Clardy's Guest House ✪

435 EAST MAIN STREET, MURFREESBORO, TENNESSEE 37130

Tel: **(615) 893-6030**
Best Time to Call: **After 10 AM**
Hosts: **Robert and Barbara Deaton**
Location: **2 mi. from I-24**
No. of Rooms: **3**
No. of Private Baths: **2**
Max. No. Sharing Bath: **4**
Double/pb: **$48**
Single/pb: **$38**
Double/sb: **$38**
Single/sb: **$32**
Open: **All year**
Breakfast: **Continental**
Pets: **Sometimes**
Children: **Welcome (crib)**
Smoking: **Restricted**
Social Drinking: **Permitted**

This Romanesque-style Victorian dates back to 1898. The 20 rooms are filled with antiques; with 40 antique dealers in town, you can guess what Murfreesboro is best known for. The world championship horse show at Shelbyville is 30 minutes away. Your hosts will be glad to advise on local tours and can direct you to the home of the Grand Ole Opry, one hour away in Nashville, and fine eating places. Middle Tennessee State University is close by.

Quilts and Croissants

2231 RILEY ROAD, MURFREESBORO, TENNESSEE 37130

Tel: **(615) 893-2933**
Hosts: **Robert and Mary Jane Roose**
Location: **28 mi. S of Nashville**
No. of Rooms: **1**
No. of Private Baths: **1**
Double/pb: **$50**
Single/pb: **$45**
Open: **All year**
Breakfast: **Continental**
Pets: **No**
Smoking: **No**
Social Drinking: **Permitted**

This unusual home, constructed out of logs hewn in 1834, combines old-fashioned country charm and modern efficiency. Stencils and folk art ornament the walls of the guest room, and patchwork quilts drape the twin beds. Don't be fooled by the appearance of the quaint icebox in the kitchenette—it's really a refrigerator stocked with juice, breakfast foods, and soda. Quilts and Croissants is less than an hour's drive from Nashville, but your hosts can steer you to the notable sights of Murfreesboro, such as Oaklands Mansion (a mid-19th-century landmark) and Canonsburgh (a restored Civil War–era village). Breakfast here is a do-it-yourself affair; take whatever you want from the refrigerator.

Bed and Breakfast Adventures ✪

P.O. BOX 150586, NASHVILLE, TENNESSEE 37215

Tel: **(615) 662-7800; (800) 947-7404; fax: (615) 662-7788**
Best Time to Call: **8:30 AM–5:30 PM Mon.–Fri.; 9 AM–1 PM Sat.**

Coordinator: **Carol Montgomery**
States/Regions Covered:
Chattanooga, Clarksville, Franklin, Gatlinburg, Jackson, Knoxville, Memphis, Monteagle, Nashville, Townsend
Descriptive Directory of B&Bs: **$1**

Rates (Single/Double):
Modest: **$45 / $60**
Average: **$65 / $85**
Luxury: **$90 / $295**
Credit Cards: **AMEX, DC, DISC, MC, VISA**
Minimum Stay: **In some areas**

Carol's worldwide travels, as well as her experience in hosting and entertaining business associates, relatives, and friends, has given her insight into people's needs and wants when traveling. The ambience of individual bed and breakfasts is very important, so Carol's policy is to see every bed and breakfast she represents, and to meet the owners/innkeepers. Her hosts are warm and gracious, knowledgeable of their area, and ready to help you have a memorable experience in Tennessee! Whether you're looking for that secluded hideaway, romantic weekend, or convenience to all the activities in a particular area, Carol will give you personalized service.

Fall Creek Falls Bed & Breakfast

ROUTE 3, BOX 298B, PIKEVILLE, TENNESSEE 37367

Tel: **(423) 881-5494**
Hosts: **Doug and Rita Pruett**
Location: **50 mi. N of Chattanooga**
No. of Rooms: **7**
No. of Private Baths: **7**
Double/pb: **$68–$103**
Single/pb: **$65**
Suite: **$118**

Open: **All year (except Jan.)**
Breakfast: **Full**
Pets: **No**
Children: **Welcome, over 10**
Smoking: **No**
Social Drinking: **Permitted**
Minimum Stay: **2 nights, weekends in October and holidays**

Enjoy the relaxing atmosphere of a new country manor home on forty acres of rolling hillside one mile from the nationally acclaimed Fall Creek Falls State Resort Park. Beautiful guest rooms have pickled oak floors and antique furniture with two common sitting areas. Lodging includes a full breakfast served in a cozy country kitchen or an elegant dining room. Doug enjoys grouse hunting and trout fishing and is a licensed Tennessee building contractor. Rita is an insurance executive who enjoys bargain hunting and antique auctions. Touring, dining, and shopping information is always available.

Ross House Bed and Breakfast ✪

504 MAIN STREET, P.O. BOX 398, SAVANNAH, TENNESSEE 38372

Tel: **(901) 925-3974; (800) 467-3174**
Best Time to Call: **9 AM–5 PM**
Hosts: **John and Harriet Ross**
Location: **110 mi. E of Memphis**
Suites: **$75–$150**
Open: **All year**
Breakfast: **Full**

Credit Cards: **AMEX, DISC, MC, VISA**
Pets: **No**
Children: **Welcome, over 10**
Smoking: **No**
Social Drinking: **Permitted**
Foreign Languages: **French, Spanish**

Part of Savannah's National Register Historic District, which contains residences from the late 1860s to the 1920s, this B&B is a Neoclassical brick house built in 1908 by John's grandparents. Inside you'll see the original owners' furniture, books, paintings, and photographs. It is a short walk to the Cherry Mansion and Tennessee River and a short drive to Shiloh National Military Park and Pickwick Lake, for fishing and boating. If you'd rather paddle your canoe, take the 45-minute drive to the Buffalo River. John practices law next door where his grandfather once did, but when time permits, he accompanies guests on bicycle tours. Harriet is a full-time hostess.

Blue Mountain Mist Country Inn & Cottages

1811 PULLEN ROAD, SEVIERVILLE, TENNESSEE 37862

Tel: **(800) 497-2335; (423) 428-2335**
Best Time to Call: **10 AM–9 PM**
Hosts: **Norman and Sarah Ball**
Location: **4 mi. E of Pigeon Forge**
No. of Rooms: **12**
No. of Private Baths: **12**
Double/pb: **$95**
Guest Cottage: **$135**
Suites: **$105–$125**
Open: **All year**
Breakfast: **Full**
Pets: **No**
Children: **Welcome (2 rooms)**
Smoking: **No**
Social Drinking: **Permitted**

This Victorian-style farmhouse inn with country cottages is located on 60 acres in the foothills of the Great Smoky Mountains. Away from the congestion you can enjoy beautiful views of rolling meadows and mountains while rocking on the huge front porch. The Inn is filled with country antiques, handmade quilts and local art. In the morning awake to a hearty Tennessee breakfast, in the evening indulge in a delicious homemade dessert. Each cottage has a large Jacuzzi and a fireplace designed for a peaceful romantic getaway. Nearby attractions include Gatlinburg, the Crafts Community, Pigeon Forge and Dollywood.

Calico Inn ✪

757 RANCH WAY, SEVIERVILLE, TENNESSEE 37862

Tel: **(423) 428-3833; (800) 235-1054**
Best Time to Call: **11 AM–9 PM**
Hosts: **Lill and Jim Katzbeck**
Location: **35 mi. N of Knoxville**
No. of Rooms: **3**
No. of Private Baths: **3**
Double/pb: **$85–$95**
Open: **All year**
Reduced Rates: **10% Jan.–Feb., 15% weekly**
Breakfast: **Full**
Pets: **No**
Children: **Welcome, over 6**
Smoking: **No**
Social Drinking: **Permitted**
Minimum Stay: **2 nights holidays and special events**

Nestled among trees atop a peaceful ridge, Calico Inn offers guests a serene panoramic view of the Smoky Mountains. Lill and Jim invite you to start your day with a delightful breakfast that may include juice, fresh fruit, homemade bread or muffins, hash browns, biscuits and gravy. The Katzbecks are only minutes from Dollywood, shopping, fishing, golfing, and hiking in the mountains. Best of all, you can take pleasure in knowing that the quiet Calico Inn awaits you each evening.

Little Greenbrier Lodge ✪

3685 LYON SPRINGS ROAD, SEVIERVILLE, TENNESSEE 37862

Tel: **(423) 429-2500**
Best Time to Call: **4–10 PM**
Hosts: **Charles and Susan LeBon**
No. of Rooms: **8**
No. of Private Baths: **2**
Max. No. Sharing Bath: **4**
Double/pb: **$95–$110**
Double/sb: **$65–$75**
Single/sb: **$55–$65**
Open: **All year**
Reduced Rates: **10% seniors**
Breakfast: **Full**
Credit Cards: **DISC, MC, VISA**
Pets: **No**
Children: **Welcome, over 12; under 12 by arrangement**
Smoking: **No**
Social Drinking: **Permitted**
Airport Pickup: **Yes**

Nestled in the hills of the Great Smoky Mountains, Little Greenbrier Lodge was built in 1939 and renovated in 1993. All rooms offer guests modern comforts with the Victorian decor. The view of the valley provides a perfect backdrop for a delicious country breakfast. Cades Cove, Dollywood, outlet malls, and numerous antique and craft shops are all within 30 minutes. If you enjoy hiking, the lodge is located right next to a park and just 150 yards from Little Greenbrier Trailhead, which will connect you to other interesting paths in the park.

TEXAS

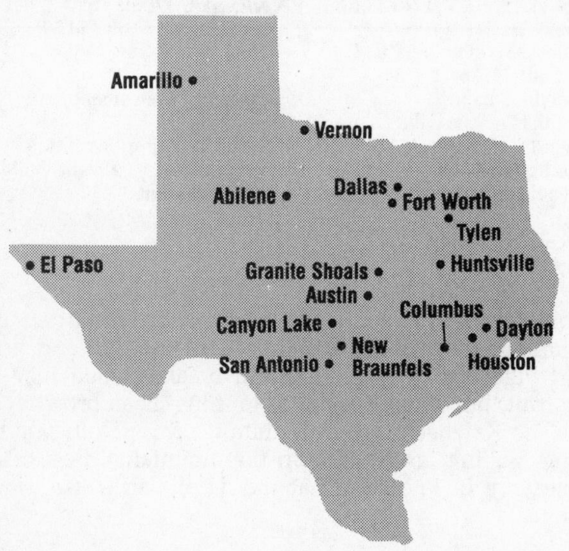

The Bed & Breakfast Reservation Service of Texas ✪

1200 SOUTHMORE AVENUE, HOUSTON, TEXAS 77004

Tel: **(713) 523-1114**
Best Time to Call: **10 AM–6 PM**
Coordinator: **Pat Thomas**
States/Regions Covered: **Statewide**

Rates (Single/Double):
Modest: **$40 / $55**
Average: **$50 / $65**
Luxury: **$75 / $125**

Whether you're traveling for business or pleasure, Pat's hosts offer the kind of friendliness and individualized care that will make your stay pleasant. The area is known for the Astrodome, Galveston Bay, NASA, and the Texas Medical Center. There are wonderful restaurants, shops, museums, and historic sights, and Baylor, Rice, and the University of Houston are nearby. Many are conveniently located urban homes, serene country houses, historic inns, and waterfront cottages.

Bed & Breakfast Texas Style ✪

4224 WEST RED BIRD LANE, DALLAS, TEXAS 75237

Tel: **(214) 298-8586; (800) 899-4538**
Best Time to Call: **9 AM–4:30 PM CST**
Coordinator: **Ruth Wilson**
States/Regions Covered: **Austin, Dallas, Houston, Lake Travis, San Antonio, Tyler**

Descriptive Directory: **$6.50**
Rates (Single/Double):
Modest: **$60 / $70**
Average: **$70 / $90**
Luxury: **$100 / $150**
Credit Cards: **MC, VISA**

The above cities are only a small sample of the locations of hosts waiting to give you plenty of warm hospitality. Ruth's register includes comfortable accommodations in condos, restored Victorians, lakeside cottages, and ranches. Texas University, Southern Methodist University, Baylor University, Rice University, and Texas Christian University are convenient to many B&Bs.

Bolin's Prairie House Bed & Breakfast ✪

508 MULBERRY, ABILENE, TEXAS 79601

Tel: **(915) 675-5855; (800) 673-5855**
Best Time to Call: **8AM–8 PM Mon.–Sat.**
Hosts: **Sam and Ginny Bolin**
Location: **180 mi. W of Dallas**
No. of Rooms: **4**
No. of Private Baths: **2**
Max. No. Sharing Bath: **4**

Double/pb: **$65**
Double/sb: **$55**
Open: **All year**
Breakfast: **Full**
Credit Cards: **AMEX, MC, VISA**
Children: **Welcome, over 12**
Smoking: **No**

Tucked into the heart of this famous frontier town is Bolin's Prairie House, a 1902 house furnished with antiques and modern luxuries. The warm, homey atmosphere puts guests at their ease. Relax in the living room with its wood-burning stove, or settle in the den for a little TV. Each of the four bedrooms—named Love, Joy, Peace, and Patience—has its own special charm. Breakfast features Ginny's delicious baked egg dishes, fresh fruit, and homemade bread, all lovingly served in the dining room, where fine china and cobalt Depression glass are displayed.

Parkview House ✪

1311 SOUTH JEFFERSON STREET, AMARILLO, TEXAS 79101
E-mail: dia1311@aol.com

Tel: **(806) 373-9464**
Best Time to Call: **10 AM–10 PM**
Hosts: **Carol and Nabil Dia**
Location: **½ mi. from I-40**
No. of Rooms: **5**
No. of Private Baths: **3**

Max. No. Sharing Bath: **4**
Double/pb: **$75**
Double/sb: **$65**
Suite: **$85**
Open: **All year**
Breakfast: **Continental**

Other Meals: **Available**
Credit Cards: **AMEX, MC, VISA**
Pets: **No**
Children: **By arrangement**
Smoking: **No**
Social Drinking: **Permitted**
Airport/Station Pickup: **Yes**
Foreign Languages: **Arabic**

This circa 1908 Prairie Victorian is located at the edge of the Historic District, and just minutes from I-27, I-40, and Old Route 66. Guest rooms are warm and inviting, with romantic draped beds, cozy reading areas, and antiques and Victoriana throughout. A gourmet breakfast is served in the dining room or the eclectic country kitchen with a view of the rose garden. The large columned porch is a wonderful place to relax and engage in conversation, or you could enjoy the hot tub and the bicycles that are available. Nabil, an engineer, and Carol, a lab technician, enjoy having guests join them for a social hour. Nearby is Palo Duro Canyon, West Texas A&M University, and city tennis.

Austin's Wildflower Inn ✪

1200 WEST 22½ STREET, AUSTIN, TEXAS 78705

Tel: **(512) 477-9639**
Best Time to Call: **Anytime**
Hosts: **Kay Jackson and Claudean Schultz**
Location: **2 mi. from Rte. IH35, Exit MLK**
No. of Rooms: **4**
No. of Private Baths: **2**
Max. No. Sharing Bath: **4**
Double/pb: **$74–$79**
Single/pb: **$65–$70**
Double/sb: **$62**
Single/sb: **$55**
Open: **All year**
Reduced Rates: **10% seniors**
Breakfast: **Full**
Credit Cards: **AMEX, MC, VISA**
Pets: **No**
Smoking: **No**
Social Drinking: **Permitted**

Nestled on a quiet, tree-lined street, this fifty-year-old central Austin home is within a few blocks of the University of Texas and within minutes of the State Capitol complex. Outdoor enthusiasts will love the hike and bike trails at Shoal Creek or tennis at Caswell Courts. Kay and Claudean pride themselves on their warm Texas hospitality and delight in serving you their hearty gourmet specialties each morning.

The McCallum House

613 WEST 32ND, AUSTIN, TEXAS 78705

Tel: **(512) 451-6744; fax: (512) 451-6744**
Best Time to Call: **10 AM–9 PM**
Hosts: **Roger and Nancy Danley**
Location: **2 mi. W of I-35**
No. of Rooms: **5**
No. of Private Baths: **5**
Double/pb: **$99**
Single/pb: **$85**
Suites: **$99–$119**
Open: **All year**
Reduced Rates: **Weekdays, $10 one night, $20 2 nights or more**
Breakfast: **Full**

Credit Cards: **MC, VISA**
Pets: **No**
Children: **Welcome, over 11**
Smoking: **No**
Social Drinking: **Permitted**

This late Victorian home is just 10 blocks north of the University of Texas and 20 blocks north of the capitol and downtown. Air-conditioned and furnished with antiques, all five guest rooms have private verandas. All facilities have phones, color TVs, sitting areas, and kitchens or mini-kitchens, irons, ironing boards, lighted mirrors, hair dryers. The garden apartment suite has a whirlpool tub and shower. McCallum House has a Texas historic marker, an Austin landmark designation and a preservation award from the Austin Heritage Society. Guests breakfast daily on fresh fruits and homemade egg dishes, muffins, and coffee cakes.

Peaceful Hill Bed & Breakfast ✪

6401 RIVER PLACE BOULEVARD, AUSTIN, TEXAS 78730-1102

Tel: **(512) 338-1817**
Best Time to Call: **Anytime**
Host: **Peninnah Thurmond**
Location: **15 min. W of Austin**
No. of Rooms: **2**
No. of Private Baths: **2**
Double/pb: **$60–$65**
Single/pb: **$60–$65**
Open: **All year**
Reduced Rates: **Stay 7 nights, $10 less per night**
Breakfast: **Full**
Credit Cards: **MC, VISA**
Pets: **No**
Children: **Welcome**
Smoking: **No**
Social Drinking: **Permitted**

Deer watch you come to a small country inn located on ranchland high in the beautiful rolling hills fifteen minutes from Austin and ten minutes from Lake Travis and the Oasis. In springtime, settle on the porch with a cup of coffee and admire the countryside and the city below. Laze away the summer in a hammock built for two, or hike and bicycle; golf, swimming, and tennis are only two miles away. In the winter, warm up by a crackling fire in the grand stone fireplace in the living room, where a glass wall looks over both the country and the city. All this and a home-cooked breakfast. Peaceful is the name and peaceful is the game. Deer watch you go.

Aunt Nora's Bed and Breakfast ✪

120 NAKED INDIAN TRAIL (NEW BRAUNFELS), CANYON LAKE, TEXAS 78132-1865

Tel: **(210) 905-3989; (800) 687-2887**
Best Time to Call: **9 AM–5 PM**
Hosts: **Iralee and Alton Haley**
Location: **15 mi. NW of New Braunfels**
Guest Cottages: **$95–$125**
Open: **All year**
Reduced Rates: **Available**
Breakfast: **Full, Continental**
Pets: **No**
Children: **Welcome**
Smoking: **No**
Social Drinking: **Permitted**

In the Texas hill country at Canyon Lake, just minutes from New Braunfels and Guadalupe River, is a country house with old-time Victorian charm, nestled on four tree-covered acres with a meadow. Walk to the top of the hill to view Canyon Lake, or breathe the fresh country air from the front porch swing. Relax amid handmade furnishings, antiques, a woodstove, and natural wood floors. Tastefully decorated Queen rooms have handmade quilts. The cottages have private decks, sofa sleepers, kitchens, beautiful decor, private baths, and a view.

Magnolia Oaks ✪

634 SPRING STREET, COLUMBUS, TEXAS 78934

Tel: **(409) 732-2726**
Best Time to Call: **Evenings**
Hosts: **Bob and Nancy Stiles**
Location: **70 mi. W of Houston**
No. of Rooms: **5**
No. of Private Baths: **5**
Efficiency Apt.: **$80–$120**
Open: **All year**

Reduced Rates: **Available**
Breakfast: **Full**
Pets: **No**
Children: **No**
Smoking: **No**
Social Drinking: **Permitted**
Minimum Stay: **Homes Tour Weekend**
Airport Pickup: **Yes**

Magnolia Oaks is an Eastlake Victorian jewel two blocks from the historic square in Columbus. This landmark home was built in 1890 by Senator Marcus Townsend. Bob and Nancy Stiles restored the house and furnished it with Victorian Texana; they opened the B&B in 1990. Featured are two fireplaces, stained glass windows, carved woodwork, gingerbread porches, a summer room, generous breakfasts, private baths, horseshoes, croquet, and a tandem bike. Columbus, on Interstate 10, is in the heart of wildflower country. It has museums, antique shops, and the Stafford Opera House.

B & G's ✪

15869 NEDRA WAY, DALLAS, TEXAS 75248

Tel: **(214) 386-4323**
Best Time to Call: **Before 8 AM**
Hosts: **George and Betty Hyde**
No. of Rooms: **2**
No. of Private Baths: **2**
Double/pb: **$60**
Single/pb: **$50**
Open: **All year**

Reduced Rates: **Available**
Breakfast: **Full**
Other Meals: **Available**
Pets: **No**
Children: **Welcome**
Smoking: **No**
Social Drinking: **Permitted**
Airport/Station Pickup: **Yes**

Betty and George are retirees who have had visitors from around the world since 1980. They want you to think of their home—furnished with "an eclectic collection of family heirlooms and junk"—as your own. Upon your arrival, they'll pour you something to drink, ascertain your interests, and direct you to appropriate activities in the Dallas–

Fort Worth area. This B&B is close to prestigious shopping malls, the University of Texas at Dallas, Southern Methodist University, and the sights of downtown Dallas, such as the Kennedy Assassination Museum and the new Arts District. You'll start the day with conversation and a three-course breakfast at a lovely table set with grandma's antique silver and good crystal.

Audubon Lodge ✪

P.O. BOX 1439, DAYTON, TEXAS 77535

Tel: **(409) 258-9141**
Best Time to Call: **9 AM–6 PM**
Hosts: **Bob and Linda Jamison**
Location: **40 mi. E of Houston**
No. of Rooms: **3**
No. of Private Baths: **2**
Max. No. Sharing Bath: **4**
Double/pb: **$75**
Double/sb: **$55–$65**
Open: **All year**
Reduced Rates: **10% weekly**
Breakfast: **Continental, plus**
Credit Cards: **MC, VISA**
Pets: **Sometimes**
Children: **Welcome, over 12**
Smoking: **No**
Social Drinking: **Permitted**
Minimum Stay: **2 nights**
Foreign Languages: **Spanish**

Here's a wonderful retreat located twenty-five miles east of Houston Intercontinental Airport, where the coastal plains meet the rolling East Texas piney woods. Audubon Lodge overlooks a private lake abundant with wildlife and a sanctuary for birds that nest nearby. The multilevel lodge is made of brick and wood, with towering glass windows that offer a panoramic view of nature's wonders. A naturalist's paradise or a romantic getaway, the lodge lies within driving distance of restaurants, theaters, museums, and antique shops.

Bergmann Inn ✪

10009 TRINIDAD DRIVE, EL PASO, TEXAS 79925

Tel: **(915) 599-1398**
Host: **David Bergmann**
No. of Rooms: **2**
Max. No. Sharing Bath: **4**
Double/sb: **$50**
Single/sb: **$35**
Open: **All year**
Breakfast: **Continental**
Other Meals: **Available**
Pets: **No**
Smoking: **No**
Social Drinking: **Permitted**
Airport Pickup: **Yes**

David has a spacious, two-story home with two large bedrooms, a sizable living room, a den with a fireplace, and air-conditioning. Guests will enjoy the back patio overlooking a yard with flower beds and fruit trees that provide shade in the summertime. Bergmann Inn offers easy access to the east–west freeway and the northbound highways leaving El Paso.

The Texas White House ✪

1417 8TH AVENUE, FORT WORTH, TEXAS 76104

Tel: **(817) 923-3597; (800) 279-6491**
Best Time to Call: **7 AM–10:30 PM**
Host: **Jamie Sexton**
Location: **2 mi. SW of downtown Fort Worth**
No. of Rooms: **3**
No. of Private Baths: **3**
Double/pb: **$105**
Open: **All year**
Reduced Rates: **Available**
Breakfast: **Full**
Other Meals: **Available**
Credit Cards: **AMEX, DISC, MC, VISA**
Pets: **No**
Children: **Welcome**
Smoking: **Restricted**
Social Drinking: **Permitted**
Airport/Station Pickup: **Yes**

Texas White House is a 1910 Colonial Revival home with a large wraparound porch on the first floor. The parlor, living room with a fireplace, and formal dining room may be rented for business conferences and luncheons. Secretarial and notary services can also be arranged. Each guest room features a queen-size bed, desk, and chair, and sitting area. You'll receive keys both to your room and the front door, so you can come and go at your leisure. Full breakfasts are served; you may eat either in your bedroom or in the dining room. Architecture buffs will want to tour the area's historical districts and landmark homes, while flora and fauna fans may prefer the Botanical Gardens and the Fort Worth Zoo.

La Casita Bed and Breakfast ✪

1908 REDWOOD DRIVE, GRANITE SHOALS, TEXAS 78654

Tel: **(800) 798-6443; (210) 598-6443**
Best Time to Call: **9 AM–9 PM**
Hosts: **Joanne and Roger Scarborough**
Location: **56 mi. NW of Austin**
Guest Cottage: **$70**
Open: **All year**
Reduced Rates: **$5 less per day weekly**
Breakfast: **Full**
Pets: **No**
Children: **Welcome**
Smoking: **No**
Social Drinking: **Permitted**
Minimum Stay: **2 nights holiday weekends**

La Casita is a private guest cottage in the Highland Lakes area of the popular Texas Hill Country. The cottage is rustic outside but thoroughly modern inside, with Persian rugs, artwork, and mementos collected from around the world by your hosts. Guests are free to enjoy the grounds, flowers, gardens, and wildlife. You can choose breakfast from a varied menu and dine in the main house with your hosts. Joanne and Roger, a retired Navy couple, are native Texans and can recommend restaurants, state parks, winery tours, lake recreation, and other activities.

The Lovett Inn ✪

501 LOVETT BOULEVARD, HOUSTON, TEXAS 77006

Tel: **(713) 522-5224; (800) 779-5224; fax: (713) 528-6708**
Best Time to Call: **10 AM–6 PM**
Host: **Tom Fricke**
Location: **Downtown Houston**
No. of Rooms: **8**
No. of Private Baths: **8**
Double/pb: **$65–$85**
Single/pb: **$65–$85**
Townhouse: **$75–$150**
Suites: **$75–$125**
Open: **All year**
Reduced Rates: **Weekly**
Breakfast: **Continental**
Credit Cards: **AMEX, MC, VISA**
Pets: **Sometimes**
Children: **By arrangement**
Smoking: **Restricted**
Social Drinking: **Permitted**

It's easy to be fooled by the Lovett Inn: although it looks far older, this stately Federalist-style mansion, attractively furnished with 19th-century reproductions, was actually built in 1924. Its convenient museum-district location puts visitors within easy striking distance of downtown Houston, the Galleria, and the Houston Medical Center. After spending the day in the city, guests are sure to appreciate a dip in the pool. Each room has a color TV.

Patrician Bed & Breakfast Inn ✪

1200 SOUTHMORE BOULEVARD, HOUSTON, TEXAS 77004

Tel: **(713) 523-1114**
Best Time to Call: **10 AM–6 PM**
Host: **Pat Thomas**
Location: **2 mi. S of Houston**
No. of Rooms: **4**
No. of Private Baths: **4**
Double/pb: **$75–$85**
Single/pb: **$55–$65**
Suites: **$75–$85**
Open: **All year**
Reduced Rates: **10% 5 nights or more**
Breakfast: **Full**
Credit Cards: **AMEX, DC, DISC, MC, VISA**
Pets: **No**
Children: **Welcome, over 5**
Smoking: **No**
Social Drinking: **Permitted**
Station Pickup: **Yes**

Built in 1919, this three-story Colonial Revival–style home was originally owned by a prominent attorney, and has been restored to its former grandeur. The Margaret Rose is a suite with an adjoining sitting room. Lottie Dee's has an adjoining private patio. All four rooms have antique queen-size beds and claw-foot baths with shower devices. Breakfast is served in the dining room or the sunny solarium. Patrician Bed & Breakfast Inn is centrally located between downtown Houston and the Texas Medical Center, within walking distance of Herman Park, Houston Zoological Gardens, Clayton Genealogical Library, Rice University, and the Houston Museum of Fine Arts. This is a perfect location for weddings, receptions, and private parties. Patricia's Fun Murder Mystery Dinners can also be arranged in advance.

Blue Bonnet Bed & Breakfast ✪

1215 AVENUE G #4, HUNTSVILLE, TEXAS 77340

Tel: **(409) 295-2072**
Hosts: **John and Bette Nelson**
Location: **70 mi. N of Houston**
No. of Rooms: **4**
No. of Private Baths: **3**
Max. No. Sharing Bath: **4**
Double/sb: **$38**
Suite: **$48**
Open: **All year**
Breakfast: **Continental**
Pets: **Sometimes**
Children: **Welcome**
Smoking: **No**
Social Drinking: **Permitted**

Seven tree-shaded acres frame this appealing blue Victorian-style house, with its white trim and wraparound porch. Try your luck fishing in the pond, sit on the porch, or play horseshoes and croquet on the lawn. The house is less than five minutes from Sam Houston State University and the adjacent Sam Houston Grave and Museum complex. Antique-lovers will find plenty of shops in the neighborhood; Bette, who owns and manages two antique malls, can give you some good suggestions. Continental breakfast may include apple fritters, poppyseed muffins, filled croissants, and fruit compote.

River Haus Bed & Breakfast ✪

817 EAST ZIPP ROAD, NEW BRAUNFELS, TEXAS 78130

Tel: **(210) 625-6411**
Hosts: **Dick and Arlene Buhl**
Location: **25 mi. NE of San Antonio**
No. of Rooms: **1**
No. of Private Baths: **1**
Double/pb: **$75**
Single/pb: **$70**
Open: **All year**
Breakfast: **Full**
Pets: **Sometimes**
Children: **No**
Smoking: **No**
Social Drinking: **No**
Foreign Languages: **German**

Historic New Braunfels, a major tourist destination, offers museums, antique shopping, and unparalleled canoeing and river sports, all in the charming setting of the German Hill Country. River Haus is a delightful hill country–style home located on the Guadalupe River at Lake Dunlap. Watch the sun set over the lake from your spacious bedroom or sitting room. On the enclosed porch, with its deck overlooking the lake, you can sip a cool drink or enjoy the warmth of a wood-stove fire. The complete gourmet breakfasts include local specialties and homemade bread and preserves.

The Rose Garden ✪

195 SOUTH ACADEMY, NEW BRAUNFELS, TEXAS 78130

Tel: **(210) 629-3296**
Best Time to Call: **Before 8 PM**
Host: **Dawn Mann**
Location: **1½ mi. from I-35, Exit 187**
No. of Rooms: **2**
Double/pb: **$65–$105**
Open: **All year**
Reduced Rates: **Available**

Breakfast: **Full**
Pets: **No**
Children: **No**
Smoking: **No**
Social Drinking: **Permitted**
Foreign Languages: **German**

This half-century-old white brick Colonial is located one block from historic downtown New Braunfels. Enjoy a movie, browse the antique shops, or stroll along the Comal Springs. Then relax by the fireplace in the parlor, or in the formal dining room with a flavored cup of coffee. The Royal Rose Room features a four-poster bed; you'll also find English and German books, pictures, and magazines concerning the royal family. The Romantic Country Rose Room has a Victorian wrought-iron and brass bed, an antique English dresser.

The White House

217 MITTMAN CIRCLE, NEW BRAUNFELS, TEXAS 78132

Tel: **(210) 629-9354**
Best Time to Call: **9 AM–9 PM**
Hosts: **Beverly and Jerry White**
Location: **20 mi. N of San Antonio**
No. of Rooms: **3**
Max. No. Sharing Bath: **4**
Double/pb: **$60–$70**
Single/pb: **$55–$65**
Double/sb: **$45–$50**
Single/sb: **$40–$45**
Open: **All year, except Thanksgiving and Christmas**
Breakfast: **Full**
Pets: **No**
Children: **Welcome (crib)**
Smoking: **No**
Social Drinking: **Permitted**

This Spanish-style white brick home is nestled among cedar and oaks in Texas Hill Country. Guests are welcomed here with tea and pastries and shown to comfortable rooms with antique beds and oak dressers. A large fishing pond is located on the premises, and a few miles away you may enjoy a refreshing tube or raft ride down the Guadalupe River. Other attractions include the Alamo, the Riverwalk, and the many old missions located nearby in San Antonio.

Beckmann Inn and Carriage House ✪

222 EAST GUENTHER STREET, SAN ANTONIO, TEXAS 78204

Tel: **(210) 229-1449; (800) 945-1449**
Best Time to Call: **8 AM–10 PM**
Hosts: **Betty Jo and Don Schwartz**
Location: **¾ mi. S of downtown San Antonio**
No. of Rooms: **5**
No. of Private Baths: **5**
Double/pb: **$80–$130**
Single/pb: **$70–$120**
Open: **All year**
Reduced Rates: **Available**
Breakfast: **Full**
Credit Cards: **AMEX, DC, DISC, MC, VISA**
Pets: **No**
Children: **Welcome, over 12**
Smoking: **No**
Social Drinking: **Permitted**
Minimum Stay: **2 nights, weekends**

Enjoy gracious hospitality in an elegant Victorian inn located in San Antonio's King William historic district. The beautiful wraparound porch welcomes guests. Inside, rooms are colorfully decorated, with high-back, queen-size, antique Victorian beds. Gourmet breakfast, complete with dessert, is served in the formal dining room on a table set with china, crystal, and silver. Then guests may stroll over to the Riverwalk or ride the trolley to the sights of San Antonio.

Rosevine Inn Bed and Breakfast ✪

415 SOUTH VINE AVENUE, TYLER, TEXAS 75702

Tel: **(903) 592-2221**
Best Time to Call: **After 9:30 AM**
Hosts: **Bert and Rebecca Powell**
Location: **100 mi. E of Dallas**
No. of Rooms: **7**
No. of Private Baths: **7**
Double/pb: **$85**
Suites: **$150**
Open: **All year**
Reduced Rates: **Available**
Breakfast: **Full**
Other Meals: **Available**
Credit Cards: **AMEX, DC, DISC, MC, VISA**
Pets: **No**
Children: **Welcome, over 3**
Smoking: **No**
Social Drinking: **Permitted**
Airport/Station Pickup: **Yes**

Rosevine Inn combines the best qualities of a bed & breakfast, offering hospitality, comfort, convenience, and a sense of history. The house sits on a hill and overlooks the Historic Brick Street District that has become a favorite of tourists because of the specialty shops and restored homes. You may also want to visit the Azalea District, where homes are notable for architectural styles representing many periods in Tyler's past. Guest rooms are cheerfully decorated with antiques and country collectibles. Guests are invited to use the living room, a denlike room upstairs with couches and a TV, the game room in the barn, or the hot tub. Breakfast is a grand affair of homemade delights served in the dining room.

Victorian Rose B&B ✪

2929 TEXAS STREET, VERNON, TEXAS 76384

Tel: **(817) 552-5354; (800) 805-8066**
Hosts: **Art and Jan Bergman**
Location: **50 mi. NW of Wichita Falls**
No. of Rooms: **4**
No. of Private Baths: **4**
Double/pb: **$39**
Suites: **$49**
Open: **All year**
Reduced Rates: **Weekly**
Breakfast: **Continental**
Other Meals: **Available**
Credit Cards: **MC, VISA**
Children: **Welcome**
Smoking: **No**
Social Drinking: **Permitted**

This beautiful three-story 1920 Victorian offers guests a great place to relax in while traveling or just getting away with friends and family. Rooms are individually heated and cooled, and each room is equipped with a microwave, coffee pot, telephone, TV, and goodies to munch on. The lower part of the house is a tea room for lunch Monday through Friday and mesquite-grilled steaks on Friday and Saturday nights. A front wraparound porch is great in the evening, with two porch swings and a pool in the back.

For key to listings, see inside front or back cover.

✪ This star means that rates are guaranteed through December 31, 1997, to any guest making a reservation as a result of reading about the B&B in *Bed & Breakfast U.S.A.*—1997 edition.

Important! To avoid misunderstandings, always ask about cancellation policies when booking.

Please enclose a self-addressed, stamped, business-size envelope when contacting reservation services.

For more details on what you can expect in a B&B, see Chapter 1.

Always mention *Bed & Breakfast U.S.A.* when making reservations!

If no B&B is listed in the area you'll be visiting, use the form on page 231 to order a copy of our "List of New B&Bs."

We want to hear from you! Use the form on page 233.

VIRGINIA

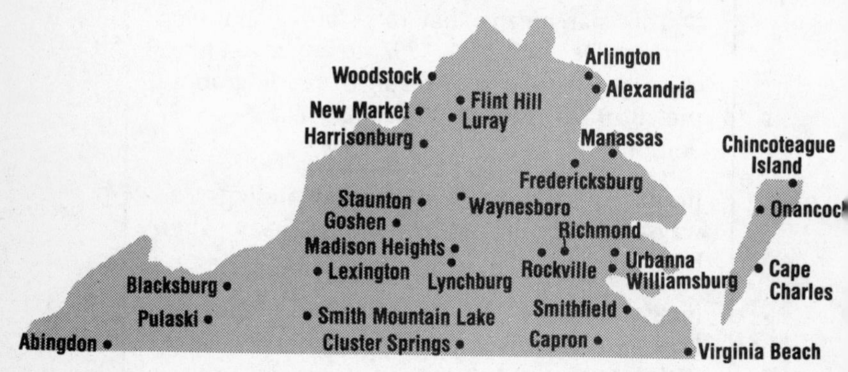

River Garden ✪

19080 NORTH FORK, RIVER ROAD, ABINGDON, VIRGINIA 24210

Tel: **(540) 676-0335; (800) 952-4296**
Best Time to Call: **Evenings and weekends**
Hosts: **Bill Crump and Carol Schoenherr-Crump**
Location: **9 mi. NE of Abingdon**
No. of Rooms: **4**
No. of Private Baths: **4**
Double/pb: **$60–$65**
Open: **All year**
Breakfast: **Full**
Pets: **Caged only**
Children: **Welcome, infants, over 4**
Smoking: **No**
Social Drinking: **Permitted**

River Garden is tucked into the foothills of the Clinch Mountains, on the bank of the Holston River's North Fork. Each room has its own riverside deck, private entrance, and a king- or queen-size bed. Guests are encouraged to try their hand at weaving on the antique loom. More contemporary challenges can be had in the recreation room, which is equipped with a Ping-Pong table, board games, and exercise equipment. Fishing equipment, a picnic table, and inner tubes are also at your disposal. The center of Abingdon, fifteen minutes away, is home to the historic Barter Theater, as well as many eateries. Lovers of the outdoors will want to head for the Virginia Creeper Trail—34 miles of scenic mountain trails for hikers, bikers, and horseback riders.

Alexandria and Arlington Bed and Breakfast Network ✪

P.O. BOX 25319, ARLINGTON, VIRGINIA 22202-9319

Tel: **(703) 549-3415**
Best Time to Call: **10 AM–2 PM Mon.–Fri.**
Coordinator: **Leslie C. and Ann L. Garrison**
States/Regions Covered: **Alexandria, Arlington, Falls Church, Fairfax; D.C.; Maryland—Patuxent River; Pennsylvania—Gettysburg, Hanover; West Virginia—Moorefield**
Rates (Single/Double):
Modest: **$65 / $75**
Average: **$75 / $85**
Luxury: **$250**
Credit Cards: **AMEX, MC, VISA**

The range listings in the Alexandria and Arlington Bed & Breakfast Network is breathtaking and can be well described as eclectic. Homes range from Colonial townhouses of Old Towne Alexandria to modern, high-rise urban dwellings. Locations outside the D.C. metro area allow travelers to experience the quiet civility of the countryside and expand sightseeing possibilities to nearby areas of historic interest. Hosts are equally eclectic, including civil servants, political activists, veterans, diplomats, and yuppies.

Princely B&B Ltd. ✪

HCR 69, BOX 17215, MATHEWS, VIRGINIA 23109

Tel: **(800) 470-5588**
Best Time to Call: **10 AM–6 PM Mon.–Fri.**
Coordinator: **Betsy Henderson**
States/Regions Covered: **Alexandria**
Rates (Single/Double):
Modest: **$75 / $125**
Minimum Stay: **2 nights**

This reservation service lists more than thirty privately owned historic homes, circa 1750 to 1890, many furnished with fine antiques, located in the heart of the Old Town area of Alexandria. All are within eight miles of the White House or Mount Vernon and afford easy access to shopping, dining, and monuments in and around Washington, D.C.

Clay Corner Inn ✪

401 CLAY STREET SOUTHWEST, BLACKSBURG, VIRGINIA 24060
E-mail: claycorner@aol.com

Tel: **(540) 953-2604; fax: (540) 951-0541**
Best Time to Call: **9 AM–9 PM**
Hosts: **John and Joanne Anderson**
Location: **35 mi. SW of Roanoke**
No. of Rooms: **8**
No. of Private Baths: **8**
Double/pb: **$75–$85**
Single/pb: **$68–$85**
Open: **All year**

Breakfast: **Full**
Credit Cards: **AMEX, MC, VISA**
Pets: **No**
Children: **Welcome, over 12**
Smoking: **No**
Social Drinking: **Permitted**

Clay Corner Inn is a cluster of houses on a corner a few blocks from downtown and the Virginia Tech campus. The main house is decorated with a mix of traditional and southwestern decors. The Huckleberry House next door, circa 1913, has four guest rooms, each with a fireplace. Each of the two Cape-style guest houses has a kitchen, dining area, living room, and four guest rooms. A heated swimming pool is located in the center of the complex and is open May through September. Wood decks with benches and rockers provide wonderful places to relax, read, visit, and enjoy coffee, tea, or breakfast.

Bay Avenue Sunset Bed & Breakfast ✪

108 BAY AVENUE, CAPE CHARLES, VIRGINIA 23310

Tel: **(757) 331-2424; (800) 331-3113 for reservations; fax: (804) 331-4877**
Hosts: **Al Longo and Joyce Tribble**
Location: **35 mi. N of Norfolk**
No of Rooms: **4**
No. of Private Baths: **4**
Double/pb: **$65–$85**
Single/pb: **$60–$80**
Open: **All year**
Reduced Rates: **Available**
Breakfast: **Full**
Credit Cards: **MC, VISA**
Pets: **No**
Children: **Welcome, over 10**
Smoking: **Restricted**
Social Drinking: **Permitted**
Minimum Stay: **2 nights, holiday weekends**
Airport Pickup: **Yes**

Enjoy a waterfront getaway on the unspoiled Eastern Shore. Cape Charles is directly on the Chesapeake Bay, at the southernmost part of the Delmarva Peninsula; this picturesque town has no traffic lights or parking meters. You'll be able to watch spectacular unobstructed sunsets from the Inn's breezy porch or common area. Sun, swim, and relax—a seasonal hot tub is available. Then walk the beach, explore the historic district, or take a bike ride. Bird-watching and charter fishing are nearby. A hearty full breakfast features homemade baked goods and fresh fruit, and delicious hot entrees.

Nottingham Ridge

28184 NOTTINGHAM RIDGE LANE, CAPE CHARLES, VIRGINIA 23310

Tel: **(804) 331-1010**
Best Time to Call: **Anytime**
Hosts: **Bonnie Nottingham and M.S. Scott**
Location: **20 mi. N of Norfolk**
No. of Rooms: **4**
No. of Private Baths: **4**
Double/pb: **$85**
Single/pb: **$60**
Open: **All year**
Breakfast: **Full**
Other Meals: **No**
Pets: **No**
Children: **Welcome, over 7**
Smoking: **No**
Social Drinking: **Permitted**
Airport/Station Pickup: **Yes**

Reflecting the beauty and charm of Virginia's historic Eastern Shore, this lovely home boasts a private secluded beach on the Chesapeake Bay, bordered by tall trees, sand dunes, and abundant wildlife. Guests can savor breakfast on the porch while watching boats and birds; at day's end, the sunsets are spectacular. Cooler times can be spent in the den by a crackling fire. Biking, fishing, tennis, golf, running, bird-watching, crabbing, swimming, and sightseeing are just a few pastimes guests can enjoy. Visitors to Nottingham Ridge can look forward to an informal, relaxed atmosphere with emphasis on the small details that create a memorable stay.

Picketts Harbor

BOX 97AA, CAPE CHARLES, VIRGINIA 23310

Tel: **(804) 331-2212**
Best Time to Call: **After 5 PM**
Hosts: **Sara and Cooke Goffigon**
Location: **21 mi. E of Virginia Beach**
No. of Rooms: **6**
Max. No. Sharing Bath: **4**
Double/pb: **$85–$125**
Single/pb: **$65–$85**
Double/sb: **$75–$85**
Single/sb: **$65–$75**
Suites: **$125**
Open: **All year**
Breakfast: **Full**
Other Meals: **Available**
Pets: **Sometimes**
Children: **Welcome**
Smoking: **No**
Social Drinking: **Permitted**
Airport/Station Pickup: **Yes**

Picketts Harbor is a real find on Virginia's Eastern Shore, with twenty-seven acres of private beach and views of the Chesapeake Bay from all rooms. Set amid pine trees, the home is built to an eighteenth-century design; central air-conditioning, fireplaces and antique pieces complement the two-hundred-year-old red heart-pine floors and cupboards. One wing of the house has a private entrance. A country breakfast is served on the porch, in the country kitchen, or in the dining room. Seasonal fruit, homemade breads with jam, and Virginia ham tempt guests. Things to do include fishing, bird-watching, and antiquing, and reasonable restaurants are nearby. Williamsburg and Chincoteague lie within a short drive.

Sandy Hill Farm B&B ✪

11307 RIVERS MILL ROAD, CAPRON, VIRGINIA 23829

Tel: **(804) 658-4381**
Best Time to Call: **6:30–8 AM; 7:30–11:30 PM**
Host: **Anne Kitchen**
Location: **11 mi. from I-95**
No. of Rooms: **2**
Double/pb: **$50**
Single/pb: **$40**
Open: **Mar. 20–Dec. 5**
Reduced Rates: **Families; 5 nights**
Breakfast: **Full**
Other Meals: **Available**
Pets: **Welcome**
Children: **Welcome**
Smoking: **Permitted**
Social Drinking: **Permitted**

Experience the pleasures of an unspoiled rural setting at this ranch-style farmhouse. There are animals to visit, quiet places to stroll, and a lighted tennis court on the grounds. This is an ideal hub from which to tour southeastern and central Virginia. Day trips to Williamsburg, Norfolk, and Richmond are possibilities. Fresh fruits and homemade breads are served at breakfast.

Guesthouses Reservation Service ✪

P.O. BOX 5737, CHARLOTTESVILLE, VIRGINIA 22905

Tel: **(804) 979-7264**
Best Time to Call: **12–5 PM Mon.–Fri.**
Coordinator: **Mary Hill Caperton**
States/Regions Covered: **Albemarle County, Charlottesville**
Descriptive Directory: **$1**
Rates (Single/Double):
Modest: **$52 / $60**
Average: **$68 / $80**
Luxury: **$100 / $150**
Estate Cottages: **$100 up**
Credit Cards: **AMEX, MC, VISA**

Charlottesville is a gracious town. The hosts in Mary's hospitality file offer you a genuine taste of Southern hospitality. All places are close to Thomas Jefferson's Monticello and James Madison's Ash Lawn, as well as the University of Virginia. Unusual local activities include ballooning, steeplechasing, and wine festivals. Reduced rates are available for extended stays, and most hosts offer a full breakfast.

Miss Molly's Inn ✪

4141 MAIN STREET, CHINCOTEAGUE ISLAND, VIRGINIA 23336

Tel: **(804) 336-6686; (800) 221-5620**
Best Time to Call: **10 AM–10 PM**
Hosts: **Barbara and David Wiedenheft**
Location: **50 mi. S of Salisbury, Maryland**
No. of Rooms: **7**

No. of Private Baths: **5**
Max. No. Sharing Bath: **4**
Double/pb: **$69–$145**
Single/pb: **$59–$109**
Double/sb: **$75–$109**
Single/sb: **$65–$99**
Open: **Mar. 1–New Year**
Reduced Rates: **10% seniors; Oct. 1–Memorial Weekend**
Breakfast: **Full**
Other Meals: **Available**
Pets: **No**
Children: **Welcome, over 8**
Smoking: **No**
Social Drinking: **Permitted**
Minimum Stay: **2 days, weekends**
Airport/Station Pickup: **Yes**
Foreign Languages: **French, Dutch, German**

This bayside Victorian inn has been lovingly restored to its nineteenth-century charm; lace curtains, stained glass windows, and period pieces add to the ambience. While writing her book *Misty of Chincoteague,* Marguerite Henry stayed here. The ponies celebrated by that story roam wild at the nearby National Wildlife Refuge close to the unspoiled beaches of Assateague Island. You, too, may find Miss Molly's cool breezes, five porches, and traditional English tea—complete with superlative scones—worth writing about.

The Watson House ✪

4240 MAIN STREET, CHINCOTEAGUE, VIRGINIA 23336

Tel: **(804) 336-1564; (800) 336-6787**
Hosts: **Tom and Jacque Derrickson, David and Joanne Snead**
Location: **180 mi. SE of Washington, D.C.**
No. of Rooms: **6**
No. of Private Baths: **6**
Double/pb: **$59–$85**
Suites: **$79–$99**
Open: **Apr.–Nov.**
Reduced Rates: **Available**
Breakfast: **Full**
Credit Cards: **MC, VISA**
Pets: **No**
Children: **Welcome, over 10**
Smoking: **No**
Social Drinking: **Permitted**
Minimum Stay: **2 nights, weekends; 3 nights, holidays**

Friendly hosts and Southern hospitality await you at this newly restored country Victorian home. Guest rooms are tastefully decorated with antiques, wicker, and nostalgic pieces; each room has a ceiling fan and air-conditioning. Watson House is within biking distance of Assateague National Wildlife Refuge, where you can enjoy numerous nature trails, guided tours, crabbing, fishing, clamming, or swimming. Your hosts will equip you with bicycles, beach chairs, and towels. In the mornings, you can mingle with other guests over a hearty breakfast which includes fruit, eggs, breads, pastries, and aromatic coffee and tea.

Oak Grove Plantation Bed & Breakfast ✪

P.O. BOX 45, 1245 CLUSTER ROAD, CLUSTER SPRINGS, VIRGINIA 24535

Tel: **(804) 575-7137**
Host: **Pickett Craddock**
Location: **60 mi. N of Durham, NC**
No. of Rooms: **3**
Max. No. Sharing Bath: **4**
Double/sb: **$60**
Single/sb: **$55**
Open: **May and Sept. weekends, full-time June–Aug.**
Breakfast: **Full**
Other Meals: **Available**
Pets: **No**
Children: **Welcome**
Smoking: **No**
Social Drinking: **Permitted**
Airport/Station Pickup: **Yes**
Foreign Languages: **Spanish**

Thomas Easley, a prominent Virginia legislator, built this estate in 1820 and it has remained in the family ever since. Pickett, the director of a preschool in Washington, D.C., is a fifth-generation descendant. She encourages guests to hike, bike, and look at the wildlife on the 400-acre grounds. All bedrooms have fireplaces and are decorated with comfortable period pieces and family heirlooms. Guests will enjoy reading or chatting in the elegant parlor or on the cheerful sunporch. Breakfast is served in the Victorian dining room. Historical Danville, Buggs Island Lake, and Richmond, the capital of the Confederacy, are within a half-hour drive. Appomattox is one hour away.

Caledonia Farm–1812 ✪

47 DEARING ROAD, FLINT HILL, VIRGINIA 22627

Tel: **(540) 675-3693; (800) BNB-1812**
Best Time to Call: **10 AM–6 PM**
Host: **Phil Irwin**
Location: **68 mi. SW of Washington, D.C.; 4 mi. N of Washington, Va.**
No. of Rooms: **3**
Max. No. Sharing Bath: **4**
Double/sb: **$80**
Suite: **$140**
Open: **All year**
Breakfast: **Full**
Credit Cards: **DISC, MC, VISA**
Pets: **No**
Children: **Welcome, over 12**
Smoking: **No**
Social Drinking: **Permitted**

This charming 1812 stone manor house and its companion "summer kitchen" are located on a working beef cattle farm adjacent to Shenandoah National Park. Each accommodation has a fireplace, period furnishings, individual temperature controls for heat or air-conditioning, and spectacular views of the Blue Ridge Mountains. A candlelight breakfast is served from a menu that offers a choice of omelette, smoked salmon, or eggs Benedict. The Skyline Drive, fine dining, caves, wineries, hayrides, hot tub, antiquing, historic sites, and sporting activities are a few of the possible diversions. Caledonia Farm is a Virginia Historic Landmark and on the National Register of Historic Places.

La Vista Plantation ✪

4420 GUINEA STATION ROAD, FREDERICKSBURG, VIRGINIA 22408

Tel: **(540) 898-8444; (800) 529-2823**
Best Time to Call: **Before 9:30 PM**
Hosts: **Michele and Edward Schiesser**
Location: **60 mi. S of Washington, D.C.; 4.5 mi. from I-95**
No. of Rooms: **2**
No. of Private Baths: **2**
Double/pb: **$95**
Single/pb: **$75**
Guest Apartment: **$95; sleeps 6**
Open: **All year**
Reduced Rates: **7th night free; families**
Breakfast: **Full**
Credit Cards: **MC, VISA**
Pets: **No**
Children: **Welcome**
Smoking: **No**
Social Drinking: **Permitted**

Built in 1838, this Classical Revival country home is nestled amidst ancient tulip poplars, cedars, and hollies, and surrounded by pastures, woods and fields. The site is close to historic Fredericksburg, but in a quiet rural area. The house retains its original charm, with intricate acorn and oak leaf moldings, high ceilings, wide pine floors and a two-story front portico. Guest rooms have private baths, air-conditioning, working fireplaces, TV, radio and refrigerator. Enjoy brown egg breakfasts from resident hens. The Schiessers also have a stocked pond.

Selby House Bed & Breakfast ✪

226 PRINCESS ANNE STREET, FREDERICKSBURG, VIRGINIA 22401

Tel: **(540) 373-7037**
Hosts: **Jerry and Virginia Selby**
Location: **54 mi. S of Washington, D.C.**
No. of Rooms: **4**
No. of Private Baths: **4**
Double/pb: **$75**
Single/pb: **$65**
Open: **All year**
Reduced Rates: **Available**
Breakfast: **Full**
Credit Cards: **MC, VISA**
Pets: **No**
Children: **Welcome**
Smoking: **No**
Social Drinking: **Permitted**
Station Pickup: **Yes**

Warm Southern hospitality is the order every day at this restored, late 19th-century Colonial located in Fredericksburg's historic district.

Selby House is decorated throughout with late American Empire furniture. Just two blocks from the railroad station and with off-street parking provided, this B&B assures easy access to good restaurants, museums, art galleries, fine antique shops, and the numerous historic attractions Fredericksburg offers. Civil War buffs will enjoy talking with Jerry and perhaps signing up for one of his Civil War seminars. Virginia, a Richmond local, will have you raving over her full Southern breakfasts with all the trimmings.

The Spooner House Bed and Breakfast

1300 CAROLINE STREET, FREDERICKSBURG, VIRGINIA 22401-3704

Tel: **(540) 371-1267**
Best Time to Call: **After 6 PM**
Hosts: **Peggy and John Roethel**
Location: **54 mi. S of Washington, D.C.**
Suites: **$95; sleeps 2, $20 additional person**
Open: **All year**
Reduced Rates: **10% weekly**
Breakfast: **Full**
Pets: **No**
Children: **Welcome**
Smoking: **No**
Social Drinking: **Permitted**
Station Pickup: **Yes**

Built in 1793 on land once owned by George Washington's youngest brother, Charles, the Spooner House operated as a general store and later a tavern. Located in Fredericksburg's historic district, it is within walking distance of museums, restaurants, shops, and the Amtrak station. The lovely two-room suite has its own private entrance and private bath. Breakfast, along with the morning paper, is delivered to guests at their convenience.

The Hummingbird Inn

WOOD LANE, P.O. BOX 147, GOSHEN, VIRGINIA 24439

Tel: **(540) 997-9065; (800) 397-3214**
Best Time to Call: **8 AM–5 PM**
Hosts: **Jeremy and Diana Robinson**
Location: **23 mi. NW of Lexington**
No. of Rooms: **5**
No. of Private Baths: **5**
Double/pb: **$85–$105**
Open: **All year**
Reduced Rates: **10% seniors; Nov. 1–Mar. 31**
Breakfast: **Full**
Other Meals: **Available**
Credit Cards: **AMEX, DISC, MC, VISA**
Pets: **Sometimes**
Children: **Welcome, over 12**
Smoking: **No**
Social Drinking: **Permitted**

Located on an acre of landscaped grounds in the Shenandoah Valley, this Victorian Carpenter Gothic villa has accommodated Eleanor Roosevelt and Efrem Zimbalist, Sr. Wraparound verandas, original pine floors, a rustic den and a solarium give Hummingbird Inn an old-fashioned ambiance. In keeping with its architecture, the B&B is decorated in an early Victorian style and furnished with antiques. Nearby recreational facilities offer golf, swimming, hiking, skiing, canoeing, tubing, fishing, and hunting. Head out in your car for scenic routes like the Blue Ridge Parkway and Skyline Drive. Or visit the Garth Newell Music Center, historic Staunton, the Museum of American Frontier Culture, Virginia Military Institute, and Washington and Lee University. Rates for MAP double: $140–$170.

Kingsway Bed & Breakfast ✪

3581 SINGERS GLEN ROAD, HARRISONBURG, VIRGINIA 22801

Tel: **(540) 867-9696**
Hosts: **Chester and Verna Leaman**
Location: **2.5 mi. NW of Harrisonburg**
No. of Rooms: **3**
No. of Private Baths: **1**
Max. No. Sharing Bath: **4**
Double/pb: **$55–$60**
Single/pb: **$45**
Double/sb: **$50**
Single/sb: **$40**
Open: **All year**
Reduced Rates: **Available**
Breakfast: **Full**
Pets: **Yes**
Children: **Welcome**
Smoking: **No**
Social Drinking: **No**
Airport Pickup: **Yes**

This modern country home reveals the carpentry and decorating skills of Chester, a cabinet builder, and Verna, a full-time homemaker. Enjoy the gardens or take a dip in the pool. If you're up for an excursion, visit George Washington National Forest, Shenandoah National Park with picturesque Skyline Drive, Thomas Jefferson's home at Monticello, or New Market Battlefield and caverns. Local sports range from hiking, skiing, to pricing the wares at the antique shops, flea markets, and the Valley Mall.

Asherowe ✪

314 SOUTH JEFFERSON STREET, LEXINGTON, VIRGINIA 24450

Tel: **(540) 463-4219**
Best Time to Call: **Early mornings, evenings**
Host: **Yvonne Emerson**
Location: **45 mi. N of Roanoke**
No. of Rooms: **4**
Max. No. Sharing Bath: **4**
Double/sb: **$53.75**
Single/sb: **$53.75**
Open: **Closed July**
Breakfast: **Continental**
Pets: **Sometimes**
Children: **Welcome, over 15**
Smoking: **No**
Social Drinking: **Permitted**
Foreign Languages: **French, German**

This comfortable 1911 wooden home lies only minutes from downtown, in the Golden Triangle section of Lexington's historic district. Sights include the Marshall Library, Washington and Lee University, the Virginia Horse Center, the Virginia Military Institute, and the home of Stonewall Jackson. Guests from both sides of the Atlantic will feel right at home here, since Yvonne speaks fluent French and German. With the Blue Ridge Parkway to the east, and the Allegheny Mountains to the west, the breathtaking scenery is sure to entice any outdoor enthusiast. Lady Calypso, the resident cat, greets all guests on arrival as any good Southern hostess would.

Brierley Hill

RT 2, BOX 21A BORDEN ROAD, LEXINGTON, VIRGINIA 24450

Tel: **(540) 464-8421; (800) 422-4925**
Best Time to Call: **8 AM–8 PM**
Hosts: **Barry and Carole Speton**
Location: **50 mi. N of Roanoke**
No. of Rooms: **6**
No. of Private Baths: **6**
Double/pb: **$75–$140**
Open: **All year**
Reduced Rates: **Available**
Breakfast: **Full**
Other Meals: **Available**
Credit Cards: **MC, VISA**
Pets: **No**
Children: **Welcome, over 14**
Smoking: **No**
Social Drinking: **Permitted**

This charming B&B sits on eight acres of farmland. Guests are sure to appreciate the spectacular views of the Blue Ridge Mountains and the Shenandoah Valley. Located nearby are Blue Ridge Parkway, the Natural Bridge area and historic Lexington. All rooms are furnished with antique brass or canopy beds, plus Laura Ashley wall coverings and linens. A TV room and a sitting room with a fireplace are at your disposal, and the dining room also has a fireplace. Barry, a retired Canadian lawyer, is interested in antique prints and refinishing furniture. Carole likes cooking, gardening, and quilting. Together, they offer relaxed comfort, wonderful food, and friendly hospitality.

Lavender Hill Farm B&B ✪

ROUTE 1, BOX 515, LEXINGTON, VIRGINIA 24450

Tel: **(540) 464-5877; (800) 446-4240**
Best Time to Call: **9 AM–6 PM**
Hosts: **Cindy and Colin Smith**
Location: **50 mi. N of Roanoke**
No. of Rooms: **3**
No. of Private Baths: **3**
Double/pb: **$64–$75**
Single/pb: **$54–$64**
Suites: **$105–$115**
Open: **All year**
Reduced Rates: **Available**
Breakfast: **Full**
Other Meals: **Available**
Credit Cards: **DISC, MC, VISA**
Pets: **No**
Children: **Welcome**
Smoking: **No**
Social Drinking: **Permitted**
Minimum Stay: **2 nights on holidays or special events**

Situated on a 20-acre working farm in the beautiful Shenandoah Valley, this restored farmhouse (circa 1790) is located five miles from historic Lexington. It has been carefully renovated to blend old and new for your comfort and relaxation. Enjoy the large front porch, fishing, hiking, bird-watching, panoramic mountain views, and lambs frolicking on the hillside. Breakfast specialties include homemade bread, stuffed French toast, fresh farm eggs, and much more. Dinner, served to guests by advance reservation, is highly recommended. Colin, the English half of the family, is the chef whose specialties involve fresh herbs and vegetables from the garden. Cindy will be glad to direct you to nearby attractions, give a spinning demonstration, or arrange a horseback riding package for you.

Llewellyn Lodge at Lexington ✪

603 SOUTH MAIN STREET, LEXINGTON, VIRGINIA 24450
E-mail: lll603@aol.com

Tel: **(540) 463-3235; (800) 882-1145**
Best Time to Call: **9:30 AM–7:30 PM**
Hosts: **Ellen and John Roberts**
Location: **50 mi. N of Roanoke**
No. of Rooms: **6**
No. of Private Baths: **6**
Double/pb: **$70–$90**
Single/pb: **$55–$80**
Open: **All year**
Breakfast: **Full**
Credit Cards: **AMEX, MC, VISA**
Pets: **No**
Children: **Welcome, over 10**
Smoking: **Restricted**
Social Drinking: **Permitted**
Airport/Station Pickup: **Yes**

A warm and friendly atmosphere, combining country charm with a touch of class, awaits you at this lovely brick Colonial furnished in traditional and antique pieces. Guests are welcomed with a cool drink on the deck in warm months, or with a refreshment by the fire in the winter. Ellen spent twenty years in the airline, travel, and hospitality business before moving to Lexington in 1985 to start her B&B. John, a native Lexingtonian, is acquainted with the hiking and biking trails and knows where the fish are hiding. A hearty gourmet breakfast is offered each morning, including omelettes, Belgian waffles, Virginia maple syrup, sausage, bacon, and Ellen's famous blueberry muffins. The lodge is an easy walk to the Robert E. Lee Chapel, the Stonewall Jackson House, Washington and Lee University, and the Virginia Military Institute.

The Woodruff House Bed & Breakfast ✪

330 MECHANIC STREET, LURAY, VIRGINIA 22835

Tel: **(540) 743-1494**
Hosts: **Lucas and Deborah Woodruff**
Location: **89 mi. W of Washington, D.C.**
No. of Rooms: **3**
No. of Private Baths: **3**
Double/pb: **$98–$125**
Suites: **$115–$145**
Open: **All year**
Reduced Rates: **20% Mon.–Thurs., 5% after 3 nights**
Breakfast: **Full**
Other meals: **Dinner, included with room rate**
Credit Cards: **DISC, MC, VISA**
Pets: **No**
Children: **Welcome, Mon.–Thurs. only**
Smoking: **No**
Social Drinking: **Permitted**
Minimum Stay: **2 nights weekends**

This fairy-tale Victorian, beautifully appointed with period antiques, hallmarked silver and fine china, is chef-owned and -operated. Escape from reality and come into this fairy tale, where the ambiance never ends. Awaken to your choice of freshly brewed coffees delivered to your door; a gourmet candlelit breakfast follows. A sumptuous candlelit high-tea buffet dinner is also included. You may want to relax in the fireside candlelit garden spa, or enjoy the canoes and bicycles provided by your hosts. Each guest room has a working fireplace and a private bath. The Woodruff House is located in the beautiful Shenandoah Valley of Virginia.

Federal Crest Inn B&B ✪

1101 FEDERAL STREET, LYNCHBURG, VIRGINIA 24504

Tel: **(804) 845-6155; (800) 818-6155**
Best Time to Call: **10 AM–10 PM**
Hosts: **Phil and Ann Ripley**
Location: **50 mi. E of Roanoke**
No. of Rooms: **5**
No. of Private Baths: **4**
Max. No. Sharing Bath: **4**
Double/pb: **$85**
Single/pb: **$80**
Double/sb: **$55**
Suites: **$100–$115**
Open: **All year**
Reduced Rates: **10% Sun.–Thurs., business rates, seniors**
Breakfast: **Full**
Other Meals: **Available**
Credit Cards: **AMEX, DISC, MC, VISA**
Pets: **No**
Children: **Welcome, over 10**
Smoking: **No**
Social Drinking: **Permitted**
Minimum Stay: **May–Oct. 2 nights weekends**
Airport/Station Pickup: **Yes**

This elegant 1909 Georgian Revival home has over 8000 square feet and is located in the Federal Hill Historic District. The original charm is seen in the woodwork and the interior columns that lead to the grand central staircase in the front foyer. Guests are invited to enjoy the antiques, the unique mantels of the seven fireplaces and the '50s cafe which offers delightful surprises. Perhaps there will be a special visitation to the third floor, where the original owner constructed a stage for his children to give plays. All rooms have queen beds, down comforters, plush robes and towels, snack baskets and clock radios. In one room, atmosphere is meant to be shared in the romantic Jacuzzi tub, as the lights dim on a painted mural of Virginia's Blue Ridge Mountains. Federal Crest lies within walking distance to many attractions.

Lynchburg Mansion Inn B&B ✪

405 MADISON STREET, LYNCHBURG, VIRGINIA 24504

Tel: **(804) 528-5400; (800) 352-1199**
Hosts: **Bob and Mauranna Sherman**
Location: **65 mi. S of Charlottesville**
No. of Rooms: **5**
No. of Private Baths: **5**
Double/pb: **$85**
Suites: **$119**
Open: **All year**
Reduced Rates: **Available**
Breakfast: **Full**
Credit Cards: **AMEX, DC, MC, VISA**
Pets: **No**
Children: **Welcome**
Smoking: **No**
Social Drinking: **Permitted**

Restored with your every comfort in mind, this Spanish Georgian mansion has pretty gardens, a spacious veranda, oak floors, tall ceilings, pocket doors, and cherry woodwork. Bedrooms are lavish, with either king- or queen-size beds, luxurious linens, fireplaces, TVs, and turn-down service. Bob and Mauranna have also added an outdoor hot tub for guests to use. Fine china, silver, and crystal complement the sumptuous full breakfasts. The mansion surveys a half-acre in downtown Lynchburg's Garland Hill Historic District, which is listed on the National Register of Historic Places; impressive Federal and Victorian homes line Madison Street, still paved in its turn-of-the-century brick. Plus there are Civil War sites, antique shops, art galleries, and countless programs offered by the city's colleges and universities.

Winridge Bed & Breakfast ✪

ROUTE 1, BOX 362, WINRIDGE DRIVE, MADISON HEIGHTS, VIRGINIA 24572

Tel: **(804) 384-7220**
Best Time to Call: **10 AM–4 PM**
Hosts: **Lois Ann and Ed Pfister**
Location: **4 mi. N of Lynchburg**
No. of Rooms: **3**
No. of Private Baths: **1**
Max. No. Sharing Bath: **4**
Double/pb: **$85**
Double/sb: **$69**

Open: **All year**
Reduced Rates: **Available**
Breakfast: **Full**
Pets: **No**
Children: **Welcome**
Smoking: **No**
Social Drinking: **No**
Airport/Station Pickup: **Yes**

Enjoy wonderful mountain views while relaxing on the large porches of this grand Colonial Southern home. Swing under the shade trees and stroll through the gardens, where you'll admire the beauty of flowers, birds, and butterflies. Spacious rooms with high ceilings, large sunny windows, and a delightful mix of modern and antique

furniture await you. Breakfasts are tempting, with offerings like oven baked pecan French toast and blueberry patch muffins. The Blue Ridge Parkway, Appomattox Courthouse, Poplar Forest, and much more are close by for your diversion.

Sunrise Hill Farm ✪

5590 OLD FARM LANE, MANASSAS, VIRGINIA 22110

Tel: **(703) 754-8309**
Best Time to Call: **Anytime**
Hosts: **Frank and Sue Boberek**
Location: **35 minutes W of Washington, D.C.**
No. of Rooms: **2**
No. of Private Baths: **1**
Max. No. Sharing Bath: **4**
Double/pb: **$85**
Double/sb: **$75**
Open: **All year**
Reduced Rates: **15% families using both rooms**
Breakfast: **Full**
Credit Cards: **MC, VISA**
Pets: **Horses boarded**
Children: **Welcome, over 10**
Smoking: **No**
Social Drinking: **Permitted**

Standing in the heart of the 6000-acre Manassas National Battlefields, this Civil War treasure overlooks Bull Run Creek. Sunrise Hill Farm is an uncommonly charming, Federal-era country home furnished in period style. This B&B is a haven for Civil War buffs and guests visiting northern Virginia and the nation's capital. Situated within the renowned Virginia hunt country, it is just 35 minutes from Washington, D.C., and close to Harpers Ferry, Antietam, Skyline Drive, Luray Caverns, and numerous historic sites and antique-filled towns.

A Touch of Country Bed & Breakfast ✪

9329 CONGRESS STREET, NEW MARKET, VIRGINIA 22844

Tel: **(703) 740-8030**
Hosts: **Jean Schoellig and Dawn Kasow**
Location: **18 mi. N of Harrisonburg**
No. of Rooms: **6**

No. of Private Baths: **6**
Double/pb: **$60–$75**
Single/pb: **$50–$65**
Open: **All year**
Breakfast: **Full**
Credit Cards: **DISC, MC, VISA**
Pets: **No**
Children: **Welcome, over 12**
Smoking: **No**
Social Drinking: **Permitted**

This restored 1870s home is located in a historic town in the beautiful Shenandoah Valley. It displays the original hardwood floors and is decorated with antiques and collectibles in a country motif. You'll start your day with a hearty breakfast of pancakes, meats, gravy, and biscuits. Daydream on the porch swings or stroll through town with its charming shops, dine at a variety of restaurants or visit the legendary New Market Battlefield and Park. Close by are Skyline Drive, George Washington National Forest, caverns, and vineyards.

The Spinning Wheel Bed & Breakfast ✪

31 NORTH STREET, ONANCOCK, VIRGINIA 23417

Tel: **(804) 787-7311; Nov. 1–March 31 (703) 684-0067**
Hosts: **David and Karen Tweedie**
Location: **60 mi. N of Virginia Beach**
No. of Rooms: **5**
No. of Private Baths: **5**
Double/pb: **$85–$95**
Open: **Apr. 1–Oct. 31**
Reduced Rates: **Over 4 nights**
Breakfast: **Full**
Credit Cards: **MC, VISA**
Pets: **No**
Children: **Welcome, over 12**
Smoking: **No**
Social Drinking: **Permitted**
Minimum Stay: **2 nights, weekends**

This 1890s folk Victorian home is in the historic waterfront town of Onancock, on the Eastern Shore peninsula separating the Chesapeake Bay from the Atlantic Ocean. The B&B is decorated with antiques and, true to its name, spinning wheels. Guest rooms have queen-size beds and air-conditioning. Kerr Place (a 1799 museum), restaurants, shops, the town wharf, and the ferry to Tangier Island are all within walking distance. David is a college professor and Karen is a teacher of the deaf. Their guests are greeted by Nelly, the resident old English sheepdog.

Count Pulaski Bed & Breakfast and Gardens ✪

821 NORTH JEFFERSON AVENUE, PULASKI, VIRGINIA 24301

Tel: **(703) 980-1163**
Host: **Dr. Flo Stevenson**
Location: **55 mi. S of Roanoke**
No. of Rooms: **3**
No. of Private Baths: **3**
Double/pb: **$75**
Single/pb: **$60**
Open: **All year**
Breakfast: **Full**
Credit Cards: **MC, VISA**
Pets: **Sometimes**
Children: **Welcome, over 15**
Smoking: **No**
Social Drinking: **No**

In a mountain village in southwest Virginia, you'll find this spacious eighty-year-old house furnished with family antiques, paintings, and pieces your host collected around the world. Guest rooms have carpeting, air-conditioning, and king- or queen-size beds; one room has a fireplace. A television, beverage center, and games and books are inside, while garden sitting areas beckon you outside. Breakfast is served by candlelight on a one-hundred-fifty-year-old table set with china, crystal, and silver. From its quiet hillside perch, this B&B overlooks the town and mountains below, yet Main Street's restaurants and antique shops are only a few blocks away. A fifty-mile bike trail originates in Pulaski; other recreational options include rafting, canoeing, and golf.

The Emmanuel Hutzler House

2036 MONUMENT AVENUE, RICHMOND, VIRGINIA 23220

Tel: **(804) 353-6900, 355-4885**
Best Time to Call: **11AM–6 PM**
Host: **John E. Richardson**
Location: **1½ mi. from Rte. I-95/64**
No. of Rooms: **4**
No. of Private Baths: **1**
Double/pb: **$85–$145**
Open: **All year**
Reduced Rates: **Corporate, 5%, seniors**
Breakfast: **Full**
Credit Cards: **AMEX, DC, DISC, MC, VISA**
Pets: **No**
Children: **Welcome, over 12**
Smoking: **No**
Social Drinking: **Permitted**

This spacious Italian Renaissance inn, built in 1914, recently received a total renovation. The classical interior has raised mahogany paneling, lavish wainscoting, leaded glass windows, and, on the first floor, coffered ceilings with dropped beams. Mahogany bookcases flank the marble fireplace in the living room, where guests can relax and converse. The generously sized guest rooms, all on the second floor, are furnished with antiques and handsome draperies; two rooms have fireplaces. The central location makes this an ideal location for either a midweek business trip or a weekend getaway.

Woodlawn ✪

2211 WILTSHIRE ROAD, ROCKVILLE, VIRGINIA 23146

Tel: **(804) 749-3759**
Best Time to Call: **3–10 PM**
Host: **Ann Nuckols**
Location: **20 mi. W of Richmond**
No. of Rooms: **2**
No. of Private Baths: **2**
Double/pb: **$75**
Open: **All year**
Breakfast: **Full**
Pets: **No**
Children: **No**
Smoking: **No**
Social Drinking: **Permitted**

An ideal hub from which to tour many historic points of interest in the area, this circa 1813 farmhouse is set on 40 acres of peaceful, grassy slopes, just 3 miles from the interstate. The interior has been completely restored, tastefully decorated, and furnished with antiques. The house has central air-conditioning for summer comfort. Each of the two guest rooms has its own fireplace. Both guest rooms are furnished with majestic hand-carved double beds and down pillows and comforters. Breakfasts with sourdough rolls, bran muffins, homemade jellies, and juice are served on the screened porch or in the dining area in the English basement.

Isle of Wight Inn ✪

1607 SOUTH CHURCH STREET, SMITHFIELD, VIRGINIA 23430

Tel: **(804) 357-3176**
Best Time to Call: **3–9 PM**
Hosts: **Bob Hart and Jackie Madrigal**
Location: **27 mi. W of Norfolk**

No. of Rooms: **9**
No. of Private Baths: **9**
Double/pb: **$59**
Single/pb: **$49**
Suites: **$79–$99**
Open: **All year**
Breakfast: **Full**
Credit Cards: **AMEX, MC, VISA**
Pets: **No**
Children: **Welcome**
Smoking: **Restricted**
Social Drinking: **Permitted**

The Isle of Wight Inn is a sprawling brick Colonial, one mile from downtown Smithfield. Inside you will find antiques, reproductions, and motifs of glass, wood, and wicker. Wake up to fresh coffee and Smithfield's own ham rolls. This riverport town has numerous historic homes that will surely delight you. Williamsburg, Norfolk, and Virginia Beach are less than an hour's drive from the house. An antique shop is on the premises.

The Manor at Taylor's Store B&B Country Inn ✪

ROUTE 1, BOX 533, SMITH MOUNTAIN LAKE, VIRGINIA 24184

Tel: **(540) 721-3951; (800) 248-6267**
Hosts: **Lee and Mary Lynn Tucker**
Location: **20 mi. E of Roanoke**
No. of Rooms: **10**
No. of Private Baths: **8**
Double/pb: **$90–$185**
Guest Cottage: **$95–$190; sleeps 2–6**
Open: **All year**
Reduced Rates: **$300–up weekly for cottage**
Breakfast: **Full**
Credit Cards: **MC, VISA**
Pets: **No**
Children: **Welcome in cottage**
Smoking: **Cottage only**
Social Drinking: **Permitted**
Airport/Station Pickup: **Yes**

Situated on 120 acres in the foothills of the Blue Ridge Mountains, this elegant manor house, circa 1799, was the focus of a prosperous tobacco plantation. It has been restored and refurbished, and you'll experience the elegance of the past combined with the comfort of tasteful modernization. The estate invites hiking, swimming, and fishing. The sunroom, parlor, and hot tub are special spots for relaxing. Smith Mountain Lake, with its seasonal sporting activity, is five miles away. Breakfast, designed for the health-conscious, features a variety of fresh gourmet selections.

Frederick House ✪

28 NORTH NEW STREET, STAUNTON, VIRGINIA 24401

Tel: **(540) 885-4220; (800) 334-5575**
Best Time to Call: **7 AM–10 PM**
Hosts: **Joe and Evy Harman**
Location: **2.7 mi. from Route I-81 exit 222**
No. of Rooms: **14**
No. of Private Baths: **14**
Double/pb: **$65–$150**
Single/pb: **$65–$135**
Suites: **$95–$150**
Open: **All year**
Reduced Rates: **Available**
Breakfast: **Full**
Credit Cards: **AMEX, DC, DISC, MC, VISA**
Pets: **No**

Children: **Welcome**
Smoking: **No**
Social Drinking: **Permitted**
Station Pickup: **Yes**

Frederick House is located across from Mary Baldwin College in downtown Staunton, the oldest city in the Shenandoah Valley. The five separate buildings that are listed in the National Register of Historic Places have been tastefully restored and furnished with antiques. The large rooms and suites feature oversize beds, modern baths, remote cable TV, air-conditioning, ceiling fans, robes, telephones, and private entrances. Some have fireplaces or balconies. A full breakfast, prepared by the owners, is served in Chumley's Tearoom between 7:30 and 10:30 AM. Breakfast choices include ham and cheese pie, apple raisin quiche, waffles, stratta, fresh fruit, juice, coffee, tea, warm bread and hot or cold cereal. Joe and Evy Harman previously worked in banking and insurance. Since 1984 they have enjoyed informing guests about the area and suggesting trips to many nearby interesting sights.

Kenwood ✪

235 EAST BEVERLEY STREET, STAUNTON, VIRGINIA 24401

Tel: **(540) 886-0524**
Hosts: **Liz and Ed Kennedy**
Location: **30 mi. W of Charlottesville**
No. of Rooms: **3**
No. of Private Baths: **3**
Double/pb: **$75–$80**
Single/pb: **$65–$70**
Open: **All year**
Breakfast: **Full**
Credit Cards: **MC, VISA**
Pets: **No**
Children: **Welcome, over 5**
Smoking: **No**
Social Drinking: **Permitted**
Airport/Station Pickup: **Yes**

Kenwood, a stately brick Colonial revival home built in 1910, has been restored and decorated with floral wallpapers and antique furniture. The Woodrow Wilson Birthplace—and its museum and research library—are next door. Staunton boasts several other museums and numerous antique shops, and it's only a half-hour drive to attractions like Monticello and the Virginia Horse Center. Select your destinations over such breakfast fare as fresh seasonal fruit and homemade baked goods.

The Sampson Eagon Inn ✪

238 EAST BEVERLEY STREET, STAUNTON, VIRGINIA 24401

Tel: **(540) 886-8200; (800) 597-9722**
Best Time to Call: **10 AM–9 PM**
Hosts: **Laura and Frank Mattingly**
Location: **35 mi. W of Charlottesville**
No. of Rooms: **5**
No. of Private Baths: **5**
Double/pb: **$89**
Suites: **$105**
Open: **All year**
Breakfast: **Full**
Pets: **No**
Children: **Welcome, over 12**
Smoking: **No**
Social Drinking: **Permitted**
Minimum Stay: **Weekends in Oct. and May**

This circa 1840 in-town Greek Revival mansion provides affordable luxury accommodations in a preservation award–winning setting. Comfort and hospitality are key. Guest rooms are spacious, air-conditioned, and have modern ensuite baths. Canopied beds and antique furnishings reflect various periods of this elegant building's past. Scrumptious, gourmet breakfasts are served daily. Within two blocks of shops and restaurants, the Inn is adjacent to the Woodrow Wilson Birthplace and Mary Baldwin College. Nearby, guests can enjoy the natural and historic attractions and recreational activities of the central Shenandoah Valley. Charlottesville and Lexington are within a 40-minute drive.

Thornrose House at Gypsy Hill ✪

531 THORNROSE AVENUE, STAUNTON, VIRGINIA 24401

Tel: **(540) 885-7026; (800) 861-4338**
Best Time to Call: **9 AM–9 PM**
Hosts: **Suzanne and Otis Huston**
Location: **3½ mi. from Rte. I-81, Exit 222**
No. of Rooms: **5**
No. of Private Baths: **5**
Double/pb: **$60–$80**
Single/pb: **$50–$70**
Open: **All year**
Reduced Rates: **Available**
Breakfast: **Full**
Pets: **No**
Children: **Welcome**
Smoking: **No**
Social Drinking: **Permitted**
Minimum Stay: **3 days over July 4th; 2 days October weekends**
Airport/Station Pickup: **Yes**

This 1912 Georgian Revival home is six blocks from the center of Victorian Staunton and adjacent to 300-acre Gypsy Hill Park, which has facilities for golf, tennis, swimming, and summer concerts. A wraparound veranda and Greek colonnades grace the exterior of the house. Inside, there's a cozy parlor with a fireplace and a grand piano. A relaxed, leisurely breakfast is set out in the dining room, which offers the comfort of a fireplace on chilly mornings. Local attractions include Blue Ridge National Park, Natural Chimneys, Skyline Drive,

Woodrow Wilson's birthplace, and the Museum of American Frontier Culture.

The Duck Farm Inn ✪

P.O. BOX 787, RTES. 227 AND 639, URBANNA, VIRGINIA 23175

Tel: **(804) 758-5685; (800) 447-1369**
Host: **Fleming Godden**
Location: **55 mi. E of Richmond**
No. of Rooms: **6**
No. of Private Baths: **2**
Max. No. Sharing Bath: **4**
Double/pb: **$85**
Single/pb: **$70**
Double/sb: **$75**
Single/sb: **$60**
Open: **All year**
Reduced Rates: **After first visit**
Breakfast: **Full**
Pets: **No**
Children: **Welcome**
Smoking: **No**
Social Drinking: **Permitted**
Airport/Station Pickup: **Yes**

This elegant, contemporary inn is situated on Virginia's middle peninsula, surrounded by 800 secluded acres and bordered by the Rappahannock River. Guests are welcome to hike along the shore or through the woods, fish in the river, sunbathe on the private beach, lounge on the deck, or retire to the cozy library with a good book. Fleming has traveled all over the world and thoroughly enjoys her role as full-time innkeeper. One of her breakfast menus consists of seasonal fresh fruit, jumbo blueberry muffins, cheese-and-egg scramble served with spiced sausage, and a variety of hot beverages.

Angie's Guest Cottage ✪

302 24TH STREET, VIRGINIA BEACH, VIRGINIA 23451

Tel: **(804) 428-4690**
Best Time to Call: **10 AM–9 PM**
Host: **Barbara G. Yates**
Location: **20 mi. E of Norfolk**
No. of Rooms: **6**
No. of Private Baths: **1**
Max. No. Sharing Bath: **4**
Double/pb: **$78**
Single/pb: **$68**
Double/sb: **$52–$72**
Single/sb: **$44–$62**
Guest Cottage: **$450–$575 weekly; sleeps 2–6**
Open: **Apr. 1–Oct. 1**
Reduced Rates: **Off-season**
Breakfast: **Continental, plus**
Pets: **Sometimes**
Children: **Welcome**
Smoking: **No**
Social Drinking: **Permitted**
Minimum Stay: **2 nights**

Just a block from the beach, shops, and restaurants is this bright and comfortable beach house. Former guests describe it as "cozy, cute, and clean." Deep-sea fishing, nature trails, and harbor tours are but a few things to keep you busy. Freshly baked croissants in various flavors are a breakfast delight. You are welcome to use the sundeck, barbecue, and picnic tables.

Barclay Cottage ✪

400 16TH STREET, VIRGINIA BEACH, VIRGINIA 23451

Tel: **(804) 422-1956**
Hosts: **Peter and Claire**
Location: **20 mi. E of Norfolk**
No. of Rooms: **6**
No. of Private Baths: **2**
Max. No. Sharing Bath: **2**
Double/pb: **$80–$90**
Double/sb: **$65–$70**
Open: **Apr.–Oct.; Special holidays**
Reduced Rates: **10% seniors**
Breakfast: **Full**
Credit Cards: **AMEX, MC, VISA**
Pets: **No**
Children: **No**
Smoking: **No**
Social Drinking: **Permitted**
Minimum Stay: **2 nights**

The Barclay is a historic building designed in turn-of-the-century, Southern Colonial style. Your hosts bring you casual sophistication in a warm, inn-like atmosphere two blocks from the beach and fishing pier. The inn has been completely restored to add the feeling of yesterday to the comfort of today. Peter and Claire look forward to welcoming you to their B&B, where the theme is, "We go where our dreams lead us."

The Iris Inn ✪

191 CHINQUAPIN DRIVE, WAYNESBORO, VIRGINIA 22980

Tel: **(540) 943-1991**
Best Time to Call: **10 AM–8 PM**
Hosts: **Wayne and Iris Karl**
Location: **25 mi. W of Charlottesville**
No. of Rooms: **7**
No. of Private Baths: **7**
Double/pb: **$75–$95**
Single/pb: **$65**
Open: **All year**
Reduced Rates: **Corporate, Sun.–Thurs.**
Breakfast: **Full**
Credit Cards: **MC, VISA**
Pets: **No**

Children: **Welcome, by arrangement**
Smoking: **No**
Social Drinking: **Permitted**
Minimum Stay: **2 nights weekends**
Airport: **Yes**

The charm and grace of Southern living in a totally modern facility, nestled in a wooded tract on the western slope of the Blue Ridge overlooking the historic Shenandoah Valley—that's what awaits you at the Iris Inn in Waynesboro. It's ideal for a weekend retreat, a refreshing change for the business traveler, and a tranquil spot for the tourist to spend a night or a week. Guest rooms are spacious, comfortably furnished, and delightfully decorated in nature and wildlife motifs. Each room has a private bath and individual temperature control.

Applewood Colonial Bed & Breakfast ✪

605 RICHMOND ROAD, WILLIAMSBURG, VIRGINIA 23185

Tel: **(800) 899-APLE (2753)**
Best Time to Call: **9:30 AM–12:30 PM; 3–10 PM**
Host: **Martha R. Jones**
Location: **5 mi. from Rte. I-64, Exit 238**
No. of Rooms: **4**
No. of Private Baths: **4**
Double/pb: **$75–$95**
Suites: **$125**
Open: **All year**
Reduced Rates: **Available**
Breakfast: **Full**
Credit Cards: **MC, VISA**
Pets: **No**
Children: **Welcome, in suite**
Smoking: **No**
Social Drinking: **Permitted**
Minimum Stay: **2 nights holiday weekends**
Airport/Station Pickup: **Yes**

The owner's apple collection is evident throughout this restored elegant Colonial home built in 1929 by the construction manager for Colonial Williamsburg. The house is located four short blocks from Colonial Williamsburg. Three guest rooms have queen canopy or poster beds, antique chests, and oriental rugs. The suite, on the first floor, has a queen poster bed with a fishnet canopy, a sitting area in front of a fireplace banked by bookcases, and a sunny breakfast room. Breakfast and afternoon refreshments are served in the formal dining room.

Blue Bird Haven B&B ✪

8691 BARHAMSVILLE ROAD, WILLIAMSBURG-TOANO, VIRGINIA 23168

Tel: **(804) 566-0177**
Best Time to Call: **Early mornings**
Host: **June Cottle**
Location: **9 mi. N of Williamsburg**
No. of Rooms: **3**
No. of Private Baths: **2**
Max. No. Sharing Bath: **4**
Double/pb: **$65**
Suites: **$76**
Open: **All year**
Breakfast: **Full**
Pets: **Sometimes**
Children: **Welcome**
Smoking: **No**
Social Drinking: **Permitted**

June welcomes you to her ranch-style home, located 20 minutes from Colonial Williamsburg. Guest accommodations, located in a private wing, feature traditional furnishings. June is interested in many kinds of handcrafts and has decorated the rooms with one-of-a-kind quilts, spreads, rugs, and pictures. Breakfast includes a Southern-style assortment of Virginia ham, spoon bread, red-eye gravy, blueberry pancakes, fresh fruits, home-baked biscuits, and granola. Blue Bird Haven is convenient to Busch Gardens, James River Plantations, and Civil War battlefields. After a full day of seeing the sights, you are welcome to enjoy some of June's evening desserts.

Candlewick Inn B&B ✪

800 JAMESTOWN ROAD, WILLIAMSBURG, VIRGINIA 23185

Tel: **(804) 253-8693; (800) 418-4949**
Best Time to Call: **Anytime**
Host: **Mary L. Peters**
Location: **2 miles from Route 64, Exit 242A**
No. of Rooms: **3**
No. of Private Baths: **3**
Double/pb: **$90–$115**
Single/pb: **$90–$95**
Open: **All year**
Reduced Rates: **Available**
Breakfast: **Full**
Credit Cards: **MC, VISA**
Pets: **No**
Children: **Welcome, over 12**
Smoking: **No**
Social Drinking: **Permitted**
Minimum Stay: **2 nights**
Station Pickup: **Yes**
Foreign Languages: **German**

Mary restored and redecorated this 1946 two-story frame house so that it looks like a farmhouse from the previous century, with beam ceilings, chair rails, and beautiful canopy beds. She also sets out wonderful country breakfasts featuring home-baked bread and muffins. Then it's an easy four-block walk or bike ride to the historic area; first stop is William and Mary College, just across the way.

Colonial Capital Bed & Breakfast ✪

501 RICHMOND ROAD, WILLIAMSBURG, VIRGINIA 23185

Tel: **(800) 776-0570; fax: (757) 253-7667; (757) 229-0233**
Hosts: **Barbara and Phil Craig**
Location: **2.5 mi. from I-64, Exit 238**
No. of Rooms: **5**
No. of Private Baths: **5**
Double/pb: **$76–$115**
Suites: **$108–$135**
Open: **All year**
Breakfast: **Full**
Credit Cards: **AMEX, DISC, MC, VISA**
Pets: **No**
Children: **Welcome, over 8**
Smoking: **Restricted**
Social Drinking: **Permitted**
Airport/Station Pickup: **Yes**

Barbara and Phil offer a warm welcome to guests in their three-story Colonial revival (c.1926) home only three blocks from the historic area. The B&B is decorated with period antiques, oriental rugs, and many of the original lighting and plumbing fixtures; all guest rooms feature four-poster beds crowned with charming canopies. In the morning you can look forward to such treats as a soufflé, French toast, fluffy omelette, or yeast waffles complemented with a choice of juices, fresh fruits, and specially blended coffees and tea. The sunny solarium or formal dining room invite guests to linger over breakfast and get to know one another as does the plantation parlor, where tea and wine are served during afternoons and evenings. Games, books, and puzzles are provided for your pleasure. Jamestown, Yorktown, some of the state's finest plantations, Busch Gardens, and Water Country USA are only a few minutes away. Personalized gift certificates are available.

For Cant Hill Guest Home

4 CANTERBURY LANE, WILLIAMSBURG, VIRGINIA 23185

Tel: **(804) 229-6623**
Best Time to Call: **Anytime**
Hosts: **Martha and Hugh Easler**
No. of Rooms: **2**
No. of Private Baths: **2**
Double/pb: **$65–$75**
Open: **All year**
Breakfast: **Continental**
Pets: **No**
Children: **Welcome, over 10**
Smoking: **No**
Social Drinking: **Permitted**
Minimum Stay: **2 nights Mar. 15–Dec. 31**

Situated in the heart of town, overlooking Lake Matoaka, a part of the campus of the College of William and Mary, the home is only a few blocks from the restored area of Colonial Williamsburg, yet very secluded and quiet in a lovely wooded setting. Both rooms are tastefully decorated, accented in winter with homemade quilts. Each room has a TV and a hearty Continental breakfast is served in the room. The hosts are happy to make dinner reservations for guests and provide very helpful information on the many attractions in the entire area.

Fox & Grape Bed & Breakfast ✪

701 MONUMENTAL AVENUE, WILLIAMSBURG, VIRGINIA 23185

Tel: **(757) 229-6914; (800) 292-3699**
Best Time to Call: **9 AM–9 PM**
Hosts: **Bob and Pat Orendorff**
Location: **2 mi. from I-64, Exit 238**
No. of Rooms: **4**
No. of Private Baths: **4**
Double/pb: **$84**
Single/pb: **$84**
Open: **All year**
Reduced Rates: **Jan. 1–Mar. 21 $90 for 2 nights**
Breakfast: **Continental**
Pets: **No**
Children: **Welcome**
Smoking: **No**
Social Drinking: **Permitted**
Station Pickup: **Yes**

Warm hospitality awaits you just a seven-minute walk north of Virginia's restored Colonial capital. Furnishings include counted cross-stitch pieces, antiques, stained glass, stenciled walls, duck decoys, and a

cup-plate collection. Pat enjoys doing counted cross-stitch. Bob carves walking sticks and makes stained glass windows.

Governor's Trace ✪

303 CAPITOL LANDING ROAD, WILLIAMSBURG, VIRGINIA 23185

Tel: **(757) 229-7552; (800) 303-7552**
Best Time to Call: **9 AM–10 PM**
Hosts: **Sue and Dick Lake**
Location: **2 mi. from I-64, exit 238**
No. of Rooms: **3**
No. of Private Baths: **3**
Double/pb: **$95**
Suites: **$95–$115**

Open: **All year**
Breakfast: **Full**
Credit Cards: **MC, VISA**
Pets: **No**
Children: **No**
Smoking: **No**
Social Drinking: **Permitted**

This Georgian brick home featured on the back cover of the 1992 edition of *Bed & Breakfast U.S.A.* is Colonial Williamsburg's closest B&B neighbor, just one door away. Hardy patriot, loyal royalist or plantation gentry travelers would have found the rooms here comfortably familiar but with modern exceptions, king- and queen-size beds and private baths. Special amenities include a fireplace in one bedroom and a screened-in porch off another. Private romantic candlelit breakfast is served in each room. Sue and Dick provide refuge from the modern world's hectic pace to let you discover unexpected treasures in an 18th-century atmosphere. Make "take away" memories at the Governor's Trace.

The Homestay Bed & Breakfast ✪

517 RICHMOND ROAD, WILLIAMSBURG, VIRGINIA 23185

Tel: **(804) 229-7468; (800) 836-7468**
Best Time to Call: **10 AM–9 PM**
Hosts: **Barbara and Jim Thomassen**
Location: **3 mi. from Rte. I-64, Exit 238**
No. of Rooms: **3**
No. of Private Baths: **3**
Double/pb: **$80–$95**
Single/pb: **$65–$75**
Open: **All year**
Reduced Rates: **20% less Jan. 2–Mar. 15**
Breakfast: **Full**
Credit Cards: **MC, VISA**
Pets: **No**
Children: **Welcome, over 10**
Smoking: **No**
Social Drinking: **Permitted**
Minimum Stay: **2 nights, weekends, holidays, and special events**
Airport/Station Pickup: **Yes**

Cozy and convenient! Enjoy the comfort of a lovely Colonial Revival home furnished with turn-of-the-century family antiques and country charm. Rooms with a Victorian double bed, king-size bed, or twin beds are available. The rooms are accented with an attention to detail. You may relax in the second floor sitting room or by the fire in the living room. A full breakfast, served in the formal dining room, features homemade breads, herb jellies (made with herbs from the garden), and delicious hot dishes. You are just four blocks from Williamsburg's famed historic area, adjacent to the College of William and Mary campus, alumni house and football stadium, and minutes away from Jamestown, Yorktown, and Busch Gardens.

Liberty Rose B&B Inn ✪

1022 JAMESTOWN ROAD, WILLIAMSBURG, VIRGINIA 23185

Tel: **(757) 253-1260; (800) 545-1825**
Best Time to Call: **9 AM–9 PM**
Hosts: **Brad and Sandi Hirz**
Location: **1 mi. from historic area**
No. of Rooms: **4**
No. of Private Baths: **4**
Double/pb: **$115–$120**
3 Suites: **$155–$185**
Open: **All year**
Reduced Rates: **5% after 3rd night**
Breakfast: **Full**
Credit Cards: **AMEX, MC, VISA**
Pets: **No**
Children: **No**
Smoking: **No**
Social Drinking: **Permitted**
Minimum Stay: **2 nights**

This enchanting old home is one of Williamsburg's most romantic—Brad and Sandi created their B&B as a honeymoon project! Antiques from all periods fill the Liberty Rose. In the guest rooms, comfortable queen-size poster beds are draped with fringed reproduction damasks and topped with silk-covered goose-down duvets. Alongside the bed, in an old-fashioned armoire, you'll find a TV/VCR. The luxurious baths have claw-footed tubs, marble showers, and ample supplies of robes, towels, and bubble bath. And everywhere you'll notice little extras, such as a dish full of chocolates, complimentary soft drinks, freshly baked chocolate chip cookies, and a long-stemmed silk rose that's yours to keep.

War Hill ✪

4560 LONG HILL ROAD, WILLIAMSBURG, VIRGINIA 23188

Tel: **(757) 565-0248; (800) 743-0248**
Best Time to Call: **9 AM–9 PM**
Hosts: **Shirley, Bill, and Will Lee**
Location: **2 mi. from Williamsburg**
No. of Rooms: **5**
No. of Private Baths: **5**
Double/pb: **$75–$95**
Suite: **$100–$145; sleeps 2–5**
Cottage: **$115–$160; sleeps 2–5**
Open: **All year**
Breakfast: **Full**
Credit Cards: **MC, VISA**
Pets: **No**
Children: **Welcome**
Smoking: **No**
Social Drinking: **Permitted**

War Hill is situated in the center of a 32-acre working farm, just three miles from the tourist attractions. Built in 1968, this Colonial replica couples the charm of yesteryear with today's contemporary conveniences. The suite is composed of two bedrooms and a bath. The wide heart-pine floors came from an old school, the stairs from a church, the overhead beams from a barn; the oak mantel is over 200 years old. Fruits from a variety of trees in the orchard are yours to pick in season. In autumn, Shirley and Bill serve delicious homemade applesauce and cider. Angus show cattle graze in the pasture, and the sounds you'll hear are crickets, frogs, owls, and the morning crowing of the rooster.

Williamsburg Sampler Bed and Breakfast ✪

922 JAMESTOWN ROAD, WILLIAMSBURG, VIRGINIA 23185

Tel: **(800) 722-1169; (757) 253-0398; fax: (757) 253-2669**
Best Time to Call: **7:30 AM–10:30 PM**
Hosts: **Helen and Ike Sisane**
Location: **Heart of Williamsburg**
No. of Rooms: **4**
No. of Private Baths: **4**
Double/pb: **$90–$140**
Open: **All year**
Breakfast: **Full**
Pets: **No**
Children: **Welcome, over 12**
Smoking: **No**
Social Drinking: **Permitted**
Airport/Station Pickup: **Yes**

Welcome to one of Williamsburg's finest 18th-century plantation-style homes. The three-story, brick Colonial B&B is richly furnished throughout with antiques, pewter, and samplers. This elegant home complements those located in the restored area and is within walking distance to historic Colonial Williamsburg. Lovely accommodations include two suites, four-poster beds in king and queen sizes, television, fireplaces, and your hosts' famous "skip lunch" breakfast. Personalized gift certificates are available.

Azalea House ✪

551 SOUTH MAIN STREET, WOODSTOCK, VIRGINIA 22664

Tel: **(540) 459-3500**
Hosts: **Margaret and Price McDonald**
Location: **35 mi. N of Harrisonburg**
No. of Rooms: **4**
No. of Private Baths: **4**
Double/pb: **$55–$75**
Open: **All year**
Breakfast: **Full**
Credit Cards: **AMEX, MC, VISA**
Pets: **No**
Children: **Welcome, over 6**
Smoking: **No**
Social Drinking: **Permitted**

This spacious home, built in the early 1890s, served as a parsonage for 70 years. It has been restored following its Victorian tradition and has porches, bay windows, and a white picket fence—in spring, one hundred blooming azaleas enhance its beauty. The interior is made particularly lovely with family heirlooms and pretty color schemes. Azalea House is within walking distance of fine restaurants, antique shops, and an art gallery. It is convenient to wineries, orchards, trails, horseback riding, and fishing. Air-conditioning assures your summer comfort.

The Country Fare ✪

402 NORTH MAIN STREET, WOODSTOCK, VIRGINIA 22664

Tel: **(540) 459-4828**
Best Time to Call: **7–11 AM; 6–10 PM**
Host: **Bette Hallgren**
Location: **35 mi. S of Winchester**
No. of Rooms: **3**
No. of Private Baths: **1**
Max. No. Sharing Bath: **3**
Double/pb: **$65**
Double/sb: **$45–$55**
Single/sb: **$35**
Open: **All year**
Breakfast: **Continental**
Pets: **No**
Children: **Welcome, by arrangement**
Smoking: **No**
Social Drinking: **Permitted**

A small cozy inn, circa 1772, The Country Fare is one of Shenandoah County's oldest homes. It is restored and carefully preserved and has wide pine floorboards upstairs, original doors and hardware, and walls hand-stenciled with original designs. Nana's Room boasts hand-painted furniture and a private bath. Two other bedrooms—one with a queen-size, the other with a full-size bed—share an old-fashioned bathroom with a claw-footed tub. Expanded Continental breakfast, served before the dining room's wood-burning stove, consists of seasonal fruits, juices, home-baked breads and muffins, and some of Nana's surprises. Your host will share information on the interesting sights and attractions of the valley.

WEST VIRGINIA

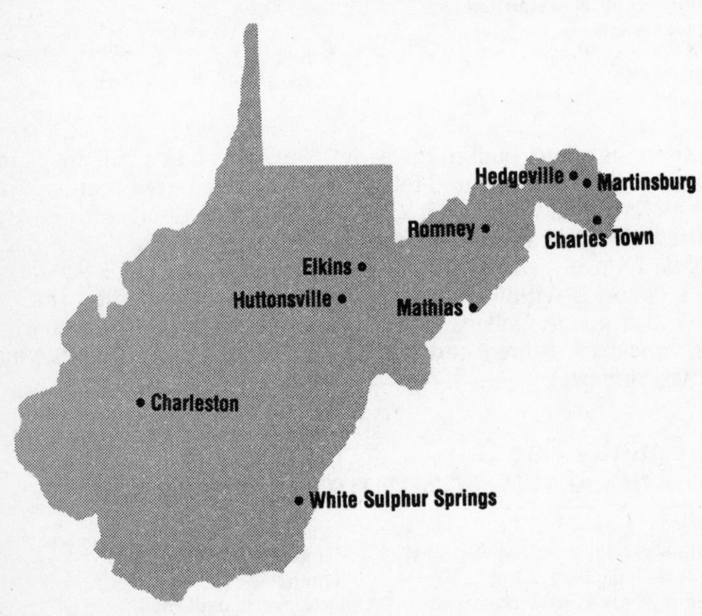

Historic Charleston Bed & Breakfast ✪

114 ELIZABETH STREET, CHARLESTON, WEST VIRGINIA 25311

Tel: **(304) 345-8156; (800) CALL-WVA; fax: (304) 342-1572**
Best Time to Call: **8 AM–11 PM**
Hosts: **Bob and Jean Lambert**
Location: **½ mi. from I-77, I-64, Exit 99**
No. of Rooms: **3**
No. of Private Baths: **3**
Double/pb: **$75**
Single/pb: **$65**
Open: **All year**
Reduced Rates: **6% seniors**
Breakfast: **Full**
Credit Cards: **AMEX, MC, VISA**
Children: **Welcome**
Smoking: **No**

The exterior of this 1905 American Foursquare home is painted gray clapboard with white trim. Most of the interior woodwork is the original natural oak. Guest accommodations are spacious—each room has a fireplace, private sitting area, and central heating and air-conditioning. The entrance hall is furnished with a Victorian loveseat, candle table, and a claw-footed desk, setting the tone for the rest of the house, which is decorated with antiques, collectibles, and handicrafts. Breakfast is served in the dining room, on an early 1930s dining suite. Then you can explore the area, starting with the state capitol and cultural center one block away.

Washington House Inn ✪

216 SOUTH GEORGE STREET, CHARLES TOWN, WEST VIRGINIA 25414

Tel: **(304) 725-7923; (800) 297-6957**
Best Time to Call: **8 AM–10 PM**
Hosts: **Nina and Mel Vogel**
Location: **60 mi. NW of Washington, D.C., and Baltimore**
No. of Rooms: **6**
No. of Private Baths: **6**
Double/pb: **$70–$125**
Open: **All year**
Reduced Rates: **Available**
Breakfast: **Full**
Credit Cards: **AMEX, MC, VISA**
Pets: **No**
Children: **Welcome, over 6**
Smoking: **No**
Social Drinking: **Permitted**
Airport/Station Pickup: **Yes**

George Washington didn't sleep here—but his relatives did. Built in 1899 by descendants of the president's brothers, John Augustine and Samuel, Washington House Inn is a wonderful example of Late Victorian architecture. From the three-story turret and wraparound porch to the carved oak mantels, this home echoes a bygone era. As you enter the main foyer, period antiques help you step back in time. In the morning, a hearty full breakfast is served in the dining room. Located in West Virginia's eastern gateway, the Inn is convenient to a host of activities. Within a ten-minute drive you will find Harpers Ferry National Park, white-water rafting, biking, and hiking on the restored C&O Canal towpath, thoroughbred horse racing, and Grand Prix–style sports car racing.

The Post House Bed and Breakfast ✪

306 ROBERT E. LEE AVENUE, ELKINS, WEST VIRGINIA 26241

Tel: **(304) 636-1792**
Hosts: **Toni Eddy, innkeeper; JoAnn Post Barlow, owner**
Location: **120 mi. S of Pittsburgh, Pa.**
No. of Rooms: **5**
No. of Private Baths: **2**
Max. No. Sharing Bath: **4**
Double/pb: **$65**
Single/pb: **$55**
Double/sb: **$60**
Single/sb: **55**
Open: **All year**
Breakfast: **Continental**
Pets: **No**
Children: **Welcome**
Smoking: **No**
Social Drinking: **Permitted**
Airport Pickup: **Yes**

Located in the heart of the mountains, the Post House Bed and Breakfast offers individual or group accommodations. Guests are invited to relax on the front porch, lounge, or in the spacious backyard complete with a children's playhouse. To really unwind, enjoy a massage by a certified masseuse. Handmade quilts are available for purchase. Nearby attractions include Monongahela Forest, Seneca Rocks, and Blackwater Falls. Cultural events are offered by Davis and Elkins College, including the world-famous six-week instruction at the Augusta Heritage Arts Center.

The Farmhouse on Tomahawk Run ✪

1 TOMAHAWK RUN PLACE, HEDGESVILLE, WEST VIRGINIA 25427

Tel: **(304) 754-7350**
Best Time to Call: **10 AM–noon, 6–9 PM**
Hosts: **Hugh and Judy Erskine**
Location: **12 mi. W of Martinsburg**
No. of Rooms: **5**
No. of Private Baths: **5**
Double/pb: **$65–$75**
Guest Cottage: **$140**
Open: **Mar.–Dec.**
Reduced Rates: **10% March**
Breakfast: **Full**
Credit Cards: **DISC, MC, VISA**
Pets: **No**
Children: **Welcome, by arrangement**
Smoking: **No**
Social Drinking: **Permitted**
Minimum Stay: **2 nights weekends**

Nestled in a quiet valley next to the historic Tomahawk-shaped spring for which the area was named, the farmhouse was built by Judy's great-grandfather during the Civil War. The land itself has been occupied by her ancestors since 1740. Two of the guest rooms inside the farmhouse have balconies. The self-contained carriage house sleeps five to seven and is available for weekend or week-long stays. A peaceful, bubbling brook winds its way through the 280 acres of woods and meadows, where walking paths are maintained for your pleasure. A Jacuzzi on the back porch of the farmhouse will ensure a restful visit.

The Hutton House ✪

ROUTES 219 AND 250, HUTTONSVILLE, WEST VIRGINIA 26273

Tel: **(304) 335-6701**
Best Time to Call: **Anytime**
Hosts: **Dean and Loretta Murray**
Location: **17 mi. S of Elkins**
No. of Rooms: **6**
No. of Private Baths: **6**
Double/pb: **$65–$70**
Single/pb: **$55–$65**
Open: **All year**
Reduced Rates: **Available**
Breakfast: **Full**
Other Meals: **Available**
Credit Cards: **MC, VISA**
Pets: **No**
Children: **Welcome**
Smoking: **No**
Social Drinking: **Permitted**
Airport/Station Pickup: **Yes**

Built in 1899 by a scion of Huttonsville's founder, Hutton House commands a broad view of the Tygart Valley and Laurel Mountain ridges. This ornate Queen Anne mansion, with its extraordinary woodwork and windows, is listed on the National Register of Historic Places. Travelers come here to ski at Snowshoe, visit Cass Railroad, and hike in the Monongahela National Forest. Civil War buffs will find plenty of battle sites to study, and the Augusta Heritage Arts Festival, in nearby Elkins, also merits a detour. For breakfast, your hosts dish out cantaloupe sorbet and whole wheat pancakes drizzled with maple syrup made from their own trees.

Pulpit & Palette Inn ✪

516 WEST JOHN STREET, MARTINSBURG, WEST VIRGINIA 25401

Tel: **(304) 263-7012**
Hosts: **Bill and Janet Starr**
Location: **20 mi. S of Hagerstown**
No. of Rooms: **2**
Max. No. Sharing Bath: **4**
Double/sb: **$75**
Single/sb: **$60**
Open: **Mar.—Dec.**
Breakfast: **Full**
Credit Cards: **DISC, MC, VISA**
Pets: **No**
Children: **Welcome, over 12**
Smoking: **No**
Social Drinking: **Permitted**
Station Pickup: **Yes**

Built in 1870, this Italianate Victorian is furnished with American antiques, Oriental objets d'art, Tibetan rugs, paintings, and stained glass work done by the hostess. Bill and Janet's objective is to give personalized attention to guests with afternoon tea, complimentary evening drinks and hors d'oeuvres, a morning bed tray, and a full gourmet breakfast. Bill and Janet are retired educators; their interests include drama production, stained glass work, art appreciation, travel, and community service. The Pulpit & Palette Inn is located 30 minutes from Harpers Ferry National Park and the Antietam National Battlefield, and 80 minutes from historic Gettysburg.

Valley View Farm ✪

ROUTE 1, BOX 467, MATHIAS, WEST VIRGINIA 26812

Tel: **(304) 897-5229**
Best Time to Call: **Evenings, 8–10PM**
Host: **Edna Shipe**
Location: **130 mi. SW of D.C.**
No. of Rooms: **4**
Max. No. Sharing Bath: **4**
Double/sb: **$40**
Single/sb: **$20**
Open: **All year**
Reduced Rates: **Weekly**
Breakfast: **Full**
Other Meals: **Available**
Pets: **Welcome**
Children: **Welcome (crib)**
Smoking: **Permitted**
Social Drinking: **Permitted**
Airport/Station Pickup: **Yes**

This 1920s farmhouse is decorated with comfortable Early American–style furniture and family mementos, and there's a nice porch for relaxed visiting. This is no place to diet because Edna is a good cook. Seasonal recreational activities are available in nearby Lost River State Park and on Rock Cliff Lake. You are certain to enjoy the local festivals, house tours, and interesting crafts shops. Bryces Ski Resort is less than an hour away.

Hampshire House 1884 ✪

165 NORTH GRAFTON STREET, ROMNEY, WEST VIRGINIA 26757

Tel: **(304) 822-7171**
Hosts: **Jane and Scott Simmons**
Location: **35 mi. W of Winchester, Va.**
No. of Rooms: **5**
No. of Private Baths: **5**
Double/pb: **$65–$85**
Single/pb: **$50–$60**
Open: **All year**
Reduced Rates: **Available**
Breakfast: **Full**
Credit Cards: **AMEX, DC, DISC, MC, VISA**
Pets: **No**
Children: **Welcome**
Smoking: **No**
Social Drinking: **Permitted**
Airport/Station Pickup: **Yes**

Only two and one half hours west of Washington, D.C., via Route 50, lies Romney, the oldest town in West Virginia. Surrounded by beautiful rolling hills, Hampshire House is conveniently located to the downtown area. You will enjoy touring the town, with its quaint shops and historic buildings, and winery tours are nearby. The bedrooms are attractively furnished with old-fashioned furniture and wallpapers and kept comfortable with central heating and air-conditioning. Jane and Scott graciously offer complimentary snacks and invite you to enjoy the old pump organ, television, VCR, or a variety of games.

The James Wylie House

208 EAST MAIN STREET, WHITE SULPHUR SPRINGS, WEST VIRGINIA 24986

Tel: **(304) 536-9444; (800) 870-1613**
Hosts: **Cheryl and Joe Griffith**
Location: **100 mi. SE of Charleston**
No. of Rooms: **4**
No. of Private Baths: **4**
Double/pb: **$55–$65**
Single/pb: **$50–$55**
Open: **All year**
Reduced Rates: **10% after 3rd night**
Breakfast: **Full or Continental**
Credit Cards: **AMEX, MC, VISA**
Pets: **No**
Children: **Welcome**
Smoking: **No**
Social Drinking: **Permitted**
Airport/Station Pickup: **Yes**

This three-story Georgian Colonial-style dwelling dating back to 1819 features large, airy rooms that are comfortably furnished and accented with antiques. Pretty quilts, iron beds, old toys, and select period pieces enhance the bedrooms' decor. Specialties such as apple pudding, homemade coffee cake, and a delicious egg-and-sausage casserole are often part of the breakfast fare. The world-famous Greenbrier Resort is less than one mile away and historic Lewisburg is less than nine miles away. Recreational opportunities abound in the nearby state parks and ski resorts.

Appendix: UNITED STATES AND CANADIAN TOURIST OFFICES

Listed here are the addresses and telephone numbers for the tourist offices of every U.S. state and Canadian province. When you write or call one of these offices, be sure to request a map of the state and a calendar of events. If you will be visiting a particular city or region, or if you have any special interests, be sure to specify them as well.

State Tourist Offices

Alabama Bureau of Tourism and Travel
401 Adams Ave.
Montgomery, Alabama 36103
(205) 242-4169; (800) ALABAMA [252-2262]

Alaska Division of Tourism
P.O. Box 110801
Juneau, Alaska 99811-0801
(907) 465-2010

Arizona Office of Tourism
1100 W. Washington Street
Phoenix, Arizona 85007
(602) 542-8687 or (800) 842-8257

Arkansas Department of Park and Tourism
1 Capitol Mall
Little Rock, Arkansas 72201
(501) 682-7777 or (800) 643-8383 or (800) 828-8974

California Office of Tourism
801 K Street, Suite 1600
Sacramento, California 95814
(800) 862-2543 or (916) 322-2881

Colorado Dept. of Tourism
1625 Broadway
Suite 1700
Denver, Colorado 80202
(303) 592-5510 or (800) 255-5550

Connecticut Department of Economic Development—Vacations
865 Brook Street
Rocky Hill, Connecticut 06067-3405
(203) 258-4355 or (800) CT-BOUND [282-6863]

Delaware Tourism Office
99 Kings Highway, P.O. Box 1401
Dover, Delaware 19903
(302) 739-4271 or (800) 441-8846

Washington, D.C. Convention and Visitors' Association
1212 New York Avenue N.W.
Suite 600
Washington, D.C. 20005
(202) 789-7000

Florida Division of Tourism
126 W. Van Buren Street
Tallahassee, Florida 32399-2000
(904) 487-1462

Georgia Tourist Division
Box 1776
Atlanta, Georgia 30301
(404) 656-3590 or (800) 847-4842

Hawaii Visitors Bureau
2270 Kalakaua Avenue
Suite 801
Honolulu, Hawaii 96815
(808) 923-1811

Idaho Travel Council
700 W. State Street
P.O. Box 83720
Hall of Mirrors, 2nd floor
Boise, Idaho 83720-0093
(800) 635-7820 or (208) 334-2470

Illinois Office of Tourism
310 South Michigan Avenue
Suite 108
Chicago, Illinois 60604
(312) 744-2400 or (312) 814-4732 or
(800) 822-0292 or
(800) 223-0121 (out of state)

Indiana Tourism Development
Division
1 North Capitol, Suite 100
Indianapolis, Indiana 46204-2288
(317) 232-8860 or (800) 759-9191

Iowa Tourism Office
200 East Grand Ave.
Des Moines, Iowa 50309
(515) 242-4705 or (800) 345-IOWA
[4692]

Kansas Travel and Tourism Division
700 SW Harrison Street, Suite 1300
Topeka, Kansas 66603-3712
(913) 296-2009 or (800) 252-6727

Kentucky Department of Travel
Development
Capitol Plaza Tower, 22nd floor
500 Mero Street
Frankfort, Kentucky 40601-1974
(502) 564-4930 or (800) 225-8747
(out of state)

Louisiana Office of Tourism
P.O. Box 94291
Baton Rouge, Louisiana 70804-9291
(504) 342-8119 (within Louisiana) or
(800) 633-6970 (out of state)

Maine Publicity Bureau
P.O. Box 2300
97 Winthrop Street
Hallowell, Maine 04347
(207) 582-9300 or (800) 533-9595

Maryland Office of Tourist
Development
217 E. Redwood Street
Baltimore, Maryland 21202
(410) 333-6611 or (800) 719-5900

Massachusetts Office of Tourism
100 Cambridge Street—13th Floor
Boston, Massachusetts 02202
(617) 727-3201 or (800) 447-MASS
[6277] (out of state)

Michigan Travel Bureau
Department of Commerce
P.O. Box 30226
Lansing, Michigan 48909
(517) 373-0670 or (800) 543-2YES [2937]

Minnesota Tourist Information Center
121 7th Place East
#100 Metro Square
St. Paul, Minnesota 55101-2112
(612) 296-5029 or (800) 657-3700
(out of state)

Mississippi Division of Tourism
P.O. Box 1705
Ocean Springs, Mississippi 39566-1705
(601) 359-3297 or (800) 927-6378

Missouri Division of Tourism
P.O. Box 1055
Jefferson City, Missouri 65102
(314) 751-4133 or (800) 877-1234

Travel Montana
1424 9th Avenue
Helena, Montana 59620
(406) 444-2654 or (800) 548-3390

Nebraska Division of Travel and
Tourism
P.O. Box 94666
Lincoln, Nebraska 68509
(402) 471-3791 or (800) 228-4307 (out of
state) or (800) 742-7595 (within
Nebraska)

Nevada Commission on Tourism
Capitol Complex
Carson City, Nevada 89710
(702) 687-4322 or (800) NEVADA 8
[638-2328]

New Hampshire Office of Travel and
Tourism Development
P.O. Box 1856
Concord, New Hampshire 03302-1856
(800) FUN-IN-NH [386-4664] or (603)
271-2666

New Jersey Division of Travel and
Tourism
C.N. 826
Trenton, New Jersey 08625
(609) 292-2470 or (800) 537-7397

New Mexico Department of Tourism
491 Old Santa Fe Trail
Santa Fe, New Mexico 87503
(505) 827-7400, (800) 545-2040, or (800) 545-2040 (out of state), (505) 827-7402 (FAX)

New York State Division of Tourism
1 Commerce Plaza
Albany, New York 12245
(518) 474-4116 or (800) 225-5697 (in the Northeast except Maine)

North Carolina Travel and Tourism Division
430 North Salisbury Street
Raleigh, North Carolina 27611
(919) 733-4171 or (800) VISIT NC [847-4862]

North Dakota Tourism Promotion
Liberty Memorial Building
604 E. Boulevard
Bismarck, North Dakota 58505
(701) 224-2525 or (800) HELLO ND [435-5663]

Ohio Division of Travel and Tourism
77 South High Street, 29th Floor
P.O. Box 1001
Columbus, Ohio 43266
(800) 282-5393

Oklahoma Division of Tourism
P.O. Box 60,000
Oklahoma City, Oklahoma 73146
(405) 521-2406 or (800) 522-8565 (within Oklahoma)

Oregon Economic Development Tourism Division
775 Summer Street N.E.
Salem, Oregon 97310
(503) 378-3451 or (800) 547-7842

Pennsylvania Bureau of Travel Marketing
Department of Commerce
453 Forum Building
Harrisburg, Pennsylvania 17120
(717) 787-5453 or (800) 847-4872

Puerto Rico Tourism Company
23rd Floor
575 Fifth Avenue
New York, New York 10017
(212) 599-6262 or (800) 223-6530 or (800) 866-STAR [7827]

Rhode Island Department of Economic Development
Tourism and Promotion Division
7 Jackson Walkway
Providence, Rhode Island 02903
(401) 277-2601 or (800) 556-2484 (East Coast from Maine to Virginia, also West Virginia and Ohio)

South Carolina Division of Tourism
1205 Pendleton St.
Columbia, South Carolina 29201
(803) 734-0122

South Dakota Division of Tourism
Capitol Lake Plaza
711 East Wells Avenue
Pierre, South Dakota 57501
(605) 773-3301 or (800) 732-5682 (out of state) or (800) 952-2217 (within South Dakota)

Tennessee Tourist Development
P.O. Box 23170
Nashville, Tennessee 37202-3170
(615) 741-2158

Texas Dept. of Commerce
Division of Tourism
P.O. Box 12728
Austin, Texas 78711-2728
(512) 462-9191 or (800) 452-9292

Utah Travel Council
Council Hall
Capitol Hill
Salt Lake City, Utah 84114
(801) 538-1030 or (800) 200-1160

Vermont Department of Travel and Tourism
134 State Street
Montpelier, Vermont 05602
(802) 828-3236 or (800) VERMONT [837-6668]

Virginia Division of Tourism
901 E. Byrd St.
Richmond, Virginia 23219
(804) 786-4484 or (800) 932-5827

Washington State Tourism Development Division
P.O. Box 42500
101 General Administration Building
Olympia, Washington 98504
(206) 586-2088 or (800) 544-1800 (out of state)

Travel West Virginia
2101 E. Washington Street
Charleston, West Virginia 25305
(800) CALL WVA [225-5982] or (304) 558-2286

Wisconsin Division of Tourism
P.O. Box 7606
Madison, Wisconsin 53707-7606
(608) 266-2161 or (800) 372-2737 (within Wisconsin and neighboring states) or (800) 432-8747 (out of state)

Wyoming Travel Commission
I-25 and College Drive
Cheyenne, Wyoming 82002
(307) 777-7777 or (800) 225-5996 (out of state)

Canadian Province Tourist Offices

Alberta Tourism, Parks, and Recreation
City Center Building
10155 102 Street
Edmonton, Alberta, Canada T5J 4L6
(403) 427-4321 (from Edmonton area) or (800) 661-8888 (from the U.S. and Canada)

Tourism British Columbia
1117 Wharf Street
Victoria, British Columbia, Canada V8W 2Z2
(604) 663-6000 or (800) 663-6000

Travel Manitoba
Department 6020
7th Floor
155 Carlton Street
Winnipeg, Manitoba, Canada R3C 3H8
(204) 945-3777 or (800) 665-0040 (from mainland U.S. and Canada)

New Brunswick Tourism
P.O. Box 12345
Fredericton, New Brunswick, Canada E3B 5C3
(506) 453-8745 or (800) 561-0123 (from mainland U.S. and Canada)

Newfoundland/Labrador Tourism Branch
Department of Tourism & Culture
P.O. Box 8730
St. John's, Newfoundland, Canada A1B 4K2
(709) 729-2830 (from St. John's area) or (800) 563-6353 (from mainland U.S. and Canada)

Northwest Territories Tourism
(403) 873-7200 or (800) 661-0788

Tourisme Quebec
C.P. 979
Montreal, Quebec H3C QW3
(800) 363-7777 (from 26 eastern states) or (514) 873-2015 (collect from all other U.S. locations)

Tourism Saskatchewan
1919 Saskatchewan Drive
Regina, Saskatchewan, Canada S4P 3V7
(306) 787-2300 or (800) 667-7191 (from Canada and mainland U.S., except Alaska)

Tourism Yukon
P.O. Box 2703
Whitehorse, Yukon, Canada Y1A 2C6
(403) 667-5340

BED AND BREAKFAST RESERVATION REQUEST FORM

Dear ____
Host's Name

I read about your home in *Bed & Breakfast U.S.A., Southeast 1997,* and would be interested in making reservations to stay with you.

My name: ____

Address: ____
street

____
city state zip

Telephone: ____
area code

Business address/telephone: __________________________

____

Number of adult guests: ______________________________

Number and ages of children: _________________________

Desired date and time of arrival: _____________________

Desired length of stay: ______________________________

Mode of transportation: ______________________________
(car, bus, train, plane)

Additional information/special requests/allergies:

____

____

____

____

____

____

I look forward to hearing from you soon.

Sincerely,

APPLICATION FOR MEMBERSHIP

(Please type or print)
(Please refer to Preface, pages xvii–xviii, for our membership criteria.)

Name of Bed & Breakfast: ______________________________

Address: ______________________________

City: __________ State: ______ Zip: ______ Phone: (   ) ______

Best Time to Call: ______________________________

Host(s): ______________________________

Located: No. of miles _____ compass direction _____ of Major

City ____________________ Geographic region __________

No. of miles ________ from major route ________ Exit: ________

No. of guest bedrooms with private bath: ______________
No. of guest bedrooms that share a bath: ______________
How many people (including *your* family) must use the shared bath? ______________
How many bedrooms, if any, have a sink in them? __________

Room Rates:

$ _____ Double—private bath	$ _____ Double—shared bath
$ _____ Single—private bath	$ _____ Single—shared bath
$ _____ Suites	
Separate Guest Cottage	$ _____ Sleeps _____

Are you open year-round? ☐ Yes ☐ No
If "No," specify when you are open: ______________

How many rooms are wheelchair accessible? ______________

Do you require a minimum stay? ______________

Do you discount rates at any time? ☐ No ☐ Yes

Do you offer a discount to senior citizens? ☐ No ☐ Yes: _____ %

Do you offer a discount for families? ☐ No ☐ Yes: _____ %

Breakfast: Type of breakfast included in rate:
☐ Full ☐ Continental

Describe breakfast specialties: ______________________________
____

Are any other meals provided? ☐ No ☐ Yes
Lunch ☐ cost: $ __________ Dinner ☐ cost: $ __________

Do you accept credit cards? ☐ No ☐ Yes:
☐ AMEX ☐ DINERS ☐ DISCOVER ☐ MASTERCARD ☐ VISA

Will you GUARANTEE your rates from January through December 1998? ☐ Yes ☐ No

Note: This Guarantee applies only to those guests making reservations having read about you in *Bed & Breakfast U.S.A., Southeast 1998*.

If you have household pets, specify how many:
☐ Dog(s) ☐ Cat(s) ☐ Other

Can you accommodate a guest's pet?
☐ No ☐ Yes ☐ Sometimes

Are children welcome? ☐ No ☐ Yes If "Yes," specify age restriction ______________________________

Do you permit smoking somewhere inside your house?
☐ No ☐ Yes

Do you permit social drinking? ☐ No ☐ Yes

Guests can be met at ☐ Airport ____ ☐ Train ____ ☐ Bus ____

Can you speak a foreign language fluently? ☐ No ☐ Yes
Describe: ______________________________

GENERAL AREA OF YOUR B&B (e.g., Boston historic district; 20 minutes from Chicago Loop):

GENERAL DESCRIPTION OF YOUR B&B (e.g., brick Colonial with white shutters; Victorian mansion with stained glass windows):

AMBIENCE OF YOUR B&B (e.g., furnished with rare antiques; lots of wood and glass):

THE QUALITIES THAT MAKE YOUR B&B SPECIAL ARE:

THINGS OF HISTORIC, SCENIC, CULTURAL, OR GENERAL INTEREST NEARBY (e.g., one mile from the San Diego Zoo; walking distance to the Lincoln Memorial):

YOUR OCCUPATION and SPECIAL INTERESTS (e.g., a retired teacher of Latin interested in woodworking; full-time host interested in quilting):

If you do welcome children, are there any special provisions for them (e.g., crib, playpen, high-chair, play area, baby-sitter)?

Do you offer snacks (e.g., complimentary wine and cheese; pretzels and chips but BYOB)?

Can guests use your kitchen for light snacks? ☐ No ☐ Yes

Do you offer the following amenities? ☐ Guest refrigerator
☐ Air-conditioning ☐ TV ☐ Piano ☐ Washing machine
☐ Dryer ☐ Hot tub ☐ Pool ☐ Tennis court
Other ______________________________

What major college or university is within 10 miles?
____

Please supply the name, address, and phone number of three personal references from people not related to you (please use a separate sheet).

Please enclose a copy of your brochure along with color photos including exterior, guest bedrooms, baths, and breakfast area. Bedroom photos should include view of the headboard(s), bedside lamps and night tables. Please show us a typical breakfast setting. Use a label to identify the name of your B&B *on each*. If you have a black-and-white line drawing, send it along. If you have an original breakfast recipe that you'd like to share, send it along, too. (Of course, credit will be given to your B&B.) **Nobody can describe your B&B better than you. Limit your description to 100 words and submit it typed, double-spaced, on a separate sheet of paper. We will of course reserve the right to edit.** As a member of the Tourist House Association of America, your B&B will be described in the next edition of our book, *Bed & Breakfast U.S.A., Southeast*, published by Plume, an imprint of Dutton Signet, a division of Penguin USA, and distributed to bookstores and libraries throughout the U.S. The book is also used as a reference for B&Bs in our country by major offices of tourism throughout the world.

Note: The following will NOT be considered for inclusion in *Bed & Breakfast U.S.A., Southeast:* Rental properties or properties where a host doesn't reside on the premises. B&Bs having more than fifteen guest rooms. Rates exceeding $35 where six people share a bath. Rates exceeding $45 where five people share a bath. Applications received after March 31, 1997. Incomplete applications, no photos, etc. Applications received in states that are overcrowded; this is due to space limitations. Higher-priced B&Bs and inns will only be included according to space availability.

Note: If the publisher or author receives negative reports from your guests regarding a deficiency in our standards of CLEANLINESS, COMFORT, and CORDIALITY, and/or failure to honor the rate guarantee, we reserve the right to cancel your membership.

This membership application has been prepared by:

____
(Signature)

Please enclose your $40 membership dues. Date: __________

I am insured by _______________________________________.

Return to:
Tourist House Association of America, Inc.
RD 1, Box 12A
Greentown, Pennsylvania 18426

To ensure that your listing will be considered for the 1998 edition of *Bed & Breakfast U.S.A., Southeast*, we MUST receive your completed application by March 31, 1997. Thereafter, listings will be considered only for the 1999 edition.

APPLICATION FOR MEMBERSHIP FOR A BED & BREAKFAST RESERVATION SERVICE

NAME OF BED & BREAKFAST SERVICE: ____________________

ADDRESS: ____________________

CITY: __________ STATE: _____ ZIP: _____ PHONE:(   ) _______

COORDINATOR: ____________________

BEST TIME TO CALL: ____________________

Do you have a telephone answering ☐ machine? ☐ service?

Names of state(s), cities, and towns where you have hosts (in alphabetical order, please, and limit to 10):

Number of hosts on your roster: ____________________

THINGS OF HISTORIC, SCENIC, CULTURAL, OR GENERAL INTEREST IN THE AREA(S) YOU SERVE:

Range of Rates:

Modest:	Single $ __________	Double $ __________
Average:	Single $ __________	Double $ __________
Luxury:	Single $ __________	Double $ __________

Will you GUARANTEE your rates through December 1998?
☐ Yes ☐ No

How often do you reinspect listings? ____________________
Do you require a minimum stay? ____________________
Surcharges for one-night stay? ____________________
Do you accept credit cards? ☐ No ☐ Yes:
☐ AMEX ☐ DINERS ☐ DISCOVER ☐ MASTERCARD
☐ VISA

Is the guest required to pay a fee to use your service?
☐ No ☐ Yes—The fee is $ ____________________

Do you publish a directory of your B&B listings?
☐ No ☐ Yes—The fee is $ ____________________

Are any of your B&Bs within 10 miles of a university? Which? ____

____

Briefly describe a sample host home in each of the previous categories: e.g., a cozy farmhouse where the host weaves rugs; a restored 1800 Victorian where the host is a retired general; a contemporary mansion with a sauna and swimming pool.

Please supply the name, address, and phone number of three personal references from people not related to you (please use a separate sheet of paper). Please enclose a copy of your brochure.

This membership application has been prepared by:

____
(Signature)

Please enclose your $40 membership dues. Date: ______________

If you have a special breakfast recipe that you'd like to share, send it along. (Of course, credit will be given to your B&B agency.) As a member of the Tourist House Association of America, Inc., your B&B agency will be described in the next edition of our book, *Bed & Breakfast U.S.A., Southeast*, published by Plume, an imprint of Dutton Signet, a division of Penguin USA. Return to: Tourist House Association of America, Inc., Greentown, PA 18426.

To ensure that your listing will be considered for the 1998 edition, we must receive your completed application by March 31, 1997. Thereafter, listings will be considered only for the 1999 edition.

INFORMATION ORDER FORM

We are constantly expanding our roster to include new members in the Tourist House Association of America, Inc. Their facilities will be fully described in the next edition of *Bed & Breakfast U.S.A., Southeast*. In the meantime, we will be happy to send you a list including the name, address, telephone number, etc.

For those of you who would like to order additional copies of the book, and perhaps send one to a friend as a gift, we will be happy to fill mail orders. If it is a gift, let us know and we'll enclose a special gift card from you.

ORDER FORM

To:
Tourist House
Association of
America, Inc.
Book Dept.
Greentown, PA
18426

From: ______________________
(Print your name)

Address: ______________________

____
City State Zip

Date: ____________

Please send:

☐ List of new B&Bs ($3.00), available August to December.

☐ ____ copies of *Bed & Breakfast U.S.A., Southeast* @ $14.00 each (includes 4th class mail)

Send to: ______________________

Address: ______________________

____
City State Zip

☐ Enclose a gift card from:

Please make check or money order payable to Tourist House Association of America, Inc.

WE WANT TO HEAR FROM YOU!

Name: ______________________________

Address: ______________________________
street

____
city state zip

____

Please contact the following B&Bs; I think that they would be great additions to the next edition of *Bed & Breakfast U.S.A.*

Name of B&B: ______________________________

Address: ______________________________
street

____
city state zip

Comments:

Name of B&B: ______________________________

Address: ______________________________
street

____
city state zip

Comments:

____

The following is our report on our visit to the home of:

Name of B&B: ____________________ Date of visit: ________

Address: ____________________ I was pleased. ☐

____________________ I was disappointed. ☐

Comments:

Just tear out this page and mail it to us. It won't ruin your book!

Return to:
Tourist House Association of America, Inc.
Greentown, Pennsylvania 18426